PLACE IN RETURN BOX to remove this checkout from your record.
TO AVOID FINES return on or before date due.
MAY BE RECALLED with earlier due date if requested.

DATE DUE	DATE DUE	DATE DUE
MAY 1 4 2001 0 4 2 6 0 1		APR 2 9 2002 042902
JAN 0 6 2003 0 1 1 6 0 3		
MAY 2 8 2005 12 2 8 0 4	FEB 2 2 2007	

1/98   c:/CIRC/DateDue.p65-p.14

ONCE
A SLAVE

The Slaves' View of Slavery

BY STANLEY FELDSTEIN

Introduction by Thomas P. Govan

19 71

William Morrow and Company, Inc., New York

Library of Congress Catalog Card Number 70-130535

In memory of my father
and for my mother
and for my wife

Acknowledgments

In preparing this manuscript, I have, of necessity, become indebted to many people. Chiefly I want to thank an outstanding scholar and teacher, Thomas P. Govan. From the inception of this study, his guidance, encouragement, and unique personal and professional contributions were essential to my efforts. I am also grateful to Bayrd Still, David Reimers and Mrs. Jane Davis Govan for their careful reading of the entire manuscript and their helpful comments and corrections. In the final stages of the study John Hope Franklin rendered much valuable advice. To my friends, colleagues and family: Roberta Robins, Samuel Forsheit, Lawrence Costello, Robert Gruber, Peter Goodman, Harold Serper, Bernard and Eleanor Koven, Howard and Gertrude Schwartz, Thelma and Irving Rahinsky and Jean and Marshall Gartman. I would like to express my heartfelt thanks for the time, interest and energy they so generously contributed to me and my work. A special and heartfelt thanks to Leonard and Carol Leibowitz for their tireless and excellent help with editorial and stenographic work.

The research for this study was facilitated by many library staffs. I am particularly grateful to Ernest Kaiser of the Schomburg Collection of the New York Public Library, Palmer A.

Brynildsen and Lillian Tutiver of the Brooklyn Public Library, Joseph Schwarz and Robert Slevin of the New York Historical Society, the staffs of the Massachusetts Historical Society and the Library of Congress.

To my wife Susan and my daughter Eileen, my thanks for their encouragement and patience.

New York City   STANLEY FELDSTEIN
May, 1970

Contents

Preface

Benjamin A. Botkin suggested in 1944 that "historians are unanimous in the conclusion that the picture of slavery will never be complete until we get the view as presented through the slave himself." [1] With these words Mr. Botkin opened a new and broad area for the study of the "peculiar institution."

Has anyone bothered to ask the slave? This is the central theme of this study, because there are approximately six thousand slave narratives extant wherein the experiences of the slaves as they saw, lived, and thought about them are recorded. Most histories of slavery have been based on other sources—primarily accounts of outsiders who injected their interpretations and their own moralities into their recording of the institution.

In this book I attempt to study the emotional and physical effect of slavery on the slaves from within, through the words of slaves themselves. It is a story told by participants, for the source of the information contained herein is the body of narratives written or dictated by slaves or ex-slaves.

The narratives are both autobiographical and semi-autobiographical. They have been preserved in book form, in church and court records, and in the files of such leading abolitionist publications as *The Liberator* and *The Liberty Bell*. They are both published and unpublished books, letters, articles, and diaries. Most of these narratives are located in the Schomburg Collection of Negro Literature and History in Harlem, and the remainder may be found at the Library of Congress, the New York Public Library, and various colleges and universities throughout the country.

I have read most of these narratives. As a group, they have certain weaknesses. A majority of them were dictated by the slaves and written down by other persons, most of whom opposed the institution and gathered the material for its use as antislavery propaganda. It is to be noted, however, that I have carefully distinguished between those narratives whose authenticity and veracity may be verified at the Schomburg Collection and those which may appear to be dictated narratives but which are, in reality, fiction. The latter group, including those whose authenticity was even suspect, have been excluded entirely from this study.

Other narratives, especially those transcribed by the members of the Federal Writers' Project of the Work Projects Administration, were dictated or written by ex-slaves, no longer in the situation, and most of whom experienced slavery only as children. As a consequence, their memories were more or less blurred depending upon the time elapsed between their departures from the plantation and the dates of the narratives.

Nevertheless a strong case may also be made for the validity of the information. The reader will note that not nearly six thousand narratives are referred to herein. Much of the material is repetitive; so many tell of basically the same conditions, the same indignities. This "parallel thinking," this similarity of description, leads me to conclude that as a general proposition with respect to the major statements, these narratives spoke for the silent millions.

It is very important for the reader to understand that, to

the fullest extent possible, this study relates only what these narratives *say* about slave-life and the institution—it is not a history of slavery, nor is it offered as the "true" story of slavery. It is exactly what the subtitle implies—that is, what the slaves whose stories were written down *said* about slavery.

Too many American students of slavery have neglected these narratives. Time and again one comes across a statement such as "the emotional character of the subject [slavery] has now sunk somewhat into the background, and one of the great difficulties in arriving at a judgment results from the fact that slaves rarely either wrote letters or kept diaries." [2] Apparently the author of this statement neglected to examine the collections of Negro literature prior to · 1900. So, too, did Samuel Eliot Morison, who asked in *The Oxford History of The American People*, "What did the Negro himself think of this system?" [3] Although Professor Morison asked the significant question, he failed to draw upon the vast amount of slave autobiography, and instead described slavery by citing Jefferson Davis, President of the Confederate States of America, and himself a slaveholder. Not one word from the slave. Indeed, if one searches the pages of most works on American slavery, he will search in vain for a trace of the slave's own narrative.

Because it was used as abolitionist propaganda, most readers are familiar with the story of Frederick Douglass, and the real-life "Uncle Tom," Josiah Henson. A handful of these and some other of the more popular narratives have been referred to in the studies of slavery. But what of the others? More than five thousand narrators experienced as much, if not more, of the institution than Douglass or Henson. I have not repeated the already familiar stories of the more popular fugitives, but rather I have attempted to present a picture using the less-known, if not completely unknown, slave narratives.

I hope that this book will contribute to the understanding of the life and thoughts of those who were once slaves; that from it will be gained knowledge of the slave's relationships with master, overseer, poor white, mulatto, and other slaves and of the attitudes of the slave toward slavery, freedom, kindness, cruelty, and white domination of his life; and finally, that through the description of the slave's heroic resistance to a system of dehumanization, the reader will gain a greater respect for his fellow man, regardless of color.

Introduction

by THOMAS P. GOVAN, University of Oregon

In 1639, thirty-three years after the English began to settle "in that part of America commonly called Virginia," the free men of Maryland, with the consent of their Lord Proprietor, stated that "all the inhabitants of this province, being Christians (slaves excepted), shall have and enjoy all such rights, liberties, immunities, privileges, and free customs within this province as any natural born subject of England hath or ought to have or enjoy in the realm of England." Like many others before and since, they were more concerned with their own freedom than the freedom of others, and the parenthetical words, "slaves excepted," were an assertion that blacks, as a Chief Justice of the Supreme Court was later to say, were "considered as a subordinate and inferior class of beings, who had been subjugated by the dominant race" and "had no rights which a white man need respect."

This view of blacks "as beings of an inferior order . . . altogether unfit to associate with the white race either in political or social relations" was accepted in all of the colonies, and their enslavement was legally permitted in Massachusetts, Rhode Island, Connecticut, New York, New Jersey, Pennsylvania, and Delaware, as well as in Maryland, Virginia, the

Carolinas, and Georgia. Only a few morally sensitive individuals protested against this explicit denial of the teachings of the English Constitution and the Christian churches, and even during the revolutionary struggle against Great Britain, John Laurens of South Carolina and Alexander Hamilton of New York could gather little support for a proposal to permit black slaves to gain their freedom through enlistment in the Continental Army.

The Declaration of Independence and the Constitution of the United States, with their common assertion that the purpose of government was to establish freedom, justice, and equality, did increase the number of whites opposed to slavery, and in the nation's first quarter century, seven of the states began the process of emancipation. The national Congress, by the Northwest Ordinance of 1787, permanently prohibited slavery in the territories north of the Ohio and west of the mountains, and many Americans thought that within a few years this unjustifiable institution would be abolished throughout the United States.

They optimistically believed that slave labor was more costly than free and that this economic fact would lead the owners to consent to emancipation. Unfortunately slavery was not unprofitable. Instead the invention of machines to spin, weave, and gin cotton created a new source of profit for the owners of slaves, and the spread of cotton culture into the newly opened areas of the Southwest provided a market for the surplus produce and slaves of earlier settled areas. The owners were unwilling to give up these profits, but, even more importantly, they became afraid to risk the dangers involved in emancipation.

One of the defenders of slavery in the Constitutional Convention had said that he "was not apprehensive of insurrections," but shortly afterwards an event occurred outside the United States that basically altered the proslavery argument.

The blacks and men of color on the island of Santo Domingo, influenced by French revolutionary doctrines, rose against the whites; and the ensuing wars and massacres sent a wave of fear through the slaveholding regions of the United States, a fear apparently confirmed in subsequent years by the plots of Gabriel Prosser and Denmark Vesey and the insurrection of Nat Turner.

Slavery became more than an economic institution. It was, in the opinion of large numbers of whites, the sole means through which the two races could peaceably occupy the same territory, and fear of the blacks became even more influential than a greedy desire for profit in inducing slaveholders to defend the institution and to insist that it must be permanent. Emancipation by legislative or judicial action stopped at the Ohio and the southern boundary of Pennsylvania, and when Missouri was admitted to the Union, slavery spread west of the Mississippi. The nation did not totally abandon its hopes for emancipation. Slavery, by the terms of the Missouri Compromise, continued as a morally condemned institution, permanently prohibited in the northern part of the national territory and begrudgingly permitted to the south only after an explicit expression of the popular will.

Some thirty years later the situation changed, and the Congress, with the approval of the President, placed slavery and freedom on an equal moral plane through what came to be called the Compromise of 1850. The doctrine of popular sovereignty which said that when territories became states, they were to be "received into the Union, with or without slavery, as their constitution may prescribe at the time of their admission," was prescribed for the territories of New Mexico and Utah. And on May 30, 1854, in the Kansas-Nebraska Act, the Congress, again with the approval of the President, not only repealed that portion of the Missouri Compromise which prohibited slavery in the northern territories, but also stated that it had become national policy "not to legislate slavery into any Territory or State, nor to exclude it therefrom, but to leave the people thereof perfectly free to form and regulate their domestic institutions in their own way, subject only to the Constitution of the United States."

The Kansas-Nebraska Act offended many whites, some because it equated freedom and slavery, but others because it permitted black slaves to be taken into territories which previously had been reserved for white settlement alone. Antiblack sentiment, it seems, was as potent a source of opposition as anti-slavery, and this white attitude was strengthened on March 6, 1857, when Chief Justice Roger B. Taney, in the case of *Dred Scott v. Sanford*, held that there was no distinction between "property in a slave and other property," and that under the Constitution a citizen of the United States could not be forbidden to take his property with him when he moved from one area of the nation to another.

The constitutionality of state laws prohibiting slavery was not an issue in the case, but the broadness of the Chief Justice's language cast doubts on their validity, and in the campaign of 1860, the Republican party received support from many whose opposition to the spread of slavery was based on their fear and hatred of blacks. These opponents of the spread of slavery also believed that blacks were "beings of an inferior order . . . altogether unfit to associate with the white race in political or social relations," and the war, when it came the following year as a result of the secession of eleven slave states, was fought for the Union, not to free the blacks. "My paramount object," President Abraham Lincoln wrote, ". . . is to save the Union, and is not either to save or to destroy slavery. . . . What I do about slavery and the colored race, I do because I believe it helps save the Union; and what I forbear, I forbear because I do not believe it would help to save the Union."

He justified the Emancipation Proclamation on military grounds, and though there is reason to believe that he objected to slavery because he knew it was wrong, he concealed these views until his second inaugural. Here, in what was to be almost his last statement to the American people, he abandoned moral neutrality, denouncing slavery as an evil, offensive to God, and pledging the nation, if it should be necessary, to continue the war "until all the wealth piled by the bondsman's two hundred and fifty years of unrequited toil shall be sunk, and until every drop of blood drawn with the lash shall be paid by another drawn with the sword."

These sacrifices were not required. The war ended a few weeks later, and during the period of reconstruction that followed, the Republican leaders of the nation, angered by the intransigence of the unrepentant rebels and seeking to find a way to strengthen their political party, not only eliminated slavery but also provided full civil rights for the freedmen by the thirteenth, fourteenth, and fifteenth amendments to the Constitution of the United States. The apparent purpose of these Republicans was to make sure that the affirmations of the Declaration of Independence would apply to blacks as well as to whites, but, if such had ever been their aim, it was abandoned in 1877, when Rutherford Hayes and his party, to gain the presidency, returned control of relations between the races to the individual states.

The nation turned back to the view first expressed in the early part of the seventeenth century, that blacks were excluded from the "liberties, immunities, privileges, and free customs" that whites rightfully enjoyed, and though many blacks, supported by a few whites, protested, their protests were not heard or read in any significant way. A legend arose that the blacks were content with their assigned subordinate place, and this legend found apparent confirmation in the writings of American historians, most of whom accepted the view that the United States, from its beginning, had been a white man's nation, and that the blacks, as a dependent and inferior race, were to be ignored except when their presence aroused disputes among the whites as had happened with the slavery controversy and during reconstruction.

Only a few of these historians were admitted racists. Most would have disavowed the name and, if asked for their personal opinion, would have admitted that slavery and also the later denial to the blacks of their constitutionally established social, political, and civil rights were both departures from the correct course of national conduct. But, as objective, detached, and uninvolved scholars, they also believed it would be improper for them to permit this disapproval to appear in their writing. They wanted to guard themselves and their accounts of the past from partisanship, an easy distinction between good and evil, right and wrong, and in the pursuit of this praiseworthy objective, they came to distrust and ignore sources that patently were partisan and self-interested, propaganda, not factual description.

In regard to much of the past, this objectivity, this avoidance of partisanship, made possible greater knowledge and understanding, but not so with slavery in the United States. For here the sources containing the viewpoint of the slave were to be found in personal narratives, written or dictated by those who passionately hated the institution, who were sure it was unjust and dehumanizing, and most of whose stories were used as abolitionist propaganda. So prevalent was the distrust of these accounts that historians of slavery almost entirely ignored them, turring instead to more neutral sources, and after a time, with a few notable exceptions such as the autobiographical writings of Frederick Douglass and other prominent blacks, their very existence was forgotten.

The present book is an effort to repair this omission, to use the more than five thousand narratives by ex-slaves as sources not for a complete description of what slavery actually was

—Stanley Feldstein is too modest a historian to make such a presumptuous claim—but rather to provide an opportunity for these previously unheeded witnesses to be heard. "It is very important for the reader to understand," Mr. Feldstein writes, "that, to the fullest extent possible, this study relates only what these narratives *say* about slave-life and the institution—it is not a history of slavery, nor is it offered as the 'true' story of slavery. It is exactly what the subtitle implies—that is, what the slaves whose stories were written down *said* about slavery."

Readers, however, will have difficulty in heeding this cautionary advice. This account of slavery has the ring of truth, and nowhere more than in its numerous descriptions of the refusal of slaves to become what the institution tried to make them be, "a chattle; a thing; a piece of property." The slaves were men, and though their masters, as many of the narratives attest, used "every instrument of cruelty" for the purpose "of obliterating the mind, of crushing the intellect, and of annihilating the soul," they did not succeed.

What the author calls "the dehumanization process—the making of a thing of a human being" was a constant characterization of the institution as described by those who experienced it; but the spirit of humanity within the slaves could not be destroyed; and despite the pain, the cruelty, and torment that appears on almost every page of this book, it yet remains a magnificent, almost joyous testimonial to the determination of men to retain not only their humanity but also their humaneness under the most adverse circumstances, to continue defiantly to say, as Aaron Siddles, a fugitive, did say, "By the law of Almighty God, I was born free."

He and all his fellows were indeed born free and were entitled to freedom. The denial of this freedom on this continent for more than three hundred years was a damnable wrong, one of the most horrid examples of man's inhumanity to man, and though Mr. Feldstein may not have written "the true story of slavery," he has done a better and more useful thing, he has made it possible for his readers to feel, to know, and to understand what it was like to be a slave.

I

The Beginnings
of Dehumanization

THE NATURE OF SLAVERY

"By the law of Almighty God, I was born free," said fugitive slave Aaron Siddles in a dictated narrative of his experiences, "by the law of man a slave." Siddles was describing not only his own condition, but that of millions of his enslaved fellows as well. His description referred not merely to the arduous physical labor to which the slave was subjected, but also to the complete emotional and moral degradation of these disenfranchised Americans.[1]

A slave, said William Wells Brown, was a chattel, a thing, a piece of personal property. The master, or owner, of this metamorphosed human being retained absolute power of disposition of the slave, his wife, and his children. The excess of abuse caused by such power, Brown passionately insisted, was beyond law or public sentiment.[2]

The system of slavery was one that struck at the foundation of civilized society and at the basis of America's civil and political institutions. It was a system that took man down from "that lofty position which his God designed that he should occupy; that drags him down, places him upon a level with the beasts of the field, and there keeps him, that it may rob him of his liberty." Slavery, he wrote, tore wife from husband, took child from mother, and sister from brother; it tore asunder the tenderest ties of nature. The system had its bloodhounds, its chains, its Negro-whips, its dungeons, and almost every other instrument of cruelty that the mind could invent. All this "for the purpose of keeping the slave in subjection; all this for the purpose of obliterating the mind, of crushing the intellect, and of annihilating the soul." [3]

The dehumanization process—making a thing of a human being—necessary to the maintenance of the slaveholding institution, was slow, deliberate, and invidious. Once instituted, the system became self-perpetuating, gathering momentum as it went, and leaving in its wake human beings living a non-human existence.

Throughout this existence, however, the slave felt, saw, and heard enough to enable him to read the characters and to question the motives of those around him. It was continually emphasized in the narratives that it was not in personal suffering or privation that the slave found the bitterest woes of the institution. More than anything else it was the stifling influence of the deep degradation of his situation that most oppressed his spirit. The moral decay resulting from his status filled him with hatred for the oppressors who engendered it; and his own consciousness of possessing higher aspirations than did those who called themselves his masters taught him that "though his skin was black, they were, in truth, beneath him in all that constitutes a man." [4]

Nonetheless, even the most militant fugitives, the individuals who dared to escape the system, carried the mark of the institution. In numerous cases fugitives, when captured and brought back to testify against the brutality of a white overseer, were afraid to bear witness against a white man. In this fear, this degradation, this loss of hope, lay the true nature of slavery. It was, the successful fugitives almost unanimously said, these moral and emotional wounds that hurt more and dug deeper than any slaveholder's lash. From the depths of this subservience come the recorded transcripts of the slaves themselves. There is woven through these narratives a discernible thread of interpretation and evaluation of the morality of the institution and its effect on the participants.[5]

In one such narrative, Linda Brent, a slave for most of her adult life, wrote of her experiences. Not, she claims, to attract attention to herself, because she would have found it more pleasant to have been silent about her sufferings, but to bring the world, especially "the women of the North to a realizing sense of the condition of two millions of women at the South, still in bondage" and suffering what she had suffered—most of them, far worse. Linda Brent writes of the masters who did their utmost to provide the slaves with distorted images of the outside world. Any concept that deviated ever so slightly from the established slave structure was stamped out, and fear substituted in its place, to insure the tranquility of the plantation.[6]

This fear, these distortions, said Linda Brent, made the slave "prematurely knowing, concerning the evil ways of the world." Forced to submit to the perverted desires of her master, unable to fight the system, she "did it, but with deliberate calculation," and in so doing was left with a mental scar which she carried throughout her life. The experience deprived her of her dignity. The shame of it is expressed in a passage of her narrative that she directs to the free white female:[7]

O, ye happy women, whose purity has been sheltered from childhood, who have been free to choose the objects of your affection, whose homes are protected by law, do not judge the poor desolate slave girl too severely![8]

If slavery had been abolished, Linda Brent claimed, "I, also, could have married the man of my choice, I could have had a home shielded by the law; and I should have been spared the painful task of confessing what I am now about to relate." [9]

However, because of the blighting influence of slavery, she was unable to protect her dignity. Constantly subjected to the most adverse circumstances, including a life as her master's unwilling mistress, preserving her self-respect proved a futile struggle: "Alone in the powerful grasp of the demon slavery; the monster proved too strong for me. I felt as if I was foresaken by God and man; as if all my efforts must be frustrated; and I became reckless in my despair." [10]

Another of the evils of the institution was described by John Brown, a fugitive slave who saw it as synonymous with cruelty and perpetuated by the overwhelming greed of the master. Slavery, according to Brown, was "kept up entirely by those who made it profitable as a system of labor." He felt that slavery would end when the profit was taken out. The master's cruelty arose out of the system, he said, no matter how much or little the cash profits for the year were.[11]

Recalling the days of his servitude, Brown shuddered at the thought of the millions left behind who might have been experiencing similar, or even greater, sufferings. The maintenance of slave labor required built-in controls and cruelties and, consequently, the laws of the slave state encouraged the severest penalties for those who opposed it. Thus, the institution bred brutality. Brown claimed that Negroes would work well enough for themselves, but that they would not work for the benefit of others unless forced to do so. According to Brown, "every slave works against his heart, because he knows he is laboring for the benefit of another man." In order to compel the slave to work for the sole advantage of the master, coercive means had to be employed, ergo the introduction of cruelty. The slave became inured to this cruelty, and would, at the master's command, perform enormous tasks. He soon became recognized as uniquely suited for tasks no free man could perform. Despite his role, the slave, as the narratives demonstrate, retained the very human desire for self-expression.[12]

As early as 1774, slaves recorded the effects of slavery on themselves. The similarities in descriptions of the institution lead to the belief that the slaves had a common bond in their view of their condition. A petition sent to Thomas Gage, Governor of Massachusetts, decries the fact that slaves "were unjustly dragged by the cruel hand of power from our dearest frinds and sum of us stolen from the bosoms of our tender Parents and from a Populous Pleasant and plentiful country and Brought hither to be made slaves for Life in a Christian land."[13]

The petition states further that the slave is a good Christian and a sincere member of the Church of Christ, anxious to fulfill the commandment of brotherly love. But, it continues, what opportunity does slavery offer to "fulfill our parte of duty to him whilst in this condition and as we cannot searve our God as we ought in this situation." Furthermore, "the laws of the Land doth not justifi but condemns slavery or if there had bin aney Law to hold us in Bondage we are Humblely of the Opinion ther never was aney to inslave our children for life when Born in a free countrey."[14]

Although most slave writers described their own experiences, many wrote of the treatment and situation of others. Fugitive slave Andrew Jackson said that he "must pass some things that are so humiliating" that he had "to blush." In pleading for his fellow slave, he decried especially the treatment that the female slave received. Insulted, abused, and humbled, she was forced into prostitution by the unlimited control of the master. Jackson deplored that "all self-respect must be thrown away. We are urged to gratify the wicked, ungodly, oppressive wretches, in all their lusts."[15]

Fugitive slave William Green either witnessed or experienced many of the cruelties of slavery. Perhaps he had not seen as much as other slaves, he said, and perhaps his condition was "not as hard as some," but just "being a slave was enough for me." [16]

When Green was nineteen years old, he watched helplessly as his older brother was put in a chain gang, to be driven off to toil on a sugar or cotton plantation. How would you feel, he asks, "if a brother or sister were taken from before your eyes and chained with a heavy iron chain and driven off where you would never hear from them again? What would be your feelings? Would not your blood boil within you and would not you visit with sudden vengeance the perpetrator of such a deed?" [17]

One of the most articulate reporters of slavery was Frederick Douglass. Douglass spent more than twenty years as a slave. He grew to manhood not as an idle spectator, not as a guest of the slaveholder, but as a slave, "eating the bread and drinking the cup of slavery with the most degraded of my brother bondmen," and sharing with them all the painful conditions that slavery imposed. Because of his hardship, he felt he had the right to speak out against the institution in the most forceful manner.[18]

It was often said, he contended, that the condition of the poverty-stricken people of Europe was more deplorable than that of the American slave. Yet, although it was impossible for him not to sympathize with the poor and oppressed of all lands, he found no analogy between the two cases. He urged, a European may be poor, "but he is *not* a slave. He *may* be in rags, but he is not a slave." He was, according to Douglass, at least, "the master of his own body." As poor as he might be, he would never be subject to a Fugitive Slave Law. He would never be liable to the shame and scandal of kidnapping, and he had the right to emigrate from his country. He could write and speak, and cooperate for the attainment of his rights and redress of his wrongs. But how was it with the American slave? Did the right to assemble exist for him? Were newspapers available to him? Where was his right to petition? Where was his right to speak out, his freedom of movement? Had you asked the slave what he thought of his condition, Douglass asserts, "you had as well address your inquiries to the *silent dead*. There comes no *voice* from the enslaved." We were "left to gather his feelings by imagining what ours would be, were our souls in his soul's stead." If there were no other description of slavery than the slave as an untrained, unintelligible being, this alone was "sufficient to mark the slave system as a grand aggregation of human horrors." [19]

THE DARK PASSAGE

The Negro, the slaves recognized, had been brought to America against his will and purely for economic reasons. Here in the "dark passage" across the Atlantic came the first step in molding the African into complete obedience to his master. Here was where the barbaric treatment commenced, the Negro's manhood stolen, and his culture destroyed.

Only a few of those who made the dark passage recorded the events they experienced, and most of these dictated their stories to anti-slavery whites. One story, however, written by Jacob and Ruth Weldon, an African couple, is the most detailed of any that have been found.

Having been captured and boarded on ship, according to the Weldons, each slave was brought upon the deck, made secure, and thrown into "such a position as was best suited to the purpose, and branded by the inhuman villain, on some part of the person, by leaving a red hot iron in the form of certain letters or signs dipped into an oily preparation, and then pressed against the naked body till it burnt a deep and ineffaceable scar, to show who was the owner." As the slaves screamed, the sailors stood over them with a cat-o'-nine-tails, and whenever their outcries or resistance became too irksome, they lashed them on the face, back, breasts, thighs, or wherever else the sailors chose to inflict the wounds. Every blow brought with "the returning lash pieces of grieving flesh." They saw "mothers with babies at their breasts basely branded and lashed, hewed and scarred, till it would seem as if the very heavens must smite the infernal tormentors with the doom that they so richly merited." [20]

The slaves were chained two by two, the right leg and arm of one to the left arm and leg of another, and crowded into the slave rooms between decks. Women were stowed in without being shackled. Packed in this fashion the ship could carry a cargo of six hundred men, women, and children—"all naked and compelled to stow themselves away, by the lash, for a voyage of eight to ten weeks under a tropical sun, and where they could not sit upright—the space between the decks being only two feet ten inches in height." The sufferings of the "cargo" in their confinement "when tarpaulins were accidentally thrown over the gratings, or when the scuttles were closed in foul weather, were utterly indescribable." [21]

On each day of fair weather, the entire cargo was permitted to come on deck, which was surrounded with high nettings to prevent them from jumping overboard and possibly escaping. For additional security a ring was attached to the shackles of each pair, through which a large chain was run, which locked them all in a body to ringbolts on the deck. At approximately three o'clock in the afternoon they were again put below, to remain until morning. While on deck they were fed twice with rice, yams, horsebeans, and occasionally a little beef and bread, and allowed a pint of water each during the day. Each day they were made to jump in their irons, an exercise which the crew called "dancing." If any of the cargo refused, they were beaten. After the first few weeks of this treatment, their ankles were worn to the bone, and many were afflicted with either flux or scurvy. Their limbs were so swollen that it became impossible for many of them to move at all.[22]

The groans and suffocating cries for air and water emanating from below deck were described as having "sickened the soul of humanity." The frequent howling and melancholy sounds of anguish caused by the reminiscences of their homeland were often followed by hysterical fits of the women and desperate imprecations from the men. The confinement and the lack of food and water caused many to sit sullen and still awaiting the blessed attack of dysentery to release them from their suffering.[23]

The ship's crew could stand to remain in the slaves' quarters no more than thirty minutes at a time. Yet "these poor creatures were there compelled to moan the long hours of night away, with no water to quench their tormenting thirst, and just air enough to prolong their misery." [24]

During the trip, while the vessel pitched and rolled, and although they suffered intensely from the closed scuttles, not a sound was heard "save the muffled groans that would involuntarily burst forth." As the days passed, many died. Fear and confinement caused dysentery among the remainder. The slaves became inured to the suffering of those around them. The weak perished and the strong fought to stay alive. In each slaveroom two or three large tubs were placed for their convenience. Often one of a shackled couple would be attacked by dysentery, while his fellow prisoner would be unable or disinclined to move, especially as he had to drag himself over the bodies of others. Thus, "the deck was soon covered with blood and mucous, emitting the horrid stench, and breeding death continually." The survivors would look down upon the motionless bodies beside them and mournfully intone, "Gone to he own country! Gone to he own friends." [25]

Sometimes the wild crowds would rush to the scuttles as

fast as their manacled limbs would permit, some dragging the dead with them in their desperate attempt to breathe the air and cry for water.* Often they would be turned back as they fainted beneath the throng that pressed for their space. Seeing this, the crew would curse them in a rage, and at times lash them for their imprudence.

Many slaves thought of suicide as a means of terminating this existence, but without means of self-destruction, they were frustrated. Many turned to starvation as a solution. When the crew saw a slave thus attempting to rid himself of the remainder of the voyage, they commanded him to eat, and upon refusal, lashed him till he fainted. After each whipping the reluctant slaves were washed in salt brine, and often subjected to a red-pepper mixture to increase the pain of the torture. After days of this treatment, many shrank in fear and prayed in desperate resolution to die, cost what pain it might. Thereafter their refusal to eat became stauncher, only to be followed by a new and more brutal method of punishment. The jaws of slaves were forced open and their mouths crammed so full that they choked, often to death. If the African survived this treatment, he was comforted only by the hope that the voyage was soon to be over.

Not even little children were spared the terrors of the voyage. The Weldons tell of a child of nine months being flogged for refusing to eat. This inducement failing, the captain of the ship then ordered the child placed feet first into a pot of boiling water. When this resulted in nothing more than the dissolving of the skin and nails, he again was flogged. As the child continued his refusal, a piece of mango-wood

* On March 9, 1783, Gustavus Vasa reported to Granville Sharp that "the master of a slave-ship trading from Africa to Jamaica, and having 440 slaves on board, had thought fit on a pretext that he might be distressed on his voyage for want of water, to lessen the consumption of it in the vessel, by throwing overboard 132 of the most sickly among the slaves." As cited in *Leeds Anti-Slavery Series No. 4, The Slave Trade, Its Extent and Horrors.* (Sold by Jane Jowett, Friends' Meeting Yard, Leeds), p. 2.

weighing fourteen pounds was tied to his neck as punishment. All else failing, the captain took him and dropped him from his arms upon the deck, and in a few moments the child was dead. At that point the captain called the mother to heave the child's body overboard, and then beat her for her refusal until she was forced to take it to the ship's side, "where, with her head averted that she might not see it, she dropped it overboard." [26]

None but "hard-hearted men," said Jacob Weldon, were captains of slave ships, "and their crew, if engaged with a knowledge of their business, will be like themselves, or if engaged on some other pretext and forced into the business, so abhorrent to all their better feelings, they will be morose and undutiful except from fear of the lash; so that the crew itself tends to make the captain still worse. Then he becomes accustomed to regard Negroes only as so much property to make money on, that he loses all thought that they are his fellow creatures." [27]

Upon arrival, the survivors of the Weldon voyage were sold by "scramble": the ship was covered with sails, the men were placed on the main deck, and the women on the quarter deck. When all was ready, the purchasers came on board, each with cards bearing his own name, and rushed through the barricaded door, some with handkerchiefs tied together with which to encircle all the slaves they wanted. Disabled slaves were sold at auction for whatever they might bring, some selling for as little as one dollar.

On shore there were erected low wooden huts for the accommodation of the unsold slaves. During the warmer weather the slaves were landed, and after being washed, were again put up for sale. In the winter months, the owners were, for their own economic advantage, obliged to furnish them with a few warm clothes.

The African was certain he had been brought to a land where he would be treated as a slave, subjected to hard work and treatment, without the slightest chance of ever seeing his home again. Yet, Zamba, another who described the tortures of the voyage, wrote of:

Negroes upon coming ashore, and being allowed to stretch their limbs, and walk about a little—to refresh themselves in the salt water, and breathe the pure air of heaven—and, above all, being furnished with fresh provisions, it was astonishing to observe how their spirits revived: a change for the better appeared in their countenances, and they expressed their delight, by capering and singing. But no wonder, after all, when we consider the difference between the hold of a ship, containing four or five hundred negroes, surrounded with filth, and suffering from suffocation, and the fresh and the grateful free air of heaven.[28]

II

Life on the Plantation — the Arena of Dehumanization

After their purchase, the slaves were taken to the homes of their new owners, which were farms, commonly known as plantations. Only a scant few of the narratives were written by slaves who lived in the cities or towns and worked in factories, shipyards, etc. It was on the plantation that the slaves lived, worked, married and raised families. It was here too that generations of human beings were treated as chattels, being intermediate between men and animals, and so in part dehumanized.

The dehumanization process was less a conscious and deliberate attempt on the part of the slaveholders to deprive the slaves of their humanity than it was a natural consequence of the system. The basic purpose of the slave system was surely not a grand design to perpetrate a horrendous crime on the black race. Notwithstanding the psychological motivations that are the source of racial prejudice and, later on, the fear of a black revolt against the masters, the system was designed primarily for its economic advantages to the masters. Nevertheless, in order to perpetuate the institution, and simply to make it work, it was essential that a strict code of rules, regulations, punishments, and controls be established and followed. The enforcement of these rules resulted in what I call the slave's dehumanization—his eventual inability to fulfill his natural human desires, needs, instincts and to maintain his integrity and dignity.

It is important to note, however, what the narratives, as described below, reveal: that this less-than-conscious attempt at dehumanization was, for the most part, staunchly and courageously resisted by the slaves. In this chapter we shall hear from the slave something of plantation life, the ways in which the dehumanization process worked, and the form, nature and success of the slaves' resistance.

SHELTER, FOOD, AND CLOTHING

The narratives, when describing the housing, feeding, and clothing of the slaves, are in substantial agreement; notwithstanding different localities, climates, and crops, these aspects of plantation life were essentially uniform.

The shelter, in almost every instance, consisted of one-room log cabins, usually without a partition, and the total furnishings were generally a bed, a bench and a few cooking utensils.

Jacob Stroyer reported that usually there were no chairs, and "tables" were packing boxes or slabs of wood. As there was no stove, all cooking was done at the fireplace, which like the chimney was made of mud and stones. One or two openings served as windows, and wooden shutters or canvas served in place of glass. Mattresses were made of straw, hay, or grass. For light, a tallow candle or pine knot was lit.[1]

Although a cabin was severely crowded, there was usually some semblance of separation of the sexes. For example, the kitchen area might be designated for males, while the young women would huddle together in the area set aside for the parents. When a child married, he or she would seek new quarters, either by building a new partition in the same cabin or by moving into a less populated one.

The commingled families were not always friendly toward each other. Anyone who was "accustomed to the way in which the slaves lived in their cabins, could tell as soon as they entered whether they were friendly or not, for when they did not agree the fires of the two families did not meet on the hearth, but there was a vacancy between them, that was a sign of disagreement." [2]

Generally, however, the slaves worked hard to make their cabins as comfortable as possible. Many worked late into the night in order to acquire some simple furniture for their homes; some spent long hours caulking the chinks between the logs of their huts or inserting mud therein so that they and their children might gain at least some protection from the storms and the cold.

The supply of food given to the slaves varied from plantation to plantation. In most cases, however, the bare minimum for a week was the peck of cornmeal.

If the cornmeal was all the slave had, it was mixed with a little water, placed in the fire, and baked. When it was "done brown," the ashes were scraped off and it was placed on a "chip," the makeshift table. The slave was then ready to sit on the ground to eat.

Charles Ball reported that he was lucky enough to receive additional rations of one gallon of syrup and three pounds of meat. But because even such a dole as this was not sufficient, raids on the smokehouse were common. Although this was considered stealing by the master and the overseer, to the slave it was merely taking what he had worked for. But if a slave were caught stealing, his punishment would, generally, be severe.

On the rare occasion when a slave was allowed to cultivate

his own garden, the produce from the garden could be used only for home consumption, unless by special privilege the slave was allowed to sell some of it. Under no circumstances was a food allotment made for children under eight years of age—they ate only what their parents did not or would not eat.

Ball also stated that on Sundays and holidays, many slaves, both adults and children, were given biscuits which they called "cake bread." Coffee was made by parching cornmeal, okra seed, or Irish potatoes. Instead of sugar, syrup was used for sweetening.

With respect to the food supply in general, Ball explained, "it is not only food, but medicine to them, and their appetites keenly court the precious morsel; whilst the children, whose senses are all acute, seem to be indued with taste and smell in a tenfold degree, and manifest a ravenous craving for fresh meat, which it is painful to witness, without being able to gratify it."

When a family was fortunate enough to have meat, it generally found its cabin surrounded by the children of fellow slaves, begging for a piece. Slave families found it "idle to think of sharing with them the contents of the board for they were often thirty or forty in number and the largest raccoon would scarcely have made a mouthful for each of them." [3]

Where the food supply actually dipped below the level of subsistence, wrote Andrew Jackson, the slave resorted to every conceivable expedient to obtain food. During opossum season —when the opossums were plentiful and fat—slaves would often be permitted to go hunting. Returning from the hunt, they would steal and kill two or three fat pigs, skin them and bury the skins and entrails. Then they would skin the opossums, bury the bodies, and put the pigs "nicely dressed" in the skins into kettles to boil. When the master came upon the party of slaves and inquired what was in the kettle, "A fat possum," was the reply, accompanied by the presentation of appropriate proof.

Jackson said that when a turkey or other bird was the stolen dish, the slave would catch, dress, and eat it, and then take care to leave the feathers so scattered around as to implicate an imaginary fox. When potatoes were stolen, the gambit was to open the hog pen to give the appearance that they had been taken by the hogs.

When caught and reprimanded, the slaves lamented, "but we were often *very hungry too*, and could see no reason why, since we were compelled to work *without* wages, why we should not eat the fruits thereof." They pointed to the free wage-earner and expressed doubt that he would deem it a very great crime to eat a pig, or even an ox that might belong to one for whom he worked without pay. With tongue in cheek, they explained that, "it could not be expected, that poor, uneducated, 'ignorant' slaves should know any better than to yield to the 'first law of nature,' self-preservation, and occasionally infringe the more *refined* rules of civilized and Christianized society." [4]

Although it was not nearly as important to the slave as food and shelter, his clothing, or the lack of it, was a source of despair.

The narratives contained in the Federal Writers' Project reveal that once a year clothing was distributed. As a general proposition, the men were given one pair of shoes, one blanket, one hat and approximately five yards of coarse, home-spun cotton. The women received a corresponding outfit, and enough additional material to make one frock for each of their children. The shoes "were made of such hard leather until the wearers' feet were usually blistered before the shoes were broken in." The slaves made their own clothes. Although the allotment was insufficient, the slave could get more only by performing additional work.[5]

THE CROPS

No discussion by a slave of life on the plantation was ever complete without a description of the crops grown there and the role of the slave in their cultivation.

In general, the consensus among the slaves was that the proprietors of most plantations did not keep their lands in good condition and that they were unskillful cultivators. Although his statement is somewhat difficult to believe, Charles Ball said that if this were not the case, "the condition of the coloured people would not be, by any means, a comparatively unhappy one." [6]

Ball was convinced that the hardship and suffering of the slave population was attributable to the poverty and distress of the owners. He recognized that as "wretched as may be the state of the negroes, in the quarter, that of the master and his wife, and daughters, is, in many instances, not much more enviable in the old apartments of the great house." The slaves quickly learned that their food supply was to be found in whatever surplus the master and his family left. [7]

For most slaves, Ball explained, the worst conditions were to be found either on the cotton plantations or in the rice fields that skirt the deep swamps and morasses of the Southern rivers. In the tobacco fields, he said, cruelties were practiced, but "not so frequently by the owners, as the overseer of the slaves; but yet, the tasks are not so excessive as in the cotton region, nor is the press of labour so incessant throughout the year." On almost every tobacco plantation, the slaves were able to complete the work of preparing the tobacco by January, and sometimes earlier, leaving the winter months for some respite from the earlier toils of the year. [8]

In those plantations where cotton was the staple, much attention was paid to its cultivation. When the price rose in the English market, the slaves immediately felt the effects, for they were harder driven. The slave often thought that if the women of the world could see the female slaves and the little children picking cotton in the fields

till the blood runs from the tips of their fingers, where they have been pricked by the hard pod; or if they could see them dragging their baskets, all trembling, to the scale, for fear their weight should be short, and they should get the flogging which in such a case they know they must expect; or if they could see them bent double with constant stooping, and scourged on their bare back when they attempted to rise to straighten themselves for a moment: or witness the infliction of what are called slight punishments on these unfortunate creatures, they would, never in their lives wear another article made of slave-grown cotton.[9]

In addition to this passionate description of the tortures of the female slaves and the children who worked the cotton fields, John Brown also depicted, somewhat less graphically, the cultivation of cotton.

In the fall season, he reported, the ground was pulverized with the plow, in order to cut up and destroy the worms and insects which infect the cotton fields. If not destroyed, these worms would burrow into the ground until springtime, when they would emerge and eat the young plants. In March, the soil, having been fallow for the winter, was ridged. In April, the ridge was split by the plow, and the cotton seed sown by hand. The experienced slave could cast the seed a distance of five to eight feet before him. He was followed by a harrowing party, which would rake the earth over the seed. Within a week, the seed would show itself, and when it came up strong, it was chopped out with the hoe, spaced ten to twelve inches apart. A small plow, called a bull-tongued plow, was then run along the furrows, so as to fill up the hoe-holes and cover the crabgrass. The cotton plant did not begin to grow very fast until the roots struck subsoil. Meanwhile, all the slaves were sent to the fields to thin and weed the plants by hand-picking —a painstaking and, due to the constant stooping, painful process. With a burning sun beating on his head and back, and the heat reflecting upwards from the ground, it took a proficient slave approximately an hour and a half to hand-pick one fifty-acre row of cotton plants without once straightening his back.

The overseer would make the rounds of the field to see that the work was being done properly. For every "sprig of grain or stray weed that had been left in the row which has been thus 'dressed,' the slave who had left it got a flogging more or less severe." [10]

The slaves would be in the field as early as 5:00 A.M. They would work until noon, when they were allowed an hour for breakfast. At 1:00 P.M., they would return to the fields and work until it was too dark to see. When the cotton was ripe, all hands were sent out to pick it. Because their fingers were more delicate and tapered, the women usually picked cleaner and better than the men. Also, it was easier for the female to "lay hold of the cotton as it lies snug in the pod." [11]

Solomon Northup, another fugitive, personalized and completed the picture of cotton cultivation. When a new slave, unaccustomed to cotton-picking, was sent into the field, he was "whipped up smartly, and made for that day to pick as fast as he can possibly." His cotton was then weighed in the evening, and his "ability" was thus judged. Thereafter, he had to bring in the same weight for the remainder of the season, for if he fell short of his first day's quota, it was considered evidence that he had been lagging, and the penalty would be fifty lashes. [12]

Some slaves, Northup stated, seemed to have a natural attribute that enabled them to pick with great celerity, and with both hands, while others were utterly unable to come up to the ordinary standard. [13]

Care was the watchword, according to Charles Ball, in working about the cotton gin. In removing the seeds from the saws of the cotton gin, slaves were known to have their entire right hands torn out.[14]

Henry Bibb said that because they were never allowed time to go to the quarters during the day to nurse their children, the slave mothers, required to pick cotton along with the men, would carry their young to the fields. Bibb felt that this was one "reason why so very few slave children are raised on these cotton plantations." "The mothers had no time to take care of them—and they are often found dead in the field and in the quarter for want of the care of their mothers." [15]

Charles Ball reported that when the cotton season had been bad and, consequently the crop light, the picking was often completed and the field cleared before the first of January. Conversely, when the crops were heavy, or if the slaves had been sickly in the fall, the picking was frequently protracted until February or even the beginning of March. It was estimated by the slaves that a good hand could cultivate and pick five acres of cotton. Five acres of cotton usually yielded ten thousand pounds of rough, or seed, cotton. Northup estimated that if the slave worked for twenty-five days a month, the picking of ten thousand pounds usually occupied him for more than six months. When the picking season ended, the harvesting of corn began. Corn was a secondary crop and received far less attention than the cotton. It was grown for the purpose of fattening hogs and feeding slaves. Very little, if any, was sent to market. As soon as the cotton and corn crops were secured, the stalks were pulled up, thrown into piles, and burned. Completing the annual cycle, the plows were started again, preparatory to another planting.[16]

Perhaps the most unhealthy occupation in which the slave was engaged, according to John Brown, was the cultivation of rice. Rice was grown in the muddy soil into which the slave sank knee-deep, his own footsteps sending up the foul-smelling vapors which inevitably caused fever and disease. The heat alone, reflected back from the water, was intolerably painful and frequently brought on sunstroke. His feet would get water poisoning or a malady they called "the toe or ground itch," when the flesh cracks and cankers. Rice plantation slaves would also attract the chigger, a small insect that punctured the skin under the toe and deposited an egg. The egg would soon hatch, producing a very minute maggot, which grew in the flesh and caused swelling and unendurable irritation. In addition, the field hand was constantly on his guard for fear of getting bitten by water moccasins. Fevers, agues, rheumatism, pleurisies, asthmas, and consumption were among the illnesses contracted in the rice swamps. It was, to say the least, "very much more trying than either cotton or tobacco cultivation." [17]

In the tobacco regions, Brown said, planting time was extremely hard. This was true for all the slaves, but it was especially so for the children. According to Brown they were considered better able than adults to creep among the plants and pick out the weeds with their little fingers. It was, too, a difficult time for the aged slaves, who, from constant stooping, "could not stand up straight to save their lives." The driver was "very sharp and active during this season; and if he sees a hand 'straighten' from his work, that is, stand up a minute to rest his back, down comes the bull whip, across the shoulders of the unfortunate man or woman, with a loud crack like a pistol shot." [18]

As the tobacco plant grew stronger, so too did the menace of the tobacco fly looking for a place to lay her eggs. This dreaded insect would come out in the evening and lay one egg on each leaf. If the egg were not picked off, it hatched by the next night, and in "two days there is a caterpiller, or grub, as big as a man's little finger." To guard against this hazard, gangs were sent around early every morning to hunt for the eggs and grubs and pick them off. The grubs were described as tough, filthy, and "blobby." In order to be removed effectively, they had to be torn in two. If, after the plants were picked, the overseer found a grub left, he "would call to the slave in whose row he had found it, and forcing his mouth open, rub the vermin against his teeth to teach him to have sharper eyes in the future." [19]

On the tobacco plantation, plowing, planting, picking, pulling, and burning stalks occupied the slave for the entire year. Although he also engaged in drawing and cutting wood, pressing cotton, and fattening and killing hogs, this was but incidental labor.

J. D. Green stated, and the Federal Writers' Project confirmed, that no matter what the crop, all except the house servants were forced to work in the fields. At an assigned hour, one slave, known as a "caller," would come to each of the cabins. He blew a cow horn, which was the signal for the slaves to get up and prepare themselves for the day's work. The hours of work depended upon the season. Often, at planting or harvest time, they would work from sunup to as late as ten or eleven at night.[20]

As described by Thomas H. Jones:

Men and women were called at three o'clock in the morning, and were worked on the plantation till it was dark at night. After that they must prepare their food for supper and for the breakfast of the next day, and attend to other duties of their own dear homes. Parents would often have to work for their children at home, after each day's protracted toil, till the middle of the night, and then snatch a few hours sleep, to get strength for the heavy burdens of the next day.[21]

Most of the narratives of the Federal Writers' Project agree that during the winter months, in addition to working in the fields, the men and women spent time clearing up new lands, chopping and burning bushes, and digging ditches. According to Thomas H. Jones, they worked on cold stormy days in the open fields, "while the piercing wind and driving storm benumbed their limbs, and almost froze the tears that came forth out of their cold desolate hearts." Children, too, he related, worked and cried, toting brush to the fires, husking the corn, watching the stock and running errands for master and mistress, receiving only scoldings and beatings as compensation.[22]

When work was done the cow horn was again blown and all hands stopped work. It was at this point in the day that one could most easily recognize one of the many ways in which the slaves displayed their resistance to dehumanization. For, one behind the other, they marched home singing, "I'm gonna wait 'til Jesus Comes"; and after dinner, they would gather in front of one of the cabins and dance to tunes played on the fiddle and the drum.[23]

MARRIAGE AND FAMILY LIFE

Perhaps the most important factor in their struggle to retain their humanity was the slaves' insistence upon maintaining the sanctity of marriage and the warmth of family life.

Marriage

Solomon Northup recognized that for him marriage, in the ordinary, legal sense, did not exist. The only requirement for entering into a marriage was the consent of the master. In most cases, slaves were encouraged to marry, for marriage was to the master like animal breeding, and had as its purpose the increase of his "stock." Unlike most Americans, slaves were permitted to have more than one mate; as many, in fact, as the owner would allow. Nevertheless, recognizing a moral law, and in defiance of the institution, many felt that it was wrong to have more than one spouse and refused, to the best of their ability, to do so. The slave was also at liberty to discard a mate with his owner's consent. Thus, asserted William Wells Brown, "there has never yet a case occurred where a slave has been tried for bigamy. The man may have as many women as he wishes, and the women as many men; and the law takes no cognizance of such acts among slaves." [24]

Kate Pickard, who recorded the experiences of Peter and Vina Still, reported that some slaves were not permitted to marry off the plantation; rather the master would manage to bring couples together locally and make a match. If either slave refused to participate, he or she was beaten into submission.[25]

Other slaves were permitted to marry "abroad" (off the plantation). Marrying abroad, they stated, required the consent of both masters. According to these accounts, physically small men were not allowed to marry large, robust women. If the male was big and healthy and the female on a nearby plantation looked as though she might be a "good breeder," the owners agreed to mutual visits, and passes were frequently given. The Georgia Narratives of the Federal Writers' Project indicate that some slaves preferred to marry abroad for they were thereby spared the sight of their mates being frequently beaten. For this reason, too, others refused to marry at all.[26]

In accordance with their desire to maintain their identities, the great majority of slaves who did marry insisted upon some celebration of the occasion. Bethany Veney related that the marriage ceremony itself was basically the same on all plantations. Usually a party was arranged for a Saturday night. A broom was placed flat down in the center of the room and the couple was directed to join hands. Together they jumped over the broom, turned around and jumped back. The ceremony thus completed, the master pronounced them husband and wife.[27]

Aside from any subconscious desire to resist the effects of the institution, most slaves married because they wanted companionship—someone with whom they could share their love. Many "yearned to have a home," even "if it was only the wretched home of the unprotected slave, to have a wife to love [him] and to love." One slave, Thomas H. Jones, recognizing the dehumanizing effects of slavery, stated that the slave who was "despised and trampled upon by a cruel race of unfeeling men" would "die in the prime of his wretched life, if he [found] no refuge in a dear home, where love and sympathy shall meet him from hearts made sacred to him by his own irrepressible affection and tenderness for them." [28]

Marriage between slaves sometimes accommodated their own personal affections, but it was always in the financial interest of the master. Therefore, the feelings of the slaves were more or less indulged as the master's interest varied. As one articulate former slave concluded:

Legally, there is no such relation as husband and wife among slaves, because the law adjudges them to be things, and not men and women. They are chattels in law, and their sexual relations in contemplation of law are the same as any other animals. The whole affair is in the hand of the master as a means of the increase and improvement of stock. Other important motives sometimes blend with it and subject it to ulterior views. But the end purpose is the same. The slave being "property to all intents," is subject of course, to the laws relating to "things" and not to "persons." [29]

The Concept of Family Life

The sanctuary of the slave's humanity was his home and family. Daniel H. Peterson conceived that the Southern slaveholder feared that real family life among slaves could undermine the foundation of slavery itself. Peterson reasoned that the master was afraid that family ties could produce loyalty to someone other than the master; such loyalty could result in insolence and disobedience. If he permitted such ties to be established, Peterson said, it could "like some alarming and death dealing infection . . . spread from plantation to plantation, until property in husbands and wives would not be worth having." Hence, the slaveholder was convinced that family life had to succumb to slavery and slavery must reign supreme over every right and every other institution, however venerable or sacred.[30]

Nevertheless, the slave married and made an attempt to raise and maintain his family. Each family had its own personal rules in the quarters, which were strictly followed by all members of that family. For example, although many parents sat up nights discussing family problems, it was the general rule not to allow their young children to enter into the conversation. Hence, most young slaves were unaware of the mental anguish of their parents.

With respect to these slave children, one slave told Benjamin Drew that if a slave married and had children, the master considered these children "of no more consequence to him [the slave] than the calf is to the cow." If the master disliked these children, he took them to the slave market and "puts them under the hammer." [31]

Nonetheless, Sarah Bradford, writing of the experiences of Harriet Tubman, stated that some slaves felt that they sacrificed and endured more for their families than the master for his. Although the threat of separation was always present, reported Sam Aleckson, the slaves patiently endured in order to teach the principles of family life. All of their pleasure came from the family and they spent what free time they had in family assemblage.[32]

Henry Bibb asserted that as for parenthood itself, the slave considered the term "father" a misnomer, for though he tried to fulfill this position, he knew he could never prevent separation from, or even flogging of, his children. He continually expressed the fear that his children were destined to share his fate. Bibb felt that if there was one act in his life that he lamented, "it was that of being a father and a husband of slaves." Some, he claimed, expressed satisfaction that they had only one child, for this would relieve them of the burden of seeing a large family in bondage. Commenting on his child,

Bibb said: "She is bone of my bone, and flesh of my flesh; poor unfortunate child. She was the first and shall be the last slave that I will ever father for chains and slavery on this earth." [33]

This feeling was also expressed by Thomas H. Jones, who wrote:

I am a father, and have had the same feelings of unspeakable anguish, as I have looked upon my precious babes, and have thought of the ignorance, degradation and woe which they must endure as slaves. The great God who knoweth all the secrets of the earth, and He only, knows the bitter sorrow I now feel, when I think of my four dear children who are slaves, torn from me and consigned to hopeless servitude by the iron hand of ruthless wrong. I love those children with all a father's fondness. [34]

Because of the masters' numerous attempts to destroy the family relationship, some slaves admitted that it was almost impossible to give a correct account of their male parentage. Many slave children had no personal knowledge of their fathers. Nevertheless, social affections were strong and extremely difficult to weaken. Indeed, brutality on the part of the master seemed to make the slave cling more closely to the family, thus intensifying his suffering when separation came. [35]

Break-up of Families

Slaves condemned the apologist of slavery and the slaveholder for denying that the separation of families, except for purposes of punishment, was practiced. In fact, separation by sale was an integral part of the system. Not only was it resorted to by severe masters, but also by those who were regarded as mild. As a punishment none was so dreaded by the refractory slave as being sold. The atrocities known to have been committed on plantations were far less feared than impending sale. [36]

The master's circumstances and not his own often determined if a slave were to be assigned to the trading block or the rice swamps. Since most slaves preferred to deal with even the most hideous circumstance so long as it was familiar, rather than the uncertainties of another plantation, they were quite concerned about the financial status and social activities and habits of their master. For example, Francis Fedric was aware that his master's continued high living was a source of danger to him and his fellow slaves and expressed the fear that his master might be killed in a duel, at a horse race, or in a drunken brawl. He reported that other slaves were terrified of a master who gambled heavily. The self-indulgent behavior of such masters could result in the sale of the master's estate, and slaves were the first property to be sold. What followed, according to Fedric, was "the blow of the auctioneer's hammer separating them perhaps for life." [37]

There were, according to Austin Steward, other reasons for the sale of slaves. If the master owed a debt, spare slaves were taken to the trader and sold. [38]

In addition, as Henry Box Brown explained, when a master died his property was inherited by his family. The human, as well as every other kind of property, was divided. Often, Brown said, no one wanted the children or the aged. Thus, the heirs made their division according to the money value of the slaves without the slightest consideration for social or family ties. The common theory, according to Brown, was that such considerations do not matter because " 'niggers' have no feelings." [39]

William Wells Brown stated that some slaves were sold because of their leadership. He asserted that there was, in every slave family, a "militant" slave. According to Brown, the master feared the influence of this slave in his quarters, and thus "such a one must take a walking ticket to the south." [40]

Peter Randolph recorded that not one word of warning was given the family of the impending sale. Husbands were seized by the trader, "wives were torn and thrust into that living grave; children were torn shrieking from their parents, never to see them more; tender maidens were dragged from the manly hearts which loved them; the ardent lover was scornfully compelled to break from the entwining arm of his loved one, and bid a final adieu to all the world held dear to his heart." [41]

Lydia Maria Child, a white woman who collected and recorded narratives dictated to her by fugitive slaves, found that some slave mothers reacted violently when their children were sold away. She tells of one instance that occurred in 1834, in Marion County, Missouri. A slave trader bought three small children from a planter. The mother became so violent that she was lashed and chained. During the night she managed to escape. She went to where the boys were sleeping, took an axe and chopped off their heads, and then ended her own life with the same instrument. The only concern of the trader whose "unrighteous bargain drove the wretched mother to this act of desperation," according to Miss Child, was his financial loss. [42]

Lewis Clarke tells of another slave mother who became so distraught upon being informed of the imminent sale of her children that she threw her three infants into a well and then jumped in after them.

Many slaves, said Clarke, experienced conflicting emotions at the death of their children. The first was one of joy, that their child was beyond the reach of the slave trader; the second was the natural grief over the loss of a loved one. Alone in the solitude of the quarters, claimed Clarke, many parents felt relieved of the burden of raising a slave. Some, he alleges, expressed a wish that their children be stillborn. [43]

Francis Fedric witnessed some mothers who were so terrified in the trader's presence that they remained absolutely silent. Fedric felt that this reaction was ordinarily the more prudent because anyone who voiced the most minor objection —that it was difficult for him to be carried away from his wife and children—would be instantly beaten. On one occasion,

Fedric reported, one planter remarked to a trader who was beating a slave he had just bought that he would kill him if he continued. "You are not going to throw away your money in that way, are you?" the planter said. The trader's response was only, "I don't care, I have bought him, he is mine, and for one cent, I would kill him. I never allow a slave to talk back to me after I have bought him." [44]

Children, according to Solomon Northup, aware of some impending danger at the trading block, instinctively fastened their hands around their mother's neck. If either mother or child were ultimately sold, one could hear such cries as, "Don't leave me, mama— Don't leave me. Don't leave me. Don't leave me—come back mama." Northup occasionally heard slave women who had been separated from their children talking to their children in the cotton fields and cabins as if they were present.[45]

Slave reaction to the sale ranged from anger to sorrow. Peter Randolph asked the defenders of the institution to place themselves in the slaves' situation:

Pro slavery men and women! for one moment only, in imagination, stand surrounded by *your* loved ones, and behold *them*, one by one, torn from your grasp, or you rudely and forcibly carried from them—how, think you, would you bear it? Would you not rejoice if one voice, even, were raised in your behalf? Were your wife, the partner of your bosom, the mother of your babes, thus ruthlessly snatched from you, were your beloved children stolen before your eyes, would you not think it sufficient cause for a nation's wail? Yea, and a nation's interference! What better are for them those poor downtrodden children of humanity? With them such scenes are constantly transpiring.[46]

Henry Box Brown also described his feelings of sorrow over the loss of his child:

These beings were marched with ropes about their necks, and staples on their arms, and, although in that respect the scene was no very novel one to me, yet the peculiarity of my own circumstances made it assume the appearance of unusual horror. The train of beings was accompanied by a number of wagons loaded with little children of many different families, which as they appeared rent the air with their shrieks and cries and vain endeavors to resist the separation which was thus forced upon them, and the cords with which they were thus bound; but what should I now see in the very foremost wagon but a little child looking towards me and pitifully calling, father! father!

And, further, the despair of his separation from his wife:

I looked from the approach of another gang in which my wife was also loaded with chains. My eye soon caught her precious face, but, gracious heaven! that glance of agony my God spare me from ever again enduring! My wife, under the influence of her feelings, jumped aside; I seized hold of her hand while my mind felt unutterable things, and my tongue was only able to say, we shall meet in heaven! I went with her for about four miles hand in hand, but both our hearts were so overpowered with feeling that we could say nothing, and when at last we were obliged to part, the look of mutual love which we exchanged was all the token which we could give each other that we should yet meet in heaven.[47]

According to Josiah Henson, some slaves voluntarily left their families. These, he said, felt that rather than remain at home to be sold away, they would escape. Sometimes these fugitives were tormented by guilt at having abandoned their families and, consequently, they returned and successfully brought their families out. Some who escaped confessed that it was one of the most self-denying acts of their lives. Taking leave of an affectionate wife and child, reported Levi Coffin, to whom many narratives were dictated, often required all the courage that they could gather. Most slaves indicated to him that the strong attachments to friends and relatives, with all the love of home and birth place which is so natural among the human family, were hard to break away from. Despite their escape, wrote Henry Bibb, most fugitives asserted that this act did not extinguish the love they bore for wife or child.[48]

EDUCATION

For those families that remained together (and even among those who did not), education was, when permitted, a prime concern.

Frederick Douglass remembered the difficulties involved in acquiring knowledge. He explained that because the danger that accompanied the acquisition of knowledge was far greater than the reward of literacy, few slaves had any desire to acquire an education, and even fewer obtained one. The slave state statute books were "covered with enactments forbidding, under severe fines and penalties, the teaching of the slave to read or to write." To educate a slave was to make him discontented with slavery, wrote Douglass, and to invest in him a power which could open the treasuries of freedom. Thus, he reasoned, since the object of the master was to maintain complete control over the slave, constant vigilance was exercised to prevent anything which would militate against or endanger the stability of his authority. One did not often hear of the enforcement of this law, or of the punishment imposed for teaching slaves to read. This was not because of a want of disposition to enforce it, claimed Douglass, for there was, among the slaveholding population, the greatest unanimity of opinion "in favor of the policy of keeping the slave in ignorance." In fact, limited enforcement of this law was due to the lack of desire on the part of the freeman to violate it. Moreover, the vast majority of slaves were in no position, financially or otherwise, to offer "temptation sufficiently strong to induce a white man to violate." Nevertheless there were freemen who were willing to risk the sacrifice of their lives or liberty by offering education to slaves. As a general rule, however, the darkness of illiteracy reigned.[49]

Booker T. Washington, the great Negro educator, reported that most educated slaves were early motivated either by innate curiosity or accident. Often, according to Washington, slaves would accompany the children of the "great house" to school and would wonder what was contained in the books they carried. The schoolroom itself, filled with apparently happy white children, made a deep and lasting impression on the servant. To many, to get into a schoolhouse and study "would be about the same as getting into paradise." Yet, to have seen a slave with the ability to read and write would have been, in the words of James Roberts, "not much short of a miracle; it would have been a very great curiosity, so much so, that hundreds would have gone fifty or a hundred miles to see such a one." [50]

Lewis Clarke was such a child. After receiving some aid from the children of the plantation, he diligently spent his free time at his newly acquired talent. When the mistress was informed that Lewis had learned spelling, she "jumped up as though she had been shot. 'Let me ever know you to spell another word,'" she screeched, "'I'll take your heart right out of you.'" [51]

Most slaves, albeit eager to learn, found themselves in similar situations. The Georgia Narratives reported that the owners who caught their sons teaching slaves to read and write would become so furious they would give their children severe beatings, and cut off the thumb and forefinger of the slave. Such mutilation became known as the sign of attempted education. [52]

Nevertheless, to many slaves education represented a positive step in their struggle to resist the institution and, therefore, some still attempted to acquire this forbidden knowledge. Jamie Parker had heard a great deal about learning to read and write. He had heard the master tell and read about the beautiful scriptural histories and he wanted to read them for himself. However, for fear of betrayal, he had never expressed his desires. He was soon to become acquainted with a fellow slave named Scipio, who had been educated while working as a hired slave in a neighboring town. Scipio agreed to teach him the fundamentals of reading and writing, but explained to the boy the necessity of secrecy. Without it, he said, they would place themselves in great danger.

After a time, Jamie was able to spell out words and read limited parts of the Bible. The two met in secrecy for many months, until one day the patrol, making its monthly rounds, came upon them. Each member of the patrol "then gave Jamie a smart cuff, by way of testifying their disapprobation of his willingness to be taught." The incident was reported to the overseer, who immediately took measures to stop Jamie from learning to read. After representing to him the enormity of this crime, he told him that hanging was in order. Acting as judge, jury, and executioner, he proceeded to take summary vengeance for the broken laws of the community by lashing the naked back and shoulders of the child. He administered his whip thoroughly so that the slave would "done forget what he learned!" Not satisfied with merely beating him, he washed his lacerated wounds in salt water. The overseer "had his *own* good reasons for insisting that 'the people' should not be instructed, for he could neither read nor write himself." For the crime of teaching, Scipio was put to death.[53]

Some slaves were so strongly motivated that despite such penalties as those inflicted upon Jamie Parker and Scipio, they managed to buy or steal spelling books, and attempted to teach themselves to read. Austin Steward's every spare moment was devoted to this self-education, and when at work he could "catch now and then a stolen glance, just to refresh the memory with the simple lesson [he was] trying to learn."

When Thomas H. Jones was discovered trying to educate himself, he was told that it was not for such as he to try to improve, that he was a slave, and "it was not proper for [him] to learn to read." He recognized this as a manifestation of the white man's need to maintain his supremacy over the poor outraged slaves.[54]

There were, of course, some whites who attempted to educate the slaves, and consequently, there were some success stories. As a child of eight, John Thompson would often be sent to the local schoolhouse with the white children, to carry their dinners; and one of them, who sought to befriend him, offered to teach him to read and write. They sometimes started out an hour or two before school time, and, in order to escape the observation of the other children, they would hold classes in the woods. John spent virtually every spare moment studying. He soon finished his first book, which was Webster's Spelling Book, and advanced to the English Reader. Next, he was introduced to writing exercises. So excited had he become with his new-found talents that he would steal away from his cabin at night to study in the open field.[55]

When John's teacher was about to leave the plantation, he said to him, "I am sorry John, that I cannot teach you longer. But you must not forget what you have learned, and try to improve what you can by yourself." Happily, John Thompson was later able to proclaim that he would forever be in debt to this slaveholder's son who gave him the rudiments of this "greatest blessing"—his education.[56]

Some slaves were driven to desire this blessing by the examples set by whites. Thomas H. Jones, for example, recalled a boyhood experience that strongly influenced his thinking. While working as a hireling, he met a young white man who could hardly read or write. Accordingly, the white youth spent a part of each day studying reading and writing. He permitted Thomas to see his books and answered all his questions about them. Thomas asked the young man why he was so diligently engaged in these activities. He answered that he was "trying to get learning enough to fit him to do a good business for himself." He said that "a man who had learning would always find friends, and get along very well in the world without having to work hard, while those with no learning would have no friends and be compelled to work very hard for a poor living all their days." [57]

These "radical" words incited the slave to thought. He became possessed of an "intense burning desire to learn to read and write." Realizing that he could not accomplish his task alone, he soon engaged a small child, ten years old, who came into the store for some candy. He beckoned the child to meet him at the rear of the store, and there they struck a bargain. They were to meet each day at noon when the slave's dinner time arrived, and in exchange for his education, he would pay the child six cents. Ultimately deprived of his teacher by discovery, Thomas continued by himself and was soon learning to read. He sensed "at night, as he went to his rest, that he was really beginning to be a *man*, preparing himself for a condition in life better and higher and happier than could belong to the ignorant *slave*." [58]

Levi Coffin reported that some slaves were fortunate enough to belong to masters who offered them the skills of writing and reading. A few benevolent individuals established Sunday schools for the instruction of such as might be permitted by their master to learn. These slaves gathered at the appointed hour, wondering at their new and unexpected privilege. They were usually arranged in separate classes and taught the alphabet. In the beginning, wrote Coffin, "they were so excited with the novelty of the situation that they accomplished little." As the lessons continued they made more progress, and in a short time some of them mastered the alphabet and began to spell words of two or three letters. These slaves, mostly adults, were dull and difficult to teach, though they tried hard. Naturally, said Coffin, when the news of this activity spread, community pressure forced most masters to abandon the scheme. In one reported case the other slaveholders were so hostile that they "threatened to put the law in force against us, and visiting those who had let their slaves attend our school, told them they were guilty as well as the teachers, and that the school must be discontinued. They said that it made their slaves discontented and uneasy, and created a desire for the privileges that others had." [59]

Kate Pickard confirmed Coffin and said that the typical master would not have his "niggers spoiled by getting learning —no indeed." He felt, according to Miss Pickard, that "niggers" were bad enough, without being upset by such rascals as these Sunday school teachers; that "they'd better not meddle with *his* property, and if he heard of one of *his* boys going near the school, he'd give him such a flogging that he'd never need any more education." [60]

Miss Pickard and Levi Coffin both reported that many slaves met secretly, and together learned to read the Bible. [61]

Austin Steward wrote:

Knowledge is power! But it is not like the withering curse of a tyrant's power; not like the degrading and brutilizing power of the slave-driver's lash, chains and thumbscrews, not like the beastly, demonical power of rum, nor like the brazen, shameless power of lust; but a power that elevates and refines the intellect; directs the affections; controls unholy passions; a power so God-like in its character, that it enables its possessor to feel for the oppressed of every clime, and prepares him to defend the weak and down trodden. [62]

Thus James Roberts was able to report that, with the aid of their secret education, his brethren *were* capable of doing what other races could do. He could demonstrate to the majority of the slaves that the Negro was as susceptible to intellectual attainment as any other people. They were, he urged, not only susceptible to high mental impressions, but also able to discharge the duties connected with any station in civilized life, even those that required the highest grade of education. [63]

According to John Hawkins Simpson, another white man

who collected and preserved slave narratives, the slaveholder claimed that the anti-education codes were enacted in self-defense against the agitation caused by the abolitionists, and that their objective was to keep from their slaves knowledge which would become a dangerous and violent power. Having enacted these codes for the purpose of maintaining ignorance, they told the nation that they were men who pitied and cared for the slaves' helpless condition, and pointed to that ignorance (of their own creation, said Simpson) as the reason why freedom would be harmful to the slave. The slaveholder argued that he wanted to keep the slave free from the "contaminating effects of an unshackled press." The slaves who dictated to Simpson generally responded to these expressions of paternal solicitude by asserting that they were completely devoid of gratitude for all its goodness, sympathy, and foresight, and that the black men fervently desired *to be left to shift for themselves.* [64]

RELIGION

One did not need an education to feel what Josiah Henson reported: when he saw the slave pens for the first time, his "faith in God utterly gave way." Henson felt that God had abandoned him, had cast him off forever, and that he could not turn to him for help. Henson saw "the foul miasmas, the emaciated frames of my negro companions; and in them saw the sure, swift, loving intervention of the one unfailing friend of the wretched, death!"

Linda Brent, on the other hand, stated that parents *did* strive to make their children feel that it was the will of God; that He had seen fit to place the Negro under such circumstances, and though it seemed futile, they ought to pray for contentment. [65]

Many slaves did not know what to think about religion. One unknown slave expressed his confusion when he stated:

They say God killed the just and unjust; I don't understand that part of it. It looks hard to think that if you ain't done nothing in the world you be punished just like the wicked. Plenty folkes went crazy trying to get that thing straightened out.[66]

In this section we will attempt to examine the nature and extent of the religious instruction which the slaves received, and, to some degree, the effectiveness and results of that instruction.

Religious Instruction

The narratives indicate that with respect to religious instruction, there were generally three basic situations extant in the slave states: (*a*) no religious instruction at all; (*b*) formal or organized instruction, more or less along the lines of the established gospel, either with or without the permission of the slaveholders; or (*c*) makeshift or fraudulent instruction designed solely to "keep the slaves in line."

Charles Ball reported that throughout the slave states the slave was discouraged, as much as possible and by all means possible, from going to places of worship and receiving instruction. The rationale behind this discouragement was that the slaves from various plantations and distant parts of the neighborhood, must be kept from getting together where they might plot conspiracies and insurrections.[67]

Another reason to discourage religious instruction, according to Ball, was not because the planter was disposed toward depriving them of the comforts of religion (provided the religious principles did not militate against the principles of slavery) but because of his fear that the slave, by attending these meetings and listening to the preachers, may come away with a morality which included the concepts of equality and liberty. Furthermore, masters who even entertained thoughts of granting their slaves permission to study the gospel would recall the oft-stated philosophy that any man "who allowed his slave to have Bibles, was not fit to own a nigger." [68]

Many masters were more direct in stifling religious instruction. James Williams reports that his master told the quarters that although there was surely a hell for the slaves, there was, however, no hell for white people, who had their punishment on earth in being obliged to take care of the slaves. He would frequently read passages from the Bible to the slaves pronouncing those he agreed with true and the balance lies. He felt that praying and singing prevented his slaves from doing their work and he would constantly interrupt the slaves who, after the day's work, were praying in their cabins. This master would make excursions at night through the slave cabins frightening the slaves engaged in prayer or psalm-singing. On one occasion, Williams reported, a slave was forced up a chimney "in order that his voice might not be heard by his brutal persecutor." Another, while praying, asked how long he would be in bondage. Suddenly, " 'as long as my whip!' cried the overseer, who had stolen behind him, giving him a blow." This same overseer had discovered an aged slave with a Bible and he thereupon declared that he would "have an end of 'nigger' preaching." He set the Bible on fire, mixed the ashes with water and forced the slave to drink it. [69]

Discouragement of religious instruction was reported by Francis Fedric to have been couched in the following language of a master: "You niggers have no souls, you are just like those cattle, when you die there is an end of you, there is nothing more for you to think about than living. White people only have souls." [70]

With respect to those areas in which there existed at least a semblance of organized or formal religious instruction, it was often the custom, recorded by Louis Hughes, to have a white minister preach to the servants on Sunday afternoon, after the morning service for the slaveholder. If no preacher was available, he said, often the master himself would fill the role.[71]

As for the services themselves, they were often held not in church, but at the plantation. On some plantations the slaves would gather in a yard or at the great house. They were generally pleased and eager to hear the instruction.[72]

According to Hughes, some masters took a certain pride in having their "gangs" appear clean and neat at the service.[73]

Sam Aleckson, reporting generally in accord with Hughes, remembered that when the meeting ended the slaves left quietly, usually not talking until they were dispersed. Then, they would go to their tasks, some fortified by those few moments of prayer and meditation.[74]

Most of the narratives received by Benjamin Drew recited that as a general rule the preacher, white or black, failed to preach the entire gospel. The slave never heard any of the passages about letting the oppressed go free, about the loosening of the bands of wickedness, or of breaking the yoke of bondage. If a black preacher were to say this, Drew recorded, he would be jailed or sold, and if a white man were to say it, "he'd have to leave, because they'd say he was 'putting too much into the niggers' heads.' "[75]

Anthony Burns reported that among the Christian slaves there were some that were regarded by both the black and white community as "quasi pastors" or preachers. Without being formally inducted to the office by any rite or ordination, they received a special kind of recognition from the church with which they were connected. Piety, ability at exhortation, and the desire to preach, were the requisite qualifications. They gathered their congregations in convenient and accessible sites, sometimes in the kitchen of a sympathetic white, sometimes in the cabin of a slave. Their meetings, as well as all other assemblies consisting exclusively of slaves, were flagrant violations of the whites' code of slavery. Consequently each of such meetings was subject to interruption, and those slaves that were caught were severely punished. The masters' patrols guarded nightly, and walked their rounds constantly on the watch for secret slave meetings. Often, while the meeting was in prayer, "the door would be suddenly burst open by a throng of profane officials, each with cord in hand, bent on securing as many victims as possible." Immediately, the lights would be extinguished and through every door, window, and chimney, the slaves would hurriedly make their escape.[76]

In order to escape detection, wrote Peter Randolph, the slaves often assembled in the swamps, out of reach of the patrols. They had various methods of communicating to their fellows the time and place of the meeting. For example, the first arrival at a selected site would, on his way, break branches from a tree and bend them in the direction of the spot.

When the group was finally assembled, the "preacher" generally began by calling himself unworthy and talking until he aroused the excitement of the group. Randolph reported that soon each member of the group would forget his own personal suffering, except occasionally to remind the others of his difficulties during the past week. They would pass from one to another shaking hands and saying, "Thank God, I shall not live here always." Then, as the meeting ended and they separated, they sang a parting hymn of praise.[77]

Some plantations had black preachers, both bond and free, who held midweek meetings in the quarters and preached to the slaves every Sunday in the master's church. According to Henry Clay Bruce, at each such meeting and sermon there was always a white man present to take note of what was preached. If the topic, or even the words used, were deemed insubordinate, or antislavery, the meeting was quickly stopped, and the preacher was lectured about his mistake, and in some cases even barred from preaching there again.

Because most slaves could not read, said Bruce, most of the slave preachers could not read their texts or any other part of the Bible. Nevertheless, "they stood in the pulpit, opened the bible, gave out the song which did not always fit the tune, and delivered prayer with much force and in language that, while not the choicest, greatly impressed its hearers." [78]

Aside from the more formal or group instruction, most slave parents, according to Henry Box Brown, would instruct their children in the principles of religion in accordance with their own notions of what was to be taught. Thus, the lessons in morality were basic and fundamental. The slave was not to steal, or lie, and was to behave himself in a manner becoming a proper human being. [79]

Anthony Burns was one such slave child who had been subjected to intensive religious training throughout his childhood. His mother, a devoutly religious person, attempted to inculcate in him her religious feelings. He had been greatly impressed by the camp meetings and the local slave preacher. During his bondage, the doctrines of William Miller (an evangelist who, in 1831, announced that Christ's second coming and the end of the world would be in 1843) had penetrated Burns's area of Virginia, and both white and black alike became alarmed. The barriers of caste were laid aside for the moment and a free and unreserved communication developed between master and slave. Burns shared this excitement and earnestly set about preparing for his future life. He received permission to be baptized and was accepted into the local Baptist Church, whose membership included both whites and slaves. Everyone in the church worshipped in the same room, and only a partition of boards separated the free from the slave. He reported:

When the Holy supper was administered, the cup was first carefully served to all of the privileged class, and afterward to their sable brethren. Those distinctions were not maintained in anticipation of heaven, but in deference to the prejudices of Virginia society. In the social religious meetings there was a somewhat nearer approach to the New Testament model, and the prayers and exhortations of the slaves were graciously suffered to intermingle with those proceeding from the master's lips.[80]

Finally, with regard to the situation in which the religious instruction was merely a guise, Peter Randolph claimed that the only prominent preaching to slaves was for the slave to obey his master; that stealing or lying was wrong; and that such conduct was a sin against the "Holy Ghost, *and is base ingratitude to your kind masters, who feed, clothe and protect you.*" In other words, to Randolph, and others who shared his sentiments, religion was merely a ploy by which the master sought to control the slave by allowing him the "wonderous privilege of such holy instruction." [81]

Randolph reported that when making their religious pronouncements, the slaveholders must surely have felt "the rebuke of the apostle" for having "betrayed the trust committed to them, or" for having "refused to bear true testimony in regard to that trust." He stated that as the slaveholder taught it, the "Gospel was so mixed with slavery, that the people could see no beauty in it, and feel no reverence for it." Randolph claimed that the preachments of the slaveholders had better be buried in oblivion, for it made the slave more a heathen than a Christian. He said that he would rather see such preachers forbidden by law to speak, than to preach the religion which "was sent as a light to the world." [82]

Josiah Henson reported that many slaves believed that there was, somewhere, a real Bible that came from God, but that the bible being used by the master was the "master's bible." Lewis Clarke thought the reason for this suspicion was that the only thing they heard from it was, "servants, obey your masters." James Roberts described a typical master's sermon as, "O, how you should love the precious truths of the lord, my servants; they are so wise and so adapted to your condition. For, by obeying your master you obey God. Do

not steal. This is another truth of equal import. How con-
descending God is, not to have forgotten you, my servants,
in his world." [83]

J. D. Green was told by the white minister how good God
was in bringing the Negro to this country from Africa, and
permitting him to listen to the sound of the gospel.

He reported that the slaveholder told the slaves that when
God was making man, he made the white man out of the best
clay, and the devil made the black man out of some black
mud, and "called him a nigger." According to Green, the
master continually impressed upon the slave the necessity of
being "a good boy," and that if he led a "good life" he might
even go to heaven. Preachers and masters reminded the slaves
of the advantages they had in bondage, for when they were
in their native country, they were destitute of the Bible, wor-
shipping idols of sticks and stones, and barbarously murdering
one another. Green was told that God had put it into the hearts
of the good masters to venture across the ocean to Africa,
"and snatch us poor negroes as brands from the eternal burning, and bring us where we might sit under the droppings of
his sanctuary, and learn the ways of industry and the way of
God. 'Oh, nigger' how happy are your eyes which see this
heavenly light; many millions of niggers desired it long, but
died without the sight." [84]

Green said that he and other slaves were frequently told
that the master envied their situation, because God's special
blessing seemed to be over them as though they were a select
people, and that their position was much happier than that of a
free man, who, if sick, had to pay doctor's fees; if hungry,
must supply his wants at his own expense; or if thirsty, must
do for himself at his own aid. They were also told that God
had commissioned the master to care for him. The master supplied their daily wants, and when they fell ill he found the
best medical skill to bring them to health as soon as possible.
It was said that the slaves' sickness was the master's care, and

his health was the master's gain. Above all, "when you die (if you are obedient to your masters, and good niggers), your black faces will shine around the throne of God." [85]

After the first rule—to obey his master—the second was to do as much work when the master or overseer was not watching as when he was. In addition to this dogma, said Lunsford Lane, the sermon was often preached "that it was the will of heaven from all eternity we should be slaves, and our masters be our owners." [86]

Although some of the slaves who dictated to William C. Emerson had a concept of heaven, for the most part they were taught about this in relation to the damnation which awaited them for their disobedience. The preacher would say, "If all you niggers be good servants and obey your master and mistress you will enter the kitchen of heaven, but never into heaven." [87]

Religious Experience and Expression

The religious tenets of the slave were taken largely from the Old Testament. Robert Anderson claimed that the slave often had his own code of religion, "not nearly so complicated as the white man's religion but more closely observed." Because of the slave's condition, wrote Anderson, slave religion dealt largely with "militarism, the fighting of the old time people, the struggles of the Israelites, the prophesies of destruction by fire and pestilence, and the pictures of hellfire and damnation. The religion was one largely of enchantment and fear, which fitted in very nicely with the old African religions of witch doctors and fear." [88]

That aspect of religion which dealt with compassion for the sick and poor was little known on the plantation. According to Anderson, the slaveholders "knew nothing of that kind of religion and it is not to be wondered at that the colored race took up the same kind of religion that was taught by the master." The great theme of the slaves' religion was condemnation, and "forgiveness was taught only as a process of escaping hellfire." The concepts of "love and charity were virtues to be taught by the 'mammies' and not by the preachers." [89]

Louis Hughes remembered that there was always a solemnity about the services—a harmony and a pathetic tone that quickened the emotions as one sang the old plantation hymn. He stated:

it mattered not what their troubles had been during the week—how much they had been lashed, the prayer-meeting on Saturday evening never failed to be held. Their faith was tried and true. On Sunday afternoons, they would all congregate again to praise God, and the congregation was enthusiastic. It was pathetic to hear them pray, from the depths of their hearts, for them who "despitefully used them and persecuted them." [90]

The slave preacher knew the hardships of his fellow slaves, for he had shared them himself. After the hymns, he would speak of the necessity for patience, urging the slaves to endure "as good soldiers." When the sermon was completed, the slaves retired to their quarters. The faces of the slaves shone with "a happy light—their very countenance showed that their souls had been refreshed and that it had been 'good for them to be there.'" Hughes concluded that these meetings were of great joy and comfort to the slave, and that even the nonreligious slaves were calm and thoughtful while the meeting was in progress.[91]

Some camp meetings were great affairs to the slaves, and were conducted on a large scale. Great numbers of slaves from the surrounding plantations would congregate to attend these meetings and religious rejoicing would be the order of the day.[92]

On rare occasions, wrote Isaac D. Williams, the patrols were ordered not to bother the slaves during these affairs, and consequently, the religious zeal was proportionately great. In the main, these very large gatherings would take place on Sundays.

These great Sunday affairs, like their midweek counterparts, were most often presided over by slave preachers from the plantation.[93]

However, according to Williams, slave ministers frequently were not permitted to preach if the master was "down on them for something." Slave preachers were often sold away because the master felt they preached too much. Such a slave, it was said, "got religion on the brain." [94]

Israel Campbell was an example of such a slave preacher. He looked forward each week to Sunday so that he could travel from plantation to plantation and hold meetings. Although he could not read, he seldom found himself at a loss for words. He learned his gospel in various ways. Blessed with a good memory, he remembered almost everything that the white children of the plantation would read to him from the Bible and almost every biblical tale told by his mistress. Often he walked miles on Sundays, and attended morning, afternoon and evening meetings. He "found that it was pleasant to wait upon the Lord." News of his preaching spread from estate to estate, and soon large crowds of people, both white and black, came to hear him. Eventually a movement began among the various masters in his area to buy him, so that they could keep him solely to preach to their slaves.[95]

If the slaveholders became enthusiastic about a slave preacher such as Israel Campbell, it was generally because he was preaching about the duty, loyalty, and obligation of the slaves to the masters, or of acceptance by the slaves of their condition. Another such slave preacher was Jupiter Hammon. He stated:

There are some things very encouraging in God's word, for such ignorant creatures as we are; for God hath not chosen the rich of this world. Not many rich, not many noble are called, but God hath chosen the weak things of this world, and things which are not, to confound the things that are: And when the great and the rich refused coming to the gospel feast, the servant was told to go into the highways, and hedges, and compel those poor creatures that he found there, to come in. Now my bretheren, it seems to me, that there are no people that ought to attend to the hope of happiness in another world so much as we. Most of us are cut off from comfort and happiness here in this world, and can expect nothing from it. Now seeing this is the case, why should we not take care to be happy after death. Why should we spend our whole lives in sinning against God: And be miserable in this world and in the world to come.[96]

Some slaves stated to Benjamin Drew that although they wished to, they were prevented from seeking the religious life. They said that a slave "cannot pray right: while on his knees, he hears his master, 'here, John!' and he must leave his God and go to his master." Such was the sentiment expressed by the slave Adam, who experienced religious inspiration and wanted to be baptized. Having been denied permission by his overseer, he bypassed the overseer and got permission from his mistress. Thereafter, he went to the stream to receive his baptism. Just as he entered the water the overseer threatened him with a hundred lashes. The slave answered, "I have but two masters to serve, my earthly and my heavenly master, and I can mind nobody else." The overseer then threatened the slave preacher if he dared baptize the slave. The slave preacher replied, "If there is a God I will baptize Adam; if not, I will not baptize him." [97] Adam was baptized and subsequently punished.

Some slaves resolved their confusion as to ethical problems by resort to the gospel. Anthony Burns wanted to escape from bondage, but a serious ethical doubt prevented him from doing so: Was it morally correct for him to leave his master? The question caused him much mental anguish, and kept him from attempting escape, for if he fled from slavery it had to be with a clear conscience. Intensive reading of the Bible convinced him that there was only one God for both black and white man, and that "He had made of one blood all the nations of the earth, that there was no divine ordinance requiring one part of the human family to be in bondage to another, and that there was no passage of Holy Writ by virtue of which Col. Suttle [his master] could claim a right of property in him, any more than he could in Col. Suttle." His doubts allayed, he "applied himself to the recovery of his inalienable right to liberty and the pursuit of happiness." [98]

Religious fervor often imbued slaves with a courage and brashness theretofore unknown. Fugitive slave Edmund Turner warned slaveholders that their institution was unnatural. He stated that God in his own time shall destroy slavery and anyone who supported it. He stated that his prayer was to slaveholders:

In the name of God who in the beginning said, let there be light, and there was light. Let my people go that they may serve me, thereby good may come unto these and to thy children's children. Slaveholders have you seriously thought upon the condition of yourselves, family and slaves, have you read where Christ has enjoined upon all his creatures to read his word, thereby that they may have no excuse when coming before his judgment seat? But you say he shall not read his word, consequently his sin will be upon your head. I think every man has as much as he can do to answer for his own sins. And now my dear slaveholders, who with you are bound and fast hastening to judgment? As one that loves your soul repent ye, therefore, and be converted, that your sins may be blotted out when the time of refreshing shall come from the presence of the Lord. [99]

The slave could not reconcile his mind to the concept of living in "boundless affection, with the white people. Heaven will be no heaven to him, if he is not to be avenged his enemies." Charles Ball claimed that this was the slaves' fundamental religious creed: a kind master would be permitted to enter heaven, but this would be a favor due to the intercession of a slave, rather than a matter of strict justice to the slaveholder. No master would be permitted to be of an equal station

...ave, once the slave, in heaven, was "raised from the
... misery, in this world." [100]

HOLIDAYS

In addition to the partial respite from work granted to them
on some Sundays, most slaves had a holiday at Christmas and
possibly two or three more at various other times during the
year. Jacob Stroyer stated that some slaveholders gave more
than three holidays, "some less; some none, not a day nor an
hour." [101]

According to Stroyer, both master and slave regarded
Christmas as a great day. On Christmas afternoon on some
plantations, the "quarters" and the master's family would get
together at the great house. The slaves would receive such
gifts as hats, tobacco and handkerchiefs, but only if the master
was satisfied with the year's work. Also, providing the plantation had produced a successful crop, the quarters were given
from five to six days additional holiday after Christmas. [102]

At the Christmas Day party at the great house, the master
would provide two or three large pails of sweetened water
mixed with a gallon or two of whiskey. This was served until
many became totally intoxicated.

Francis Fedric reported that it was considered a disgrace
by both master and slave for a slave not to get drunk on
Christmas. The slave who did not provide himself with enough
whiskey to last through Christmas was regarded as lazy. Occasionally a master would even force the slaves to drink against
their protests. After they were all sufficiently inebriated, he
would call them together and say,

Now, you slaves, don't you see what bad use you have been
making of your liberty? Don't you think you had better have a
master, to look after you, to make you work, and keep you from
such a brutal state, which is a disgrace to you, and would ultimately be an injury to the community at large? [103]

In response, they would reply, "yees, Massa; if we go on in dis way, no good at all." Thus by contrived plan, the slave was made to put the seal of approval upon his own servitude.[104]

Despite such cruelties, there were slaves who reported some happier holiday events.

Linda Brent recalled that slave children rose early in the morning of Christmas Day to see the "Johnkannaus." The Johnkannaus consisted of slaves wrapped in calico with a multicolored net thrown over them. Cow tails were fastened to their backs and their heads were decorated with horns. Some used a gumbo box covered with sheepskin as a drum, while others would strike triangles. The Johnkannaus was allowed to go from plantation to plantation begging for gifts. No plantation was left unvisited where there was the slightest chance of obtaining a penny or a glass of whiskey. The total of the Christmas donations frequently amounted to twenty or thirty dollars. It was seldom that any white man refused to give a gift. If the Johnkannaus *was* refused, they would sing:

> Poor massa, so dey say;
> Down in de heel, so dey say
> Got no money, so dey say;
> Not one shillin, so dey say;
> God A'mighty bress you,
> So dey say.[105]

Slaveholders would sometimes also give a Christmas supper. On this occasion, described Solomon Northup, slaves from neighboring plantations were invited, and sometimes three or four hundred would attend. Tables were spread outdoors with varieties of vegetables and meats. The regular staple of corn meal was conspicuously absent. At some dinners, ditches were dug and filled with coals, over which chickens, ducks, turkeys, pigs, and sometimes the entire body of an ox, were roasted. The slave was given flour to make biscuits and preserves for dessert.

During the holidays after Christmas, said Northup, slaves were given "passes" and permitted to go where they pleased within a limited distance. Some stayed on the plantation and were given the opportunity to work for wages, although it was rare that such an alternative was chosen.[106]

During this period, wrote Charles Ball, slaves could be seen happily scurrying in all directions, in a frenetic attempt to use all of this unusual free time at their disposal. They were described to C. G. Parsons as different beings from what they were in the field; the temporary relaxation, and the brief deliverance from fear, produced a metamorphosis in their appearance and demeanor.[107]

The industrious slave would engage himself in making brooms, mats, horse-collars, and baskets; others would spend their time hunting and fishing. Most of the slaves enjoyed sports and amusements such as playing ball, wrestling, running footraces, fiddling, dancing, and drinking whiskey. Frederick Douglass said that this frivolous way of spending the time was "by far the most agreeable to the feeling of our masters." [108]

The holiday was among the most effective means of preventing insurrection. Holidays served as conductors, or safety valves, to dispel the rebellious spirit of the "quarters." Frederick Douglass proclaimed, "woe betide the slaveholder, the day he ventures to remove or hinder the operation of these conductors." Douglass warned that if the holiday were eliminated, "a spirit [would] go forth in their midst, more to be dreaded than the most appalling earthquake." [109]

LEISURE TIME AND RECREATION

No matter what the condition of man, after a sufficient period of time he will become so accustomed to it that it will eventually become bearable—bearable, that is, to the extent that he will eventually find or create moments of laughter, relaxation, and even frivolity. Thus we find in the narratives descriptions of leisure-time activities, relaxation, and even parties.

As with all other aspects of the slave's life, however, leisure time, too, was in the main regulated by the master. William Henry Singleton reported that on some plantations the master actually created and encouraged moments of relaxation and recreation. This was done, however, mostly for the purpose of achieving a social or financial end.[110]

For example, some masters would have occasional parties at the plantation, to which they would invite slaves from other plantations for the purpose of having the young ones meet and, hopefully, mate.[111]

Sometimes, when the master had guests, he would gather the slaves at the house to provide entertainment. The banjo-pickers would play the liveliest tunes, and the little boys and girls, as well as the men and women, would dance and sing.

Sometimes, according to the Arkansas Narratives of the Federal Writers' Project, a clever master would combine leisure time with work, in order to keep the slaves happy. One such narrative, for example, reported that the master would have "corn shuckings," or parties, where a big pile of corn was laid out and everyone would kneel and throw the corn as they shucked it. One slave was made "general," and he would walk from one person to another, seeing to it that each slave was working as hard as he could. A prize was given at the end of the evening to the first one who finished his pile. After the shucking was over all the slaves would get pies, beef, biscuits, corn bread, and whiskey as a reward.[112]

On most plantations, however, there was little leisure. James Williams reported that after it was too dark for work in the field, the men were kept busy in burning brush, while the women were made to spin and weave cotton for their clothing.[113]

On these plantations, according to most of the stories told to Benjamin Drew, Sunday was the only day the slave could count on receiving any leisure time. Some masters would give the slave all or part of the day for himself; sometimes slaves were allowed to hire themselves out on this day. But of course, if the master were angry with them for any reason, they had to work all day.[114]

For many, however, not even Sunday represented a respite from toil. James Williams recalled that those who had not been able to complete their chores during the week were forced to finish them on the Sabbath, in order to save themselves from a whipping on Monday.[115]

Despite the restrictions, the Georgia Narratives contain instances of slaves slipping away to the woods to indulge in a frolic. In order to protect themselves from being caught they tied ropes across the paths leading to their hideaway. The ropes were placed at a height sufficient to knock a man from his horse. The device stopped any intruder long enough to give the slaves time to flee to safety.[116]

There were, claimed Robert Anderson, some masters who regularly permitted their slaves leisure time, and even parties, for no selfish reason, so long as they did not interfere with the work. During nonproductive periods in the fields, slaves would be permitted to visit each other and engage in social affairs.[117]

Some slaves whose stories were recorded by the Federal Writers' Project remembered being given special holidays, as for instance, at "laying-by time," that is, after the cultivating of the crops was finished or before harvest. These masters would provide a big barbecue, where music was furnished by a slave who could play banjo or fiddle, and the others would sing and dance. The slaves bought instruments with the extra money they could earn on Sundays or other free time they had. Some made their fiddles "out of a large-sized gourd—a long wooden handle was used as a neck, and the hair from a horse's tail was used for a bow. The strings were made of cat gut." [118]

Robert Anderson compared the slaves' social gatherings to those of their masters. They danced some of the dances the whites danced, e.g., the minuet and the reel. Most, however, preferred their own dances in which they tried to express, in motion, their own particular feelings. These were solo or partner dances, consisting of a shuffling of the feet, and a swinging of the arms and shoulders. The slave became quite proficient in such dances, and could eventually even play a tune with his feet, dancing mostly to an inward music which was, according to Anderson, felt, but not heard. Religious dances were also part of the repertoire. These were usually "expressions of the weird, the fantastic, the mysterious, that was felt in all our religious ceremonies." [119]

Anderson concluded that "the colored people are naturally musical. They have a peculiar music of their own, which is largely a process of rhythm, rather than written music." He described the music of the slaves as basically a rhythmical chant. It often had much to do with religion and the lyrics were largely on religious themes. Practically all of their music was accompanied by motion. Music, said Isaac D. Williams, was something we

colored people had in our souls. It may not have been very fine, but the heart was there and it expressed all our best emotions, Thank the Lord for instilling in our souls this taste for the harmonious and for making us naturally lighthearted and cheerful under so many afflictions.[120]

DEATH

In death as in life, tradition and custom were carefully observed. Usually, Anthony Burns recalled, burial took place on the day of death, while the funeral would be preached one year later. Crudely constructed coffins were painted with whatever kind or color of paint was available. Laid to rest in a potter's field, the "dead bodies of the slaves never mingled their dust with that of the sovereign race." A rough stone gathered from the roadside was the deceased's only monument.

Henry Bibb felt that less care was "taken of their dead bodies than if they were dumb beasts." [121]

For example, Henry Watson wrote that before the burial, straw was placed in the makeshift coffin, and if available, white cloth was wrapped around the body. The coffin would be nailed closed, placed in a cart, and carried to the grave. Sometimes the body was left in the blanket in which it had died, placed in a handbarrow and carried to the graveyard.[122]

On some plantations, after the death of a slave, the "quarters" would sing and pray throughout the night. If the deceased was a Christian, his fellow Christians felt, as did Peter Randolph, "very glad, and thank God that brother Charles, or brother Ned or sister Betsy, is at last free, and gone to heaven where bondage is never known. Some who are left behind, cry and grieve that they, too, cannot die and throw off their yoke of slavery, and join the company of the brother or sister who has just gone." [123]

After a last look at the deceased, the funeral procession was formed. Austin Steward recalled that first came the minister and the coffin, followed by the dead slave's family and the master's household. Behind the master were the slaves belonging to the plantation. The last group were the friends, both black and white.[124]

If several slaves had died a mass funeral was held. On Peter Randolph's plantation all work was suspended until the dead were buried. Any slave from an adjoining plantation who could obtain a pass would come.[125]

Anthony Burns poetically summarized it: For two centuries, the "long and ever swelling procession has been moving on in its weary path to the grave, but no name of them all survive, save where, here and there, one has escaped out of the American Egypt, or Spartacus-like, has risen to take bloody vengence on his oppressors." [126]

III

The Master's Business

In addition to the operation and maintenance of the plantation, the master's business included the rearing, "rental," purchase, and sale of slaves.

Slaves wrote and dictated as extensively about their experiences with these aspects of their existence as they did about life on the plantation.

SLAVE REARING

According to the Arkansas Narratives, the breeding of slave children for the sole purpose of sale did not exist on a large scale, but it certainly did exist.[1]

The Fisk University Narratives reported that some masters would buy one female and one male and put them together as though they were cattle. There were also masters who had breeding farms, where they would raise slaves to sell on a regular basis.[2]

As an example of the former situation, Frederick Douglass told of the case of a master who was financially able to purchase only one slave. Therefore, he bought her as a "breeder," and then hired a married man to live with her for one year. Every night he would place the man and woman together in a room, and at the end of the year, the woman gave birth to twins. The children were regarded by the master as an important addition to his wealth, and his joy was such that the breeder was kept in the finest of material comfort in the hope that she would continue providing good fortune to the master and his family.[3]

James Roberts also reported that on his plantation fifty to sixty females were kept solely for breeding. No other slave was allowed near them, for they were reserved for whites. From twenty to twenty-five children a year were bred on this plantation and as soon as they were ready for market, they would be taken away and sold.[4]

Because of this practice of breeding, or rearing, some female slaves reported that they had refused to marry for it would only lead to their children being held in bondage, and they were unwilling to breed slaves for any master. If, said Jane Blake, "all the bond women had been of the same mind, how soon the institution could have vanished from the earth, and all the misery belonging to it, been lifted from the hearts of the holders of slaves."[5]

TRADING IN SLAVES

Because of its relative rarity, slave rearing or breeding, was not a subject of extensive discussion in the narratives. However, another feature of the master's business, slave trading, was described in great detail. An analysis of the narratives dealing with slave trading reveals that the activity may be conveniently broken down into three stages: the "coffle," or slave train; the slave pen, and the auction block.

The Coffle

According to Jamie Parker, when a number of slaves were to be sold away they would sometimes be herded together into groups of five hundred or more, all handcuffed two by two, with a long chain running through the middle of the line, collecting them as one mass. This train of slaves which, after a forced march, eventually arrived at the auction block, was known as the coffle.[6]

On the coffle, women and men were treated alike. After the day's walk, they would lie down together by the woodside and sleep. If any lagged along the way, there were numerous overseers known as "nigger drivers" who would lay the lash on unsparingly, and in the words of Isaac Williams, "the poor fainting victims would often lie bleeding on the road and die from sheer exhaustion." Although there were wagons for the sick and the children, many nevertheless died on the road, where graves were hastily dug and the bodies dumped.[7]

Henry Watson reported that the coffle would, on occasion, stop for a quick sale of one of the gang. If a stop was made at a house, visitors from the neighborhood would come to examine the "flock." Signs were sometimes placed along the road which informed the planters that the trader had in his gang blacksmiths, carpenters, and field-hands. The sign might also contain the inducement that in the group there were "also several sickley ones," whom he would sell "very cheap."[8]

Watson claimed that many slaves wished to be sold during the trip, for they were no longer able to endure the remainder of the journey. If the trader was at all displeased by a slave, he would order him to be stripped and tied hand and foot. A paddle—a board approximately two feet long and one inch wide, with fourteen holes bored through it—would be applied to the slave on parts of his body which a purchaser would not be likely to examine. The flesh protruded through these holes at every blow, and blisters the size of each hole would form, causing pain and soreness to the victim. Punishment was usually inflicted in the morning, before visitors came to examine the slaves.[9]

William Wells Brown also described the plight of women and children in the coffle. Often, he wrote, young children grew very noisy, being too young or unsophisticated to understand the gravity of the situation. The driver would complain of a child's crying and warn the mother to stop the noise. If the crying persisted, the driver would take the child away from its mother and give it away to the first home the gang came across. The mother would run up to the driver and fall on her knees begging for him to return her child to her. Clinging to his legs she might cry, "Oh, my child! my child! master, do let me have my child! Oh, do, do, do. I will stop its crying, if you will only let me have it again." After one such occurrence, a feeling of horror would shoot through every mother on the coffle, as each would imagine this happening to her.[10]

The Fisk Collection of Narratives noted that sales were often made along the roads, and it was not uncommon for a mother to have her nursing child taken from her and sold along the roadside, as easily separated as a mother pig from her litter.[11]

Although such treatment was the norm, Jermain W. Loguen recalled that some "nigger drivers" exercised restraint on these trips, for they felt that the trip might be expedited and that it was better to amuse, coax and flatter their " 'stock', than cross their tempers . . . by unnecessary violence." Thus, what sometimes appeared to the slaves as favorable treatment was often merely a means of expedition, rather than a manifestation of humane feeling. Loguen noted however that mild treatment was not the only means employed to hasten the coffle along. The drivers' whips, followed by the groans of the sufferers, informed the weary slaves that whatever the inconvenience, their steps had to respond to the will of their drivers.[12]

Loguen stated that slaves were encouraged to greater speed during the day upon which they arrived at their destination by the promise of a few moments of rest and refreshment when they arrived. Some slaves were told that they would be met by their old master or their husbands, or that they would be reunited with their children. Experience had taught the slaves that a slaveholder's word, and especially the trader's word, was meaningless; nevertheless they appreciated the pretense, and hope itself was some relief.[13]

Charles Ball was one of the many slaves who experienced the coffle. As he was hitching his oxen to a cart on the plantation, several men gathered around him. One of them was a stranger whom he had seen speaking with his master. This man came up to him and seized him by the collar, shook him violently, and announced that he was his property and must go with him to Georgia. At the sound of these words, thoughts of his wife and children rushed through Ball's mind. He immediately knew his situation was hopeless, and that resistance was in vain. His purchaser ordered him to cross his hands, which were quickly bound with a strong cord. He asked if he could be allowed to see his wife and children, or if not, if they might not have permission to come and see him. He was told only that he would be able to get another wife in Georgia.[14]

Ball was placed with a group of thirty-two other slaves, both men and women. The women were held together with a rope "about the size of a bed cord, which was tied like a halter round the neck of each." A strong iron collar was fitted closely by means of a padlock around the neck of each man, and a chain of iron approximately a hundred feet in length was passed through the harps of the padlocks, except at each end, where the harp of a padlock passed through a link of chain. They were handcuffed with iron staples and bolts, with a short chain about a foot long. The slave to whom Ball was chained "wept like an infant when the blacksmith, with his heavy hammer, fastened the ends of the bolts that kept the staples from slipping from [their] arms." [15]

They took up the line of march, traveling five miles until they reached "one of those miserable public houses [something of an inn], so frequent in lower parts of Maryland and Virginia, called 'ordinaries.' " The master ordered a pot of mush for their supper, and after eating, they rested on the floor in their handcuffs and chains until it was time to sleep. Although they usually all slept together, this time the women slept on one side of the room and the men, who were chained, occupied the other.[16]

Although the passage of time did not reconcile Ball to his chains, it did make him familiar with them. In a few days the horrible sensation attendant upon his separation from wife and children subsided somewhat. He began to reflect upon his hopeless and desperate situation, and sought to devise some means of escaping from his new master. He examined the long chain to see if there might not be some place where it could be severed, but he found it completely secured, and its separation impossible. From that time on he endeavored to beguile his sorrows by examining the state of the countryside through which he traveled, observing the condition of his fellow slaves on the plantations along the road he walked, and thinking of the slave pen.[17]

The Slave Pen

Ultimately the coffle reached its destination. The slaves were then taken to a trade yard or slave pen. The slaves were kept here to await sale, and the narratives contain vivid descriptions of both the physical setting and the experiences of those imprisoned therein.

John Brown described the accommodations. They consisted of a block of houses forming a square, and covering a full acre of land. The center of the square within which the slaves exercised was a solid floor of gravel.[18]

The housing quarters for the slaves consisted of three floors of rooms in each building. There were two entrances to the pen—one for the slaves, the other for visitors and buyers. The windows in front, which overlooked the street, were heavily barred, as were those overlooking the yard. It was an "awfully gloomy place, notwithstanding the bustle that was always going on in it." [19]

A "confidential slave" in the "employ" of the trader was in charge of the arrangements. He had great power and did what he liked to make the approximately five hundred slaves comfortable or otherwise. Men and women were separated and both were segregated from the children. The youngest and prettiest females were set apart as the concubines of the masters, who might change mistresses as often as every week. The degree of immorality in the pen was extremely high, yet many slaves felt that the beautiful females dreaded the fate that awaited them when sold away even more than life in the pen. [20]

Henry Bibb reported that when the coffle reached its destination, the gang was examined by a city official whose business it was to inspect slave property brought for sale. He examined their backs for scars and their limbs to see whether they were inferior. As it was often difficult to tell the ages of slaves, the examiner opened their mouths and checked their teeth as one would a horse. He might also "prick up the skin in the back of their hands, since if the person was very far advanced in life, when the skin was pricked up, the pucker would stand so many seconds on the back of the hand." [21]

The most rigorous examinations of slaves were made to determine mental capacity. Intelligence, they said, undermined the fabric of the slave's chattelhood; such a quality made him prone to what the slaveholder considered the most unpardonable sin—escape. In addition, such a slave could be led easily into insurrection, bloodshed, and an exterminating war against slavery. [22]

According to John Brown, conditions quickly improved for the slaves in the pen as compared to the coffle. They were regularly fed, washed, shaved, combed, and "plucked" (an activity performed upon the old slaves which consisted in pulling out gray hairs). Those who were too gray to be plucked without making them bald had their hair dyed. For breakfast they would receive enough bread, bacon, and coffee that they might soon become healthy looking. They would be given instructions by the confidential slave as to how to display themselves, after which they were formed into groups, according to size, sex, and age. As a consequence of this alignment, the members of families were separated, and would often see the last of one another at the auction block.[23]

Brown also described the "flogging room." Screwed into the floor of this room were several rows of wooden cleats, through which was passed a long cord. There were floggings every day; men, women, and children were punished alike. They were brought in, stripped naked, laid flat on the floor with their face down and their hands tied to the cleats with the cords. Their feet were similarly bound, as the whipper punished for half an hour or more. It was a rule among "nigger dealers" (traders) not to flog with any instrument that would cut the skin, in order not to depreciate the value of the "property." Punishment was therefore inflicted with a flogging paddle, which contained the flogs of leather, about a foot and a half long. Although no blood was drawn the punishment was severe. Flogging was inflicted for various reasons, but especially for "not speaking up and looking bright and smart" in the presence of a potential buyer.[24]

William Anderson noted that some traders had private slave pens, run by confidential slaves. Anderson said that what went on in these slave pens was "too wicked to mention."[25]

Henry Watson described the scene: Men and women stood separate. Certain women were selected and taken into another room for a special and unique examination. A slaveholder would "take a poor female slave, . . . make her strip, then feel and examine her, as though she were a pig, or a hen, or merchandise." [26]

The Auction Block

The final step in the trading process was, of course, the sale. The narratives contain descriptions of these sales and the attendant horror, fear, degradation, and sometimes, after weeks in the coffle and the slave pen, relief.

Josiah Henson described the feelings of the slaves as follows:

[The] knowledge that all ties of the past are to be sundered; the frantic terror at the idea of being sent down "South"; the almost certainty that one member of their family will be torn from another; the anxious scanning of purchaser's faces; the agony at parting, often forever, with husband, wife, child—these must be seen and felt to be fully understood.[27]

The sales were generally conducted in a large hall or at an open-air auction block. The interested planters or traders would be seated around the block upon which the slave was placed, with the auctioneer standing beside them. Solomon Northup reported that prospective buyers would approach the slave up for sale and ask him what he could do. The customers would dwell upon the several good or bad qualities of the slave, and many would make the "merchandise" hold his head up and walk briskly back and forth. They might feel the hands, arms, and body, or order the slave to open his mouth and show his teeth, "precisely as a jockey examines a horse which he is about to barter for a purchase." Sometimes a man or woman was taken back to a private room in the yard, stripped, and inspected more minutely. Scars found on a slave's back were considered evidence of a slave's rebellious or unruly spirit, and would hurt the sale.[28]

John Brown recalled that despite the emotional impact of

the proceedings, the slave was forced to look bright and lively, for his price depended to a great extent on his general appearance. Brown claimed that men or women may be "well made, and physically faultless in every respect, yet their value be impaired by a sour look or a dull, vacant stare, or a general dullness of demeanor." For this reason the slaves who were to be sold were instructed to look "spry and smart," to hold themselves up well, and put on a smiling, cheerful face. They were also told to speak for, and recommend themselves; to conceal any defects they might have, and never to tell their age when they were past the active period of life.[29]

Charles Ball noted that during the progress of the sale, planters often requested good "breeding slaves." The auctioneer would reply that he was selling some of the best breeding slaves and he might exaggerate, that, for example, a particular female had twenty-two children and could produce as many for the new master.[30]

According to Milton Clarke, females who were expected to bring a high price were often furnished with new gowns and sent to the barber to have their hair done. Jamie Parker recorded the reaction of one slaveholder who, viewing a particularly attractive female, whispered to his friend, "that article is a little bit of magnificent. A rare beautiful piece of ebony." [31]

Zamba witnessed truly harrowing scenes at auctions, especially those involving females. Some women became so agitated that auctioneers were forced to put off the sale until the following day, by which time they would have been beaten into submission. Zamba recorded his feelings in the following words: "What would ladies in civilized Christian England think of the *fair* and gentle ladies of free and Christian America—to see, these ladies of the creation at an auction table, putting questions to victims of their own sex, such as no modest *man* would repeat, and that too, in the presence of a crowd of men?" Zamba saw masters order these black women to pull down their stockings, and, if they hesitated, assist them in doing so. The purpose of this examination, the slave was told, was to ascertain if the individual offered for sale was diseased or had ulcerated legs. This "was done with the utmost coolness; just in the same manner as a butcher handles his four-legged victims." [32]

When the sale began, some slaves were in tears; others appeared to be relieved. When the auctioneer finished examining his "merchandise," the commerce in human flesh began. Henry Watson gave an account of the auction. The auctioneer would start,

"Gentlemen, here is a likely boy; how much? He is sold for no fault; the owner wants money. His age is forty. Three hundred dollars is all that I am offered for him. Please to examine him; he is warranteed sound. Boy, pull off your shirt—roll up your pants —for we want to see if you have been whipped." If they discover any scars, they will not buy; saying that the nigger is a bad one. The auctioneer seeing this, cries, "three hundred dollars, gentlemen, three hundred dollars. Shall I sell him for three hundred dollars? I have just been informed by his master that he is an honest boy and belongs to the same church that he does." This turns the tide frequently, and the bids go up fast; and he is knocked off for a good sum. After the men and women are sold, the children are put on the stand.[33]

Louis Hughes described the scene this way: The women were placed in a row on one side of the room or block, and the men on the other. Customers who were so inclined passed between the lines looking them over and questioning them: "What can you do? Are you a good cook? seamstress? dairymaid?" Or, "Can you plow? Are you a blacksmith? Have you ever cared for horses? Can you pick cotton rapidly?" [34]

Many of the narratives report that families would sometimes be sold to plantations hundreds of miles apart. Women were whipped for begging the new master for an opportunity to say good-bye to a child. Some slaves were sold as "guaranteed niggers"; that is, warranted not to run away. In such cases, should the man "bolt," the seller was obliged to refund the sum he received for him.[35]

Slaves who did not wish to be sold to a particular planter might purposely present an appearance that was distasteful. Others might whisper to the prospective buyer that they had killed an overseer and for that reason were being sold away. The slaveholder knew that if a "good nigger killed a white overseer, they wouldn't do nothing to him. If he was a bad nigger they'd sell him." The Arkansas Narratives reported that light skinned slaves did not sell as well as the darker ones as it was believed that the "black nigger stood the climate better." [36]

Zamba saw husbands and wives, and sometimes infants, upon the auction table:

The husband with his arms around the neck of his faithful and long-loved, although black partner, imploring, in the most moving language, while tears trickled down his sable cheeks, that they would not separate him from all that he cared for upon earth; and the poor woman equally moved, and in many cases more so, beseeching with all the eloquence of nature's own giving, that she might be allowed to toil the remainder of her earthly existence with the only one her heart ever loved.[37]

John Brown suggested that "nigger trading was as much a business as any other," and that there was an enormous amount of cheating perpetrated. Many tricks were employed to sell a bad or an unsound slave, and the man who succeeded in "shoving off a used up nigger" was considered a clever business man. The tricks of the trader were known and the buyer used every means at his disposal to defeat them. For example, the testing of the soundness of a slave often led to the most distorted expedients by the buyer. The slave was handled in the grossest manner and inspected with the most elaborate and disgusting minuteness.[38]

HIRING OUT

The narratives also discuss another aspect of the master's business—that of renting or hiring slaves out.

Anthony Burns reported that many slaveholders, having more slaves than they could use, found it profitable to hire them out. In addition, some slaveholders felt that it was better to give consideration to the slave's desire to earn some money than to risk rebellion and possible loss by thwarting his inclination. Many were taught by long and bitter experience that "one willing slave is worth half-a-dozen refractory ones." This custom of hiring-out was found in every slave state.[39]

According to Burns, if an owner decided to hire out, he usually summoned the "quarters" before him and designated by name those whom he had chosen to go. He generally issued passes to those chosen, and left them to find their own way to the "hiring-ground." [40]

Burns described the hiring-ground as an area which, by custom or pronouncement, had been designated as the place where a slave or slaves could be leased or rented for a specific period of time. Whatever the distance to the hiring-ground, it was at the slave's peril that he failed to appear at the appointed time. En route to the hiring-ground, and until leased, the slaves were to make their own way. The master rarely provided food or shelter, but gave each one a small amount of money with which he was expected to survive. If they were not able to find shelter with a friendly black in the city or town, they would sleep and eat in the street or open field.[41]

The hiring-out itself was usually done by contract, written or oral, and consummated either between the slave and the lessee or the slaveholder and the lessee. Most contracts were entered into around Christmas-time each year, and one year was the usual term.[42]

Burns reported that the slave played an important role in the hiring-out transaction. He had to be as active as his owner in finding employment. He was instructed to praise his ability and honesty and give complete assurances to the potential lessee that he was capable of performing all manner and degrees of labor.[43]

The contract usually required that the hired slave pay a fixed percentage or amount of his earnings to the master. If the slave lost time through sickness within the year, he was obliged to make it up. Whatever the weather or the availability of work, at the end of each month the master had to receive his stated amount. If not, many masters would withdraw the hiring-out privilege. Obviously, wrote Frederick Douglass, the entire arrangement was decidedly in the master's favor. It relieved the master of the burden of caring for the slave, while nevertheless insuring his investment. Douglass noted that the master "received all the benefits of slaveholding without its evils; while I endured all the evils of a slave, and suffered all the care and anxiety of a freeman." [44]

According to the Georgia Narratives, many masters owned no plantation at all. They kept slaves for the sole purpose of hiring them out either to those who owned no slaves, or to masters who needed more help but were not able to own as many slaves as their work required. In some cases, slaves would be hired out by the day.[45]

The collection of narratives recorded by William Still reported that the slave had to find his own room and supply himself with board and clothes. But difficult as this arrangement was, it was generally considered better than plantation life. To many, to be allowed these responsibilities was a step toward freedom.[46]

Sometimes, as leasehold property, the slave found himself in poorer straits than he had been in the service of his master. The interest of his owner, according to Jermain Loguen, "regards his health and strength as of the greatest pecuniary importance, but if he is held by a mortgagee or lessee, the interest changes from the person of the slave to the amount of labor to be obtained from him." [47]

According to William Still, however, the living conditions of the hired slave were generally good. Some slaves were even able to purchase clothes for themselves, "which they usually valued highly, so much so, that after escaping they would not be contented until they had tried every possible scheme to secure them." Because of the newly gained affluence, the hired slave often began to develop attitudes which deviated from common slave thought. Not only did the desire for freedom intensify, but he soon questioned the sharing of his earnings with his master. The fact that the slave was permitted to retain a percentage of his wages was proof that he was entitled to the whole of them. Discontent among this class of slaves grew, and many began looking for means of escape. Frederick Douglass claimed that instead of increasing contentment, improved conditions tended to add to dissatisfaction. In order to have a contented slave, it was necessary to make an unthinking one. In this connection, Douglass wrote, "It is necessary to darken his moral and mental vision, and, as far as possible, to annihilate the power of reason. He [the slave] must be able to detect no inconsistencies in slavery; he must be made to feel that slavery is right; and he can be brought to that only when he ceases to be a man." [48]

In addition to domestic and plantation work, hired slaves were also found working in industrial capacities. Young slaves from ten to fifteen years of age found employment in the hemp or bagging factories. Their wages varied between twenty and thirty dollars a year. Due to their lack of skill, they were often subjected to cruel treatment, which, in turn, caused them to commit even greater errors. Aside from being whipped, many were "yoked" with pronged iron collars, with the owner's name imprinted thereon. [49]

Milton Clarke reported that working in these factories often took the life and spirit out of a young slave, "and he soon becomes little more than an idiot." When they were no longer useful in the factories (usually at about the age of nineteen or twenty), they were sold to the trader. When presented to a potential buyer who inquired as to his ability, the broken slave would be forced to lie and make great pretensions to avoid a severe beating by the trader. The slave who was forced to lie to his new master for the benefit of his former one generally atoned for it by many a cruel flogging. When the new owner would find "one that is very awkward and ignorant, the master tells the overseer to 'put him through for what he is worth,' 'use him up as soon as you can'; 'get what you can out of him in a short time and let him die.' " [50]

Peter Randolph noted that the slave in the cities did not fare as badly as the plantation slave. Most were hired out. Many of them were employed in factories or worked at trades. The city slaves dressed well, had what was considered comfortable homes and, in many instances, learned to read and write. Generally, they did well, and if they were industrious they could earn considerably more than was exacted of them by their owners. Often, one was able to buy his own freedom with the extra money he was able to earn. [51]

That the slave preferred city life to the plantation is borne out by the reports related to Wilson Armistead that a city master's common reaction to some violation would be the threat, "I shall sell you into the country, you rascal, the very next time you do so and so." Such threats were not lightly regarded by city slaves. [52]

For the most part, the city slave owner seemed anxious to be known as a gentleman. There appeared to be, in the words of Frederick Douglass, a "vestige of decency, a sense of shame," that did "much to curb and check those outbreaks of atrocious cruelty so commonly enacted upon the plantation." Few city masters were willing to have a reputation as brutes, and above all, of not providing their slaves with proper meals. [53]

Although the city was preferable to the plantation, slavery, said Peter Randolph, was still slavery. The city slave might have escaped the cruel lash of the overseer, but if he offended the master, or any other citizen, his offense would not go unpunished. Punishment was usually meted out by hardened professionals. Having been "convicted" of wrongdoing, the slave would be told, " 'Hand this note to Captain Heart or Captain Thwing'—and well does the shrinking slave know what is to follow. These last-mentioned gentlemen *give* their time to, and improve their talents by, laying the lash upon the naked backs of men and women!" Whipping posts were the slave cities' monuments.[54]

Peter Still recalled that during the winter months, slaves located in port cities found many opportunities to earn extra money. Wet or damp raw cotton, which was considered unfit for market, often became the means of earning a windfall. On Sundays, the slaves would carefully spread the wet cotton in the sun, turning and shaking it frequently until it was dry and ready to be repacked. For this they sometimes received as much as a dollar a day—thus supplying themselves with the means of procuring many little otherwise unobtainable comforts.[55]

The plantation slave, too, had opportunities to earn money. Peter Still claimed that sometimes a good master would divide a large field into many little patches, and each slave could work nights and Sundays cultivating one patch. If all was going well with the plantation work, the overseer, if he were so inclined, might give the slave an additional half-day or even Saturday to work his own plot. Whatever was produced on this small patch, was sold to the master—"*at his price*, which was seldom more than half the market value." [56]

If the slave retained any semblance of hope for the future, said Henry Box Brown, it was that by some means he might eventually attain his freedom. Those who had the opportunity labored unusually hard in the hopes of earning the price of their own redemption. Those who were given the opportunity to work with skilled white men from whom they could eventually learn a trade, were very eager. They knew that they could one day hire out and, with the money earned, buy their liberty. According to the Georgia Narratives, the white man rarely objected to slave assistance, for even though he was somewhat disgruntled about slaves learning his trade, "he was able to place all the hard work on the slave which made his job easier." [57]

Peter Still claimed that the plan to buy one's freedom was too often ended by a rude awakening to the master's deceit. The slave would propose the subject to the master, who would fix a price for his liberty. Now he had something for which to work. Within a short number of years he would be able to pay the agreed price. He would pay his hard-earned wages to the master only to find to his amazement that the master would keep the payment, deny ever having promised the slave his liberty and bid "him never mention the subject more." Sometimes, however, slaves who paid for their freedom in installments took precautions against this deception by demanding written receipts for each payment. This method too was often unsuccessful, for suddenly the master would leave the city, and "before the poor slave was aware of any approaching change, an agent to whose care he had been consigned, had sold him to another master." [58]

The slave documents collected by *The Liberator* reported that many masters enticed their slaves into harder work by promising them the chance to purchase their freedom. Although there were some slaveholders who kept their word, most merely used this as a device. The question of the morality of buying one's freedom was raised by Frederick Douglass when he was presented with the opportunity. It was charged that to buy one's freedom recognized and reinforced the very principle of slavery. Douglass replied that the purchase of his freedom was not to compensate the slaveholder, but to release himself from his power; not to establish his natural right to freedom, but to be released from all legal liabilities to slavery. He asserted that "the error of those, who condemn this transaction, consists in their confounding the crime of buying men *into slavery*, with the meritorious act of buying men out of slavery, and the purchase of legal freedom with abstract right and natural freedom." He analogized, "there is now, in this country a heavy duty on corn. The government of this country has imposed it and though I regard it a most unjust and wicked imposition, no man of common sense will charge me with endorsing or recognizing the right of this government to impose this duty, simply because, to prevent myself and family from starving, I buy and eat this corn." [59]

KIDNAPPING

Slaves reported that kidnapping and reselling slaves was a thriving business. The men who engaged in this activity were called "nigger stealers" and while some belonged to groups, others operated individually.

John Brown reported that the groups were composed of men stationed in various parts of the slave areas, and when one member succeeded in stealing a Negro he would pass him on as quickly as possible to the nearest "station," from which point the slave would be forwarded to another until he was safely disposed of. Brown stated that many of these men would come to the quarters at night trying to entice slaves away. Some slaves cooperated with these agents for money and regularly ran off from one master to another, to be sold several times. [60]

Free Negroes and the slaves were both victims of nigger stealers. Levin Tilmon reported that in the state of New Jersey kidnappers were prowling about in several communities, wherein they secured the services of a white man who went "with the band of man-stealers, and at a late hour of the night, rapped at the door of this colored family's house, when the lady from within asked, who was there? the reply was 'a friend.' They continued by asking 'is your husband at home?' When she wished to know what he wanted with him, his reply was, to see him about going to work to-morrow." When she finally opened the door an entire gang rushed in and her husband was headed back to the slave pen within the hour.[61]

Incidents of slave kidnapping right on the edge of the quarters or plantations were reported in the Texas Narratives of the Federal Writers' Project. Spence Johnson reported that he and his family were on the plantation when some men rode up in a carriage to water their horses:

By'n by, a man coaxes de two bigges' chillun to de carriage and give dem some kind-a candy. Other chillun see dis and goes too. Two other men was walkin' round smokin and gettin' closer to mammy all de time. When he kin, de man in de carriage go de two big step-chillun in with him and me and sis' climb in too, to see how come. Den de man holler, 'Get de ole one and let's get from here.' With dat de two big men grab mammy and she fought and screeched and bit and cry, but de hit her on de head with something and drug her in, and throwed her on de floor. De big chillun begin to fight for mammy, but one of de men hit 'em hard and off dey driv, with de horses under whip.[62]

Many slaves, like Solomon Northup, who could not produce "free papers" (a document given by a master to a freed slave) fell victim to the kidnapping business. They, like Northup, were placed in confinement and beaten until they learned the "virtue" of silence. Austin Steward reported that many were snatched without warning from their homes and friends, and crowded into the slave wagons, "like sheep for the slaughter, to be carried they knew not whither; but, doubtless to the dismal rice swamp of the South." [63]

Steward also stated that dealers would capture Negroes from free territory, run them into a slave state, and there sell them for the market. He wrote of men who would lure the unsuspecting slaves away from their quarters and as quickly as possible transport them into another part of the state. Free Negroes were sometimes enticed back to the plantation by being told that their family was being sold and wanted to bid him farewell. According to Steward, the "sorrow and fearful apprehension of these wretched recaptured slaves can not be described nor imagined by any one except those who have experienced a like affliction." [64]

Charles Ball was a free Negro kidnapped into slavery. Unlike most, he was determined to claim protection under Georgia law, and after speaking to an attorney, he was disillusioned to find that he had to prove himself a free man rather than, as would appear more rational, that his master should be required to prove him to be a slave. Nevertheless his case was eventually tried and after several weeks the Court declared that the law was "well settled in Georgia, that every negro was presumed to be a slave until he proved his freedom by the clearest evidence." The Court continued, as follows:

Where a negro was found in the custody or keeping of a white man, the law declared that white man to be his master, without any evidence on the subject. But the case before the court, was exceedingly plain and free from all doubt or difficulty. Here the master has brought this slave into the state of Georgia, as his property, has held him as a slave ever since, and still holds him as a slave. The title of the master in this case, is the best title that a man can have to any property, and the order of the court is that the slave Charles be returned to the custody of his master.[65]

CONTROL OVER THE SLAVES

The key element in the operation and continuance of the master's business was the maintenance of control over the slaves. This control was achieved by various means ranging from brute force to subtle psychology. Lewis Clarke, in discussing the reasons a master might have for punishing, and even killing, a valuable slave in order to set an example to the others and thereby maintain control, said that

This must be done, cost what it may. Some say a man will not kill a horse worth a hundred dollars, much less a slave worth several hundred dollars. A horse has no such will of his own, as the slave has; he does not provoke the man, as a slave does. The master knows there is *contrivance* with the slave to outwit him, the horse has no such contrivance.[66]

This section will deal with three methods referred to most often in the narratives and utilized by the master to control the slaves, i.e., fear, the slave patrols, and the "black driver."

Fear as a Weapon of Control

Although actual murder of slaves merely to set an example was fairly uncommon, Frederick Douglass reported that slaveholders punished slaves for the smallest offenses, to prevent the commission of large ones. Masters could always find some excuse for whipping a slave. Douglass claimed that an individual unaccustomed to slave life would be astonished to see with what ease a slaveholder could make occasion to punish a slave. "A mere look, word, or motion—a mistake, accident, or want of power—are all matters for which a slave may be whipped at any time." If the slave looked dissatisfied, it was said that he had the devil in him, and it must be whipped out. If he spoke too loudly when spoken to by his master, it was said that he was getting high-minded. If he forgot to remove his hat at the approach of a white person, he was wanting in reverence, and had to be whipped for it. If he ventured to vindicate his conduct when censured for it, he was guilty of impudence. If he, while plowing, broke a plow, he was considered careless. Masters seldom failed to take advantage of such opportunities.[67]

Douglass reported that on his plantation the savage barbarity was equalled only by the consummate coolness with which the overseer committed the grossest and most vile tortures upon the slaves. One slave, he reported, who was being whipped, ran to the creek and plunged in, in order to escape the punishment. Having refused to come out after being ordered to do so, the overseer, without consultation or deliberation, shot the slave to death. The horror of this scene flashed through the mind of every slave on the plantation. In explaining why he acted thus, the overseer told the master that the slave had set a dangerous example to the others—one which, if let go unpunished, would lead to the total subversion of all rule and order on the plantation. He argued that if one slave refused to be punished, and escaped with his life, the others would follow the example, and the result would be "the freedom of the slaves, and the enslavement of the whites." The overseer's explanation was accepted by the master, and the overseer was continued in his position. The murder was committed in the presence of the slaves, and they could neither institute suit, nor testify against him; thus, wrote Douglass, "the guilty perpetrator of one of the bloodiest and most foul murders goes unwhipped of justice, and uncensured by the community in which he lives." [68]

Douglass claimed that this treatment was an integral part of the system of fraud and inhumanity which was used to perpetuate slavery. He wrote also of methods adopted to disgust the slave with freedom, by allowing him to see only the abuse of it. For example, if a slave enjoyed molasses, and if he were caught stealing some, the master would force him to eat massive quantities of it until he became sick at the mere mention of the word. Similar treatment was accorded to teach the slaves to refrain from asking for more food than that granted in their regular allowance. If a slave consumed his allowance and asked for more, the master would give him a great deal more than was necessary, and force him to eat it all within a given time. If the slave complained that he could not eat it all, he was said to be "satisfied neither full nor fasting, and [was] whipped for being hard to please." [69]

Peter Still asserted that many masters believed that there was nothing as effective as frequent floggings to make a slave a "good nigger," and to set an example to the others. Such masters might "buck" a slave for several hours by tying the slave's hands together, drawing them over his knees, and confining them by means of a stock thrust under his knees. The slave was frequently left in the "buck" for several hours —sometimes all night—and, in such cases, the protracted straining of the muscles caused intense pain.[70]

Harriet Tubman noted that many masters would often whip slaves in advance of their "deserving" it, in order to alarm their fears, and strike terror into those who planned to escape. Some slaves were beaten immediately after their purchase and when the slave asked why he was being punished, the reply might be, "I have no complaint to make of you. You're a good nigger, an' you've always worked well. But you belong to me now; you're *my* nigger, and the first lesson my niggers have to learn is that I am the master and they belong to me, and are never to resist anything I order them to do. So I always begin by giving them a good licking. Now strip and take it." [71]

Although he was not beaten by his new master, Charles Ball was forced to witness a punishment intended to instill fear of misbehavior in him. He was ordered to the "great house" to become acquainted with the methods by which slaves were chastised. The master showed him a pump. One of the female slaves had committed an offense for which she was to be punished, and the opportunity was used to exhibit to Ball the nature of this punishment. The slave was stripped naked, and tied to a post so situated that the stream of water fell from the spout of the pump onto the girl as would a shower. Water was then pumped upon the head and shoulders of the victim, and in a short time the woman fell unconscious. Eventually she was removed in a state of insensibility. The "punishment of the pump," as it was called, was described by Ball as follows:

When the water first strikes the head and arms, it is not at all painful; but in a very short time, it produces the sensation that is felt when heavy blows are inflicted with large rods. This perception becomes more and more painful, until the skull bone and shoulder blades appear to be broken in pieces. Finally, all the faculties become oppressed; breathing becomes more and more difficult; until the eye-sight becomes dim, and animation ceases. This punishment is in fact a temporary murder; as all the pains are endured, that can be felt by a person who is deprived of life by being beaten with bludgeons.[72]

The narratives collected by John Hawkins Simpson contain the story of one slave girl who died under the lash for praying. The slave, Jessie, had been consumptive for several months. From weakness and consequent apathy, she failed to complete her appointed task. She had been warned by the master to stop wasting her time praying, and to better utilize her time as the plantation's clothes maker. The master was determined that such a dangerous example as praying when one should be working should not be set to the rest of the slaves and he was watchful to see that she obeyed his orders. The master had occasion to catch the slave girl in prayer and decided to instill in her and the other slaves a lesson that they would not forget. He rang the plantation's bell to call all the slaves and the children to see a practical warning by which they were to profit. In the presence of the entire "quarters" the master beat the girl to death. The narrative reports that the "slaves stood horrified, as if rooted in the ground." [73]

Such cases were not isolated. Charles Ball reports that when a severe beating was given to him, such was the terror of his fellow-slaves, that, although they loved and pitied him, not one of them dared to approach his cabin for several days thereafter.[74]

Ball reported that the vast majority of slaves felt that it was a mistake to assume that the master could ever retain his property, or live among his slaves, if those slaves were not kept in terror of the punishment that would follow acts of violence and disorder. There was no difference, he claimed, between the feelings of black and white men, so far as their personal rights were concerned. The slave was as anxious to possess and to enjoy liberty as the master would be, were he deprived of his freedom. "Low ignorance, moral degradation of character, and mental depravity, are inseparable companions; and in the breast of an ignorant man, the passions of envy and revenge hold unbridled dominion." [75]

In this regard, Ball claimed that the sentiments that bind together the many members of society in a state of freedom and social equality being absent, the slaveholder had to resort to physical restraint and "rules of mental coercion, unknown in another and a different condition of the social compact." [76]

The Slave Patrols

Another method employed to maintain control over the slaves was the use of slave patrols. The narratives relate that it was the general function of these groups to enforce strict obedience by the slaves to all the laws, rules, regulations, and customs of the community, and that their special duty was to search the quarters and the homes of free Negroes to uncover fugitives or slaves visiting without a pass.

Solomon Northup reported that the patrols which rode on horseback were armed and accompanied by dogs. The dogs were trained to seize a man on orders and tear him to pieces. The patrols had the right, according to Northup, either by law or general consent, to inflict punishment upon a slave caught beyond the boundaries of his master's estate without a pass, and even to shoot him if he attempted to escape their questions. Northup recalled that they were compensated by the slaveholders, who would contribute in proportion to the number of slaves they owned. [77]

Henry Clay Bruce noted that some patrols had jurisdiction covering the city or town limits only, and had no legal rights outside of it. Often, however, their desire to whip a particular slave or group of slaves was so great that they left their designated area and gathered secretly in the woods without the knowledge or consent of the city officials.[78]

On New Year's Day in Francis Fedric's community, ten or more whites were chosen to man the patrols. The group was usually composed of slaveholders, poor whites, and professional "nigger-baiters." They were sworn in at the local courthouse, and the leader was called the captain.[79]

The patrols, and especially the captain, had almost unlimited power over the slaves. Lewis Clarke expressed his specific hatred of the captain of the patrols in the following ringing denunciation:

[The] greatest scoundrel is always captain of the band of patrols. They are the off-scouring of all things; the refuse, the fag end, the ears and tails of slavery; the scales and fins of fish; the tooth and tongues of serpents. They are the very fool's cap of baboons, the echo of parrots, the wallet and satchel of polecats, the scum of stagnant pool, the exuvial, the worn-out skins of slaveholders. They are, emphatically, the servants of servants, and slaves of the devil; they are the meanest, and lowest and worst of all creation. Like starved wharf rats, they are out nights, creeping into slave cabins, to see if they have an old bone there; drive out husbands from their own beds, and then take their places. They get up all sorts of pretences, false as their lying tongues can make them, and then whip the slaves and carry a gory lash to the master, for a piece of bread.[80]

Patrols also made a business of whipping slaves for a fee. Moses Grandy recalled that they would ride about informing persons who kept no overseers that if there was a slave to be whipped, whether man or woman, they would be available when called, for a fee of half a dollar. According to Grandy, widows and other females got their slaves whipped in this manner.[81]

Grandy also stated that if a slave had offended the patrol,

even by so innocent a matter as dressing tidily to go to a place of worship, he would be seized, his pass destroyed, and he flogged, while the remainder of the patrol looked the other way. When his master made a complaint of his slave having been beaten without cause, the others would swear they saw no one beat him. The slave's oath would stand for nothing, and in such a case, "his tormentors are safe, for they were the only whites present." [82]

According to Henry Clay Bruce the patrols took great pride and pleasure in whipping slaves. They whipped some so unmercifully that some masters issued orders to the patrols, that in punishing a captured slave, no skin should be broken, no blood brought out by the lash. There was no established law of patrolling, it having originated as a custom to please a few slaveholders and to help them control their stock. Therefore, in certain communities, masters threatened to punish any man interfering with their slaves, even if found off their lands, and the patrols carefully avoided such men's slaves. [83]

Austin Steward wrote of masters who had a reputation for kindness and indulgence. Steward reported that they were looked upon with suspicion, and sometimes hatred, by their neighbors, and their slaves were watched more closely than others. The patrol was often anxious to flog some of "these pampered niggers, who were spoiled by the indulgence of a weak, inefficient, but well-meaning owner." A narrative contained in Benjamin Drew's collection stated that the other slaveholders felt that "*his* niggers spoil *our* niggers." [84]

Solomon Northup reported that although the patrol was specifically established to guard the slaves, any white man could seize a Negro without a pass and whip him. Generally, said Northup, those whites "having the air and appearance of gentlemen, whose dress indicated the possession of wealth," usually took no notice of the Negro; but the poor white never failed to do so. They would thoroughly scrutinize and examine almost every slave, because catching runaways was a money-making business. If, after advertising, no owner appeared, they were sold to the highest bidder, and fees were given to the finder for his services. In Northup's words, "A mean white, therefore—a name applied to the species loafer—considers it a god-send to meet an unknown Negro without a pass." [85]

The Arkansas Narratives, as did the Georgia Narratives, stated that slaves would sometimes tie ropes across roads that were frequented by the patrols, causing the patrollers and their horses to fall. This type of "warfare" was constant in the slave states, and Henry Clay Bruce reported other deceptions practiced on the patrols. He claimed that it was easy to fool them, "because they were, as a rule illiterate, and of course could not read writing." Knowing this, slaves would take a portion of a letter that they had found, and present it to the captain as a pass. The captain would take it, look it over wisely, and return it. Others would secure a pass from the master, find a slave who could read to erase the day and month, and then use it indefinitely. Other slaves would get their young master or mistress to sign their father's name on a pass whenever they wanted to go out. According to Moses Grandy, patrols were so numerous that they could not be easily escaped, and therefore, it was imperative that the slave present some written document to prevent a beating.[86]

On rare occasions, said Linda Brent, a free Negro was recruited into a patrol. This person was often of mixed blood and previously set free by a slaveholder. The community generally knew that this person was a former slave who, for the sake of passing himself off as white, was "ready to kiss the slaveholders' feet." According to Miss Brent, the slaves despised this person more than the members of the patrol. The duties of the patrollers were despicable, but they were considered superior to the black man who was their companion, a companion who held the office only to exercise the authority of a white.[87]

The Black Driver

Perhaps the most invidious method of control was the use of the black driver: the slave who was trained and employed by the master to supervise, lead and punish the other slaves. This turning of black against black was one of the most degrading and dehumanizing aspects of the institution.

Peter Still reported that sometimes the master would want to raise one of his young slave children to be a black driver. These slaves would ultimately receive better treatment than the rest of the "quarters," and the master was usually "not displeased either, with saving the expense of a large salary for a white superintendent," or as was often the case, with the superior job that the slave did for him.[88]

In other cases, according to Jamie Parker, the most trusted and likely of the adult slaves was selected for this position. If he proved himself well qualified he was permitted to keep the job for life, or until he was worn out. Parker noted, however, that when these slaves got too old for this function they were "laid aside, like an old garment, labeled in the inventory 'old and useless.' "[89]

Parker explained that during the planting season it was the driver's function to lead the slave gang. In hoeing he took the "fore row," and saw to it that every slave kept up the pace. If they loitered he was authorized to whip them, or give the information to the overseer, if there was one, who would administer the punishment. The driver was generally considered "the boss of the plantation" and was expected to participate in various types of work.[90]

Parker claimed that the amount of labor performed on the plantation was largely dependent upon the driver. If he was of top quality he worked the slave gang hard. If he was easy and "fond of resting on his hoe," the slaves had an easy time, especially when the overseer was out of sight.[91]

The driver almost always felt his importance, and at times

e considered himself equal to the aristocracy of his race, i.e.,
he house servants. He was looked up to by the "quarters" as
"*slave of consequence.*" The other slaves found it to their
advantage to keep in his good graces, for as a result they
vere less likely to be turned over to the overseer for punishment. Many slaves reported that power in the hands of a
river was dangerous; for power was something he did not
now how to exercise. The driver had the power to make
eople work, and very often for the sake of exercising his
ower he would work until exhausted. The slave gang was
orced to labor with him and were therefore at his mercy.
Those who hung back would always face the driver's whip.[92]
In most cases, wrote Parker, the young slave had to be
roken in by the driver. The young field hands, he said, being
naccustomed to the "yoke of patiently enduring hard toil—
nd working simply because they *must* (although they know
hat this is the only way of drawing 'lowance, or rations),
vork just as little as they can." Thus the driver generally
ound it necessary to "train them in," as one broke in horses.
The overseer would constantly urge the driver, who in turn
vould urge the gang to keep up the pace.[93]
In most instances the driver was under the supervision of
white overseer. Nevertheless, Jacob Stroyer reported that in
many cases, the driver treated his fellow slaves worse than
he white overseer and sometimes masters thought more of the
river than of the overseer. Stroyer wrote of Uncle Esau, who
vas one such driver. Many of the slaves on his plantation had
o fear of the white overseer, but would run from him. Some
ayed in hiding for as long as ten months because of the treatment they received from him. They were so afraid of Esau
nat, according to Stroyer, "they would rather see the devil
nan to see him; they were glad when he died." [94]
When Lewis Clarke was asked why a black driver was
vorse than a white one, he replied, "he must be very strict and
evere, or else he will be turned out. The master selects the

hardest-hearted and the most unprincipled slave upon the plantation." [95]

Some plantations had no overseer, only a driver. Anthony Burns served in this capacity. His master trusted him to operate the entire estate without white supervision. As Burns matured, his ability was recognized by his owner and he was asked to supervise the farm in the absence of the master or overseer. The master would return once a year for a reunion with his driver and his slaves. On his annual visit, he would meet with them, see their physical condition, and review the events that had transpired during the previous year. If any slave had been sick, gotten into difficulty, or had been punished by the authorities, this was the opportunity for explanation. The interview ended with each slave receiving a dime or some smaller coin, and when the master left, Burns once again became the sole authority on the plantation.[96]

According to the Alabama Narratives of the Federal Writers' Project, few slaves were fortunate enough to have a driver like Burns, or to be in the position of the slaves he supervised. For the most part, they hated the driver, and many vowed that when they "growed up dat" they "was agoin' to kill dat nigger iffen it was de las' thing" that they "efer done." [97]

On the other hand, Solomon Northup claimed that some drivers treated their slave gangs well. One learned to handle a whip with such dexterity and precision, that he could throw the lash within an inch of the slave's body without touching him. If he was being observed from a distance, he pretended to apply the lash vigorously, and the slave who was being punished, according to a prearranged plan, would squirm and scream, as if he were receiving a beating.[98]

William Grimes reported that when the driver was ordered to whip a slave, the master would watch to see that it was well executed. Sometimes if the master felt that the whipping was not severe enough, he would order the punished slave to beat the driver. Then he would order the driver to whip the slave

harder than he did before and what would ensue was the most
severe and brutal whipping. In this second trial, the driver
would exert all his strength and agility to make the slave suffer.
Thus, said Grimes, "the Negro drivers and indeed the slaves,
show much less humanity in punishment than the masters." [99]

The Texas Narratives tell of drivers being brutal purely
for the sake of brutality. These drivers would report a theft
that the master would never have been concerned about, or
an infraction of the rules passed over by the severest overseer.
One slave said, "we might a done very well if de ole driver
hadn' been so mean, but de least little thing we do he beat us
for it, and put big, chains 'round our ankles and make us work
and dem on till de blood be cut out all around our ankles."
This same driver was said to have placed slaves in stocks,
chained to the ground, face up to the sun, and "leaves 'em dere
'till dez nearly dies." [100]

IV

Types of Slaves

In the preceding chapter there was some discussion in detail of what the narratives say about life on the plantation in general, and the ways in which the slaves survived and even resisted the effects of the system.

The narratives, however, also contain descriptions of the various types, classes, and categories of slaves, the ways in which slavery affected each, and some of the reasons for the assumption of certain roles adopted by the slaves; and in this chapter the more recognizable of these categories of slaves and what the narratives say about each will be set forth.

THE AGED SLAVE

One of the shabbier characteristics of slavery described in the slave narratives, and one which tended to deepen the slave's conviction of the infernal character of the institution and to fill him with utter loathing of slaveholders, was the master's alleged lack of gratitude to the aged slave. According to Frederick Douglass, many of these elder slaves had served the plantation faithfully for all of their lives. Often they had been major factors in the accumulation of the master's wealth. Many had, over the years, nursed the master through infancy, "attended him in childhood, served him through life, and at his death wiped from his icy brow the cold death-sweat, and closed his eyes forever." [1]

In an effort to extract the last ounce of value from these old slaves, the master would make use of them, in various ways, until the last hours of life. They would be made to shell corn, pack tobacco, or remain at home to nurse the sick. One of their more common chores, said Douglass, was to attend to the needs of the children too young for field work.

If no work of any value could be found for them, or if they outlived their original masters and fell into the hands of strangers, they would either be sold for any price they would bring, or be simply turned out to fend for themselves. William Wells Brown reported cases of aged slaves being sold for one dollar "to men not worth one cent." Even at that price, Brown noted, there were slaves who had to be discarded after the master received no bids at all. [2]

The old slave who was turned out did as best he could to survive. After a losing battle with cold and hunger, and, in the words of Lewis Clarke, racked with the pains of old age, he was often found, "*starved* to death, out of doors, and half eaten up by animals." [3] Zangara and Maquama claimed that many of the elderly were forced to beg for food and shelter from the neighboring slave quarters or from free Negroes. These slaves wandered around the countryside until they died either from exposure, starvation, or a slaveholder's rifle. An example of the attitude of the typical white toward these "slaves in exile" and the sense of futility which pervaded these discarded slaves is the following incident recorded by Zangara:

Two white men seeing a discarded slave in the field began to joke about his condition. One of them said, "Tom I'll wager you a dollar that I wing that old good-for-nothing nigger the first shot, at fifty yards." The second agreed to the wager and they paced off the distance. The old slave, aware of what was happening, but unable to move, expressed only the desire that they might kill him.[4] They left him wounded, and he survived.

Some aged slaves became so embittered at being replaced by younger men that their contempt was directed toward their fellow slaves. Charles Ball's grandfather, for example, considered the younger slaves to be "a mean and vulgar race, quite beneath his rank, and the dignity of his former station." [5]

There were, according to certain of the narratives, more fortunate elder slaves who were given cabins of their own, with half an acre or so to cultivate for themselves and from which they were able to draw their subsistence.

Indeed, the Arkansas Narratives reported:

They [the masters] did't make the old people in slavery work when they was my age. My daddy when he was my age, they turned him out. They give him a rice patch where he could make his rice. When he died, he had a whole lot of rice. They stopped putting all the slaves out at hard labor when they got old. That's one thing white folks will take care of their old ones.[6]

Nonetheless, in general, in the inventory of the plantation, the slave who was labeled old and useless had all light of hope dimmed. Lacking any consolation, slavery became even more galling to him; not only was he helpless, but he was now useless as well. These elderly slaves were, in the most real sense, the end result of the dehumanization process. Frederick Douglass's grandmother presented an illustrative example of the situation of the aged slave. Douglass described her, as follows:

And now, when weighed down by the pains and aches of old age, when the head inclines to the feet, when the beginning and ending of human existence meet, and helpless infancy and painful old age combine together—at this time, the most needful time, the time for the exercise of that tenderness and affection which children only can exercise towards a declining parent—my poor old grandmother, the devoted mother of twelve children, is left all alone, in yonder little hut, before a few dim embers. She stands —she sits—she staggers—she falls—she groans—she dies—and there are none of her children or grandchildren present, to wipe from her wrinkled brow the cold sweat of death, or to place beneath the sod her fallen remains. Will not a righteous God visit for these things? [7]

THE FEMALE SLAVE

Slaves wrote widely about the condition of the female in bondage. Although slavery was generally considered to be a universal nightmare for all involved, the female slave received special and additional tortures peculiar to her sex. William J. Anderson wrote of a female slave who, upon learning that her new-born babe was a girl, expressed no other wish for the child than its death. [8]

As with men, the lash was also freely used on women, young and old. Anderson alleged that it was not an uncommon scene on the plantation to see a female stripped naked, tied to a stake, and whipped with a hard saw or club, which was eventually broken over her body. [9]

James Williams noted that many of the female slaves were by nature delicate and never became accustomed to field labor. They suffered from the extreme heat and the severity of the toil. One could observe these women at day's end, "dragging their weary limbs from the cotton field at nightfall, faint and exhausted. The overseers would laugh at such sufferings and quip that they were "Virginia ladies, and altogether too delicate for Alabama use; but they must be made to do their tasks notwithstanding." At times, Williams claimed, the treatment of these women was so horrid that the men would volunteer to take their places in the fields. [10]

In addition to their use as farmhands, according to several of the North Carolina Narratives of the Federal Writers' Project, slave women were to the master as the cows were to the stock raiser. If she gave birth frequently she was considered valuable. (Females who resisted forced mating were beaten or sold.) Many were separated from their families and sold to distant slave states, as punishment and as a lesson to the others.[11]

Isaac D. Williams swore that if he had not seen and experienced slavery, he would not believe one-half of the evils inflicted upon women. The white man, he claimed, had from the first taken advantage, abused his power, and striven to keep the female slave in the cruelest subjugation.[12]

Williams told of a young slave mother sold by her master to a distant plantation. She was forced to leave her infant son who was just beginning to walk. Nineteen years later, all ties between the two having been broken, her child was sold to the same plantation. Working near each other in the field, the two "strangers" became attached and after a time were married. Some time thereafter, the mother noticed a peculiar scar on her husband's head and asked him how he got it. He told her that as a child he fell out of his mother's arms into a fire and got badly burned. He said that it happened when he was on Judge Campbell's plantation. "'Why!' screamed the poor woman, 'you are my own son!' and she fainted away." When the true relationship was discovered, the master sold the male away to a distant farm and the two never met again. Williams reported that episodes such as this "were of frequent occurrence."[13]

Much of the punishment inflicted on the female was due to the irresponsibility of the slaveholder. Few owners took the time to train or instruct their slaves. Harriet Tubman related a typical case to Sarah Bradford: a slave was engaged to do housework by day and to mind the master's children at night. Her first task was to sweep and dust a parlor. No instructions

were given as to how this was to be done. After sweeping the
parlor, she took the dusting cloth and wiped the other objects
in the room. There being no escape for it, the dust merely
settled in the room again. When the mistress came to see how
the work had progressed, she cursed the slave for neglecting
her duty. The slave repeated the entire process, but the result
was the same. This mistress proceeded to beat the slave for
not following orders. The screams of the slave were heard by
the mistress's sister, who, being advised of the problem, asked
if the slave had been given any instruction whatever. Receiving a negative reply, the sister told the slave to open the
windows and sweep, and then to wipe the dust. Thereafter
there was no more trouble. This incident caused Tubman to
decry the fact that "many a poor slave suffered for the stu-
pidity and obstinacy of a master or mistress, more stupid than
themselves." [14]

The most despicable area of female slave treatment was that
of sexual abuse. William Anderson claimed that such treatment
was "carried on to an alarming extent in the far South."
According to Anderson, the slave plantation of the old South
was a virtual hotbed of incest and bigamy. [15]

Linda Brent reported that, generally, the secrets of the
master-female relationship were guarded and concealed from
the outside world. The slaves were sure, however, that the
masters were the fathers of many slave children. Although,
according to Miss Brent, it was common knowledge in the
slave quarters, the mothers would not dare reveal who the
father was. No slave in the quarters, or around the great house,
would even allude to it. [16]

One slave whose story was transcribed by James Redpath
was asked, "Are the wives of slaves respected as married
women?" His reply was, "No mass'r, dey don't make no
diff'rence wedder de colored women is married or not. White
folks jest do what dey have a mind to wid dem." In response
to the question "Do white people ever act immorally to col-

ored women on the plantation?" he answered, "Yes, mass'r, *bery of 'em, indeed.*" The master "would catch young colored girls and whip them and make them do what they wanted." [17]

Louisa Picquet revealed the shame of the institution in a brief analysis of the master-female relationship. She said that because she was forced to become a concubine, the female slave was often the cause of marital difficulties between master and mistress. The end result of such a situation was usually the sale of the slave. She reported that slaves had as many as six or seven white children, some having light hair and blue eyes, but none having an acknowledged father. Miss Picquet suggested that the same master who forced his attentions on the slave, might, nevertheless, very well be recognized as a "gentleman" and freely admitted into white female society, "as if he were as pure as Joseph." [18]

Many masters who feared carrying on their illicit sexual activities at home boarded out their concubines in the city. As a consequence of the multitude of master-slave relationships, Miss Picquet estimated that there were 300,000 mulattoes in the slaves states, "to a great extent the contribution of slave-holders and their sons to the common stock of southern chattels." [19]

In this connection, James Pennington told of one master who owned a twenty-four-year-old female. Within one year of her purchase his son became attached to her, "for no honorable purposes; a fact which was not only well-known among all the slaves, but which became a source of unhappiness to his mother and sisters." The family's concern over this relationship resulted in the sale of the slave. That same son who had degraded her, and who was the cause of her being sold, was designated to be the salesman. [20]

Pennington suggested that this incident reflected the operation of the chattel principle; that slavery could not exist without this principle; and that the end result of this case was inevitable. Slavery, he claimed, made it difficult to speak of kind or Christian masters, for the slaveholders were not the masters of the system, but rather the system was their master, "and the slaves are their vassals." [21]

The Kentucky Narratives of the Federal Writers' Project contain the story of one occasion, indicative of many, wherein a slave trader took a beautiful mulatto slave to his room and attempted "to satisfy his bestial nature." This particular girl, however, could not be coerced or forced, and, consequently, she was violently attacked and beaten. In the struggle, she grabbed a knife "and with it she sterilized him, and from the result of the injury he died the next day:" It was said that the attack was the result of merely being pretty, a dubious distinction among female slaves. The girl was put to death.[22]

Kate Pickard told of similar experiences of a slave girl named Maria. Maria was a thirteen-year-old house servant. One day, receiving no response to her call, the mistress began searching the house for her. Finally, she opened the parlor door, and there was the child with her master. The master ran out of the room, mounted his horse and rode off to escape, "though well he knew that [his wife's] full fury would fall upon the young head of his victim." The mistress beat the child and locked her in a smokehouse. For two weeks the girl was constantly whipped. Some of the elderly servants attempted to plead with the mistress on Maria's behalf, and even hinted that "it was mass'r that was to blame." The mistress's reply was typical: "She'll know better in the future. After I've done with her, she'll never do the like again, through ignorance." [23]

After Maria had been kept imprisoned for two weeks, the mistress's eldest son came to visit. Upon arrival he was told by his mother of "*Maria's depravity,* and [she] begged him to take her [Maria] away with him." Her orders to her son were to sell the child to the hardest master he could find, for "If she stays, I shall certainly kill her." [24]

Fugitive slave John Thompson tells another such story, albeit with a different ending. During his wife's absence, the master tried to force his attentions upon Thompson's sister. She resisted him, and the master, becoming enraged, ordered the girl beaten "until the blood stood in puddles under her feet." After a while, this became a recurring scene, but only during the wife's absences. Learning of the beatings and knowing her husband's inclinations, the wife became suspicious and began asking for the reasons for the whippings. When she asked her maid about the punishment, the slave, despite the fact that she knew it could mean her death, answered, "I must not tell you, but you may know what it is all for. If I have done anything, Madam, contrary to your wishes, and do not suit you, please tell me, but do not kill me without cause." After hearing the full story, the mistress was so shocked that she fainted and had to spend six weeks in bed. Despite her illness and her complaints, the master's conduct persisted, and, it was said, the situation finally caused her death.[25]

Many slaveholders were known to go into the slave cabin and make the husband sit outside while he would, according to William Anderson, "carry on the same sport with the colored man's wife at the same time."[26] In one case recorded in the Fisk University collection of narratives, a husband whose wife was often the object of the master's desires could no longer remain mute. One morning he waited outside for the master and, when he emerged, the slave bludgeoned him to death. The slave, of course, was subsequently hanged.[27]

Some slaves who dictated the Fisk University autobiographical accounts of slavery claimed that there were females who were not really forced to have relations with white men; that, in reality, they did it of their own volition. Other females, they said, engaged in these affairs out of fear of being sent to the deep south, "and they would do anything to keep from it." It was also reported that some white mistresses kept beautiful black maids in the house to "entertain" their sons and to keep them from marrying. Many of these young masters would have children by these slaves. Such children found it difficult, if not impossible, to find acceptance either in the master's family or in the slave quarters.[28]

Most slaves who were interviewed for the North Carolina Narratives displayed contempt for the female who was willing to become the concubine of the master, especially if she submitted without a struggle. This group of submissive females, some of them half white, were used not only by the master, but by his friends as well. They were usually granted special privileges and worked very little. They had private quarters which were well furnished and in some cases they had great influence over the master. Some of these slave girls, according to one reporter, broke up families by "getting the master so enmeshed in their net that his wife, perhaps an older woman, was greatly neglected." [29]

Louisa Picquet analyzed the stories of the role of the female in bondage. She felt that if such was the *exposed* life under slavery, what must the hidden life be? The telltale mulatto (half white, half black), quadroon (one-quarter black), and octoroon (one-eighth black) faces stood out as testimony to the deep moral pollution of the slave states. The people of America, she suggested, might shudder at the "heathenism of a Turkish harem," and "stand aghast at the idea of twenty thousand Syrian women sold to supply the harems of the Mussulmans," but, she asked, "is all this whit worse than what is constantly practiced, with scarce a word of unfavorable comment, in our own Christian land?" She claimed that if there were any difference, it was in favor of the Turks, for neither his concubines, nor his children by them, were slaves, while in the United States "our chivalrous 'southern gentlemen' beget thousands of slaves; and hundreds of the children of our free white citizens are sold in the southern slave markets every year." [30]

THE CONTENTED SLAVE

There were, indeed, "contented" slaves. One may speculate on the basis of their contentment, or the reasons therefor—whether it was because they had deceived themselves into believing they were happy, or had merely given up hope of escaping or of changing their way of life and had therefore given only an appearance of satisfaction, or any number of other reasons—but the fact of the matter is that according to the narratives there was a group or type of slave who *appeared* to be completely and wholly contented with the institution and his way of life within it.

To be sure, in some cases, it was, in the words of William Wells Brown, a "low kind of happiness existing only where masters were disposed to treat their servants kindly, and where the proverbial lightheartedness of the latter prevailed." [31]

In most cases, however, those slaves whom we herein classify as contended appeared to be, without qualification, genuinely happy. Brown himself tells of the slave Charlotte, who was freed. After some time, she began thinking on her former life with such longing that she sought to return. Finding this impossible to accomplish, she asked that, at least, none of her children, who were still in bondage, be set free. [32]

Other narratives tell similar stories of contented slaves. One finds, in analyzing these narratives, that the heading "Contented Slave" may be further broken down into two basic subheadings: that of the "loyal slave," whose satisfaction with the institution manifested itself in his fervent fealty to the master, and that of the "pious slave" who because of religion found what appeared to the observer to be respect, dignity, and true happiness in his station.

In any event, and whatever the reasons therefor, these contented slaves represented the ultimate success of the dehumanization process. In them there was no longer resistance. They had succumbed completely to the needs and desires of the master and the institution. They were able to find contentment in a situation which was totally foreign to any rational definition of what is noble, genuine, and, above all, human in mankind.

The Loyal Slave

The loyal slaves were generally found to be the "reliables": the ones whom the master trusted and seldom had occasion to scold for neglect of duty. They spent their lives in the service of the master, and brought up their children in the same tradition. The loyal slave not only looked after his own interest, but was quite concerned with the master's as well.[33]

For example, Josiah Henson reported that the loyal slave often served as a protector or bodyguard of his master. A master might spend his nights drinking in local taverns, and at times he would be aware that he would not be able to find his way home at night. Thus he would order the slave to come after him and help him home. Only the most loyal slave was chosen for this confidential duty. At times quarrels and brawls would occur at the tavern. Whenever they became too dangerous for the master, it was the function of this slave to rush in and drag his master from the fight to his home.[34]

Henson reported that many a loyal slave refused to take advantage of opportunities for obtaining freedom. He did not wish to leave his master because of what Henson described as a "perception of [his] own strength of character, the feeling of integrity, and the sentiment of high honor." [35]

When Henson's master found himself in financial difficulty he told Henson to take the other slaves beyond the slave states and wait for him in Ohio. Thus he would be able to start again in another slave area, while keeping his creditors away from his slaves. When Henson reached Ohio, he was told that he and the others were no longer slaves but, if they chose, free men. Freedom had always been an ambition of his, but he wanted it only if he had purchased it himself. He felt that the duties of the slave to his master should be obeyed. To run away seemed like stealing, and his "notions of right were against it." He had made a promise to his master and he felt that he had undertaken a great thing. The motivating force behind Henson's decision was his loyalty and the immense admiration and respect with which his master regarded him.[36]

Slaves like Henson reported that their loyalty prevented them from betraying a specific trust. An illustration of such loyalty was given by Bethany Veney, who told of a slave who had made a contract with his master prior to the Civil War to buy his freedom. While he was paying for himself, he was permitted to live and work where he pleased. The slave found that he could earn more in Ohio, so that is where he lived. When he was emancipated, he was still in debt to his master for three hundred dollars. Although by the passage of the Thirteenth Amendment he was freed from any obligation to his master, this ex-slave "walked the greater portion of the distance back to where his old master lived in Virginia, and placed the last dollar, with interest, in his hands." Although not required to pay the balance of the debt, he had given his master his word. He said that he could not enjoy his liberty unless he fulfilled his promise.[37]

The loyalty of these slaves was sometimes rewarded by the masters. Abigail Mott wrote of Robert, a slave of another master who found himself in financial difficulty. One day the master called him in and told him that because of his faithful service he was setting him free, for he was no longer able to maintain him. The slave replied, "No, massa, me no leave you; you maintain me many years, me now try what I can do for you." Robert procured employment as a laborer, and regularly brought his salary to his master. Both men managed to subsist on this income until the master was able to gain possession of a considerable amount of property and restore himself to his former status. Grateful to this faithful servant, one of the first acts of the master was to create an annuity for the slave for the remainder of his life.[38]

In another similar case, dictated by a slave to Ralph Roberts, the master was compelled by circumstances to move to a new area and to sell some of his slaves. One such slave found his relationship with his new master quite difficult. Instead of trying to escape to freedom, he fled from his hard master and attempted to find his former master for protection. He journeyed one hundred and fifty miles on foot, through an area which was entirely unknown to him. Only the hope that he would reach his old master encouraged him to go on. When his food and money were exhausted, he begged food from other slaves, and received directions to his destination. He finally reached the house of his former master, and told him of the flight from his legal owner. The old master, knowing that he was liable to prosecution for harboring a runaway, nevertheless took his former slave into his house and kept him.[39]

Loyal slaves like this one, even if sometimes infirm or aged, were often valuable to the slaveholder for their loyalty alone. Whenever such a slave was sold on the auction block, the price was invariably higher than his worth as a worker. Henry Bibb told of one master who caused the price of such a slave to rise by describing him in the following manner:

He is not able to accomplish much manual labor, from his extreme age and hard labor in early life. Yet I would rather have him than many of those that are young and vigorous; who are able to perform twice as much labor—because I know him to be faithful and trustworthy, a Christian in good standing in every church. I can trust him anywhere with confidence. He has toiled many long years on my plantation and I have always found him faithful.[40]

The Pious Slave

Like his "loyal" brother, the "pious" slave, who either preached the word of God or lived the religious life, appeared to find comfort and contentment within the institution. According to the pious slave, wrote Daniel H. Peterson, a great many blacks brought trouble upon themselves by their own malingering and disloyalty to the master. Uncle Jack, a slave preacher, who dictated his story to William White, claimed that if the slave did his job, was loyal to the master and fearful of God, he had no better friend than the slaveholder.[41]

These pious slaves were never known to offend the slaveholder, and according to Uncle Jack, they were "entirely removed from all want and grievance." The pious slave was generally welcome to preach to the quarters on all neighboring plantations, and was sometimes sent long distances to conduct services. Wherever he went he would receive the most polite and friendly attention of the whites on the plantation.[42]

White wrote of Uncle Jack that the respect and "attention bestowed upon him by persons of the highest standings were remarkable." He was invited into the master's home, sat with the family, took part in the family's worship and sometimes led the family in prayer. Many of the leading slaveholders of the community attended his meetings and listened to his sermons. He was considered by the whites the best preacher in the community, and it was said of him that his "opinions were respected, his advice followed, and yet he never betrayed the least symptom of arrogance or self-conceit." When in the presence of the slaveholder, he seldom began a conversation, and when he did, it was done by modestly asking some pertinent question on an important subject. When no opportunity for a question existed, he was silent.[43]

When Uncle Jack spoke of the American Colonization Society (see Chapter VII), he said it would be successful if the "natives were duly restrained." In discussing the superstitious practices and conditions of the African, he asserted that they could never compare with the superior Christian system. White said that he "was often heard to thank God that he had been brought to America," for "coming to the white man's country as a slave, was the means of making me free in Christ Jesus." [44]

Jupiter Hammon, another pious slave, asserted that whether it was right or lawful in the sight of God for the white to enslave the black man, it was the slaves' duty to obey their masters "in all their lawful commands, and mind them unless we are bid to do that which we know to be sin, or forbidden in God's word." He felt that it was God's commandment for the slave to obey his master. Although he personally thought slavery was wrong, he refused to question the dictates of God. He reported that if a servant pleased his master, the slaveholder would do the same for the servant. Hammon claimed that good servants made good masters. If, he said,

your master is really hard, unreasonable and cruel, there is no way so likely for you to convince him of it, as always to obey his commands, and try to serve him, and take care of his interest, and try to promote it in all your power. If you are proud and stubborn and always finding fault, your master will think the fault was wholly on your side; but if you are humble, and meek, and bear all things patiently, your master may think he is wrong; if he does not, his neighbors will be apt to see it, and will befriend you, and try to alter his conduct. [45]

Because of this kind of philosophy, the slaveholder respected the pious slave. The narratives indicate, however, that the blacks had mixed emotions; they variously loved, feared, and obeyed him. In either event, though, his influence among the slaves was usually unbounded, and his authority over the members of his own church often greater than that of the master or the overseer. [46]

THE INFORMER

Throughout history, Judas has been a familiar figure. The informer is both a melancholy and classic character whose appearance among the slaves was neither unusual nor un-expected.

As the contented slave was able to make his way and find satisfaction in his situation through the various means discussed in the previous section, so too, the type of slave we discuss in this section was able to relate to his master and the institution and thereby maintain at least a somewhat less painful physical existence than his brethren.

In many instances, especially among the free Negroes, the informer's motivation was financial reward; in some it was out of genuine affection for the master, as in the cases of saving the master from insurrection. In most cases, however, his activities were motivated by a desire to exist within the institution as painlessly as possible, and reflected another manifestation of the dehumanizing effect of slavery.

Austin Steward described the informer as one who, for the sake of currying favor with the master, would betray his fellow slave and

by tattling, get him severely whipped; and for these acts of perfidy, and sometimes downright falsehood, he is often rewarded by his master, who knows it is for his interest to keep such ones about him; though he is sometimes obliged, in addition to a reward, to send him away, for fear of the vengeance of the betrayed slaves.[47]

The informer was always treated with more affability than the others, for the slaveholder was well aware that without the information he got from him, his family could be destroyed through an insurrection.[48]

Black men of this character were sometimes sent into free states to spy and inform on fugitives. One such incident was related to Levi Coffin. An informer was sent as a spy from Kentucky, asking for help and protection, and appearing to be fearful that he would be captured. As infiltration by in-formers was common among the fugitives, they were ever watchful and guarded about the information they released and

to whom they granted sanctuary. The false fugitive was tem-
porarily given protection by the fugitive community and was
guarded until it could be ascertained whether the man was an
actual fugitive. When it was discovered that he was an informer, "the colored people, among whom he had been stay-
ing, arose in their indignation, took him out of the city, and
administered punishment in the shape of a severe whipping.
After this he returned to Kentucky, and was never known to
play such a part again." [49]

William Nell tells of another "black betrayer" in Cincinnati,
Ohio, who was placed on "trial" by the free colored population. He escaped with his life only after three hundred blows
were inflicted on him—"one blow for each dollar of blood
money which he had received for doing the infamous work of
these Kentucky hunters of men." [50]

In another of Coffin's narratives, a black man who had been
employed by some slaveholders to act as an informer journeyed to Ohio dressed as a woman. He presented himself at
the basement of a Negro church in Cincinnati where fugitives
were known to assemble. One female fugitive became suspicious and sent for some of the men. The suspect was questioned and cross-questioned. When they were almost certain
that he was a man in disguise, he was turned over to the leaders
of the fugitive community, who stripped him of the female
garments, and inflicted such a severe punishment upon him
that he was fortunate to escape with his life. [51]

The narratives report that, in addition to spying on fugitives
and aiding in their recapture, slave informers were also known
to reveal incipient insurrection, both real and fabricated.

A petition to the Virginia Legislature in 1824 for entrance
and residence into that state relates the story of one such informer, a freed slave who was originally a native of Richmond,
Virginia, but who had been living in New Orleans. In 1812,
he had exposed a plot of insurrection which "would have ex-
hibited a spectacle of ruin and desolation exceeding anything

which formerly transpired in St. Domingo." The information about the plot which the petitioner had given to the authorities resulted in the execution of countless slaves. The petition alleged that he could not remain in "safety as he had every reason to believe that he might be the victim of disappointed treason." He claimed that because of his behavior he would be the object of persecution by Negroes of New Orleans, both bond and free.[52]

Although the sabotaged insurrection which was the subject of the petitioner's information may have been a real one, the narratives indicate that, for various reasons, informers would also "invent" insurrections about which they could confess. In one such incident reported in the Fisk University collection of narratives, a group of slaves were having a dance without the master's consent. A slave patrol caught one slave and threatened to whip him if he did not disclose who was there. The slave, who had invented and then revealed a possible uprising in order to escape punishment, reported that

It was around the time when the niggers was rising, and they asked me did I hear them shooting? "Did you see any guns?" And I said, "No, I didn't see no guns, but I heard them shooting." I hadn't heard a thing, but I knowed what they wanted to hear, so I said I did.[53]

In a similar incident, Solomon Northup told of a concerted movement among a number of slaves in Louisiana to escape to the neighboring territory of Mexico. Their avowed hope was to encounter no opposition, and thereby avoid any bloodshed. Northup reported that the leader of the plot became convinced of the ultimate failure of the project, and in order to curry favor with his master and avoid the consequences which he imagined would follow their failure, he told the slaveholders that a group of slaves had collected in the swamps and, although he knew that they wished no violence, that they were going to emerge from the swamps at the first favorable opportunity and murder every white person in the community.[54]

The words of the informer, exaggerated even more as they passed from master to master, filled the community with terror. The fugitives were captured and hanged. Not only were those who were involved executed, but because of the leader's infidelity, many slaves who were suspected, though entirely innocent, were likewise taken from the quarters and murdered. The informer not only escaped this fate, he "was even rewarded for his treachery." [55]

The narratives indicate that not all informers were slaves, but that, albeit for different reasons, usually financial, many free Negroes were engaged in betraying their slave brothers. These freemen would invite fugitives fresh from bondage to their homes on various pretexts, and, by pretending to befriend them, get the name of their master, his residence, and other needed information. He would then communicate with the master and make arrangements for the recapture. Joseph Vance Lewis described the treachery of one free Negro who had been luring fugitives to his home and then reselling them to a group of kidnappers who would return them to their masters. The slaves eventually discovered the betrayer's scheme, and his connections with these transactions were clearly proved. It was decided by the slaves "to force him to quit the nefarious business," and six men were chosen to kill him. [56]

Because of these and other betrayals, the fugitives determined to protect themselves from the slave kidnapper and informer. Frederick Douglass wrote of a fugitive and a free Negro who were on unfriendly terms. The freeman was heard to threaten the fugitive with exposure. A meeting of the black community was immediately called and the potential betrayer was asked to attend. The first order of business was the election of a "religious gentleman" as president of the meeting. He addressed the assemblage: "Friends, we have got him here, and I would recommend that you young men just take him outside the door, and kill him!" [57] Although this particular potential informer escaped without injury, Douglass reported that after this meeting no such threats were ever heard and if they had been made, he did not doubt "that death would be the consequence." [58]

The narratives also indicate that many slaves never betrayed a friend. Most would stand severe punishment rather than give away a fugitive or a white friend who favored freedom for all. Levi Coffin was told by one slave of an instance in which a slave refused to reveal the identity of a free Negro who had written a pass for him. The master threatened, but the slave persisted in his refusal. Finally the master placed the slave's hand on a blacksmith's anvil and struck it "with a hammer until the blood settled under the finger nails. The negro winced under each cruel blow, but said not a word." [59]

Frederick Douglass confirmed the fact that informers were in the minority. He stated that he had never confided in anyone so much as in his fellow-slaves. He claimed that many slaves would rather die before they would turn informer. On his plantation, he said, the slaves never did anything important without mutual consultation. He wrote, "we never moved separately. We were one; and as much so by our tempers and dispositions, as by the mutual hardships to which we were necessarily subjected by our conditions as slaves." [60]

THE MILITANT

In previous sections—notably "The Informer" and "The Contented Slave"—we have seen from the narratives clear examples of the dehumanizing effect of slavery. In this section and the next, we examine what the narratives indicate are the purest and most basic examples of slave resistance to dehumanization; for surely the most noble and self-respecting reaction to the slave situation was to fight back (the militant) and to attempt to escape to freedom (the fugitive). It is to be noted that in this section we discuss only what the narratives say about the "physically" militant slave, that is, the one who rebelled physically and often violently against beatings or torture. In a later chapter we shall discuss what may be termed the "intellectual" militant who revolted against the system and his condition by speaking and writing.

Ironically, but not surprisingly, the narratives reveal that in most cases the slave who refused to submit voluntarily to beatings, received, for his rebellious attitude and lack of cooperation, more frequent and harsher punishment than the others.

Henry Clay Bruce recalled that usually the militant could be beaten only when overcome by greater numbers. He generally could be taken only dead. However, because many of these militants were young, strong, and, when they wanted to be, quite industrious, the militant was often worth too much money alive to be killed in order to conquer him. Instead, slaveholders would gather several friends, surround such slaves, and punish them. Bruce also claimed that there were thousands of militants who spent their lives in their master's service, doing their work undisturbed, "because the master understood the slave." [61]

As a general rule, when militants were sold, it was for insubordination, resisting the master, or beating the overseer. Sometimes they were sold to the trader for less than they were worth and the trader would attempt to speculate on them. Many of these slaves were also sold because they had committed crimes not deserving the death penalty, for there were no prisons for slaves. Isaac Williams observed that militants were known to steal away at night and visit other slaves, creating discontent and making them sullen and disobedient by disseminating rebellious ideas. Neighboring slaveholders often demanded that the master of such a slave sell him away or kill him. [62]

John Brown spoke of the "brave look" about many of these militants, and when a slave's look offended the master he might swear to "flog his nigger pride out of him." The Fisk University collection of narratives contains the story of the slave Jack, who was one such militant. Everyone, both white and black, feared him. He was a fine worker but he did not allow anybody to whip him. The narratives reveal that the only time he was punished was through the master's deception. The master had a gang of patrollers hide in a thicket, while he told the slave that he had to be whipped. The slave responded that he would not willingly submit. The master proceeded to get the slave drunk and soon he was so intoxicated that he could hardly stand. At that point the master called to the hiding patrol and the slave was whipped almost to death.[63]

Another illustrative example of the militant was reported by John Thompson. The slave Aaron was a carpenter by trade, an excellent workman and a man of great physical strength. He never submitted to being flogged, unless taken by superior force. Whenever his master did attempt to whip him, it was never without the assistance of at least five or six other men. Aaron was too valuable to kill, and his master did not want to sell him. Nevertheless, the master grew tired of calling on help to whip this slave, and realizing that failing to punish him would be interpreted by the other slaves as submission, he finally decided to get rid of him.

One day while Aaron was at work repairing his master's barn, he observed several strangers approaching him. He was asked to come down from the scaffold, as one of the men wanted to talk with him about building a barn. He refused to comply with the request, for having recognized one of the men as a slave trader he "surmised his business and supposed that he, himself, was sold." [64]

When he refused, he was pelted with stones until he could remain aloft no longer. He jumped from the scaffold, axe in hand, and tried to cut his way through them. He was soon restrained, knocked down, put in irons, taken to the slave pen, and beaten severely; but not until he had badly wounded two of his captors. He was kept in confinement for two weeks during which time he was whipped each morning, until he finally made his escape to the free states.[65]

Finally, there is the William Wells Brown narrative about the slave called Randall. Randall declared that no white man would ever whip him—that he would die first. The newly arrived overseer announced that he could, and would, flog any slave that was put to work under him. The master had left the plantation and the overseer thought the time had come to put his threats into execution. He began to find fault with Randall, and threatened to whip him. One morning he gave the slave a difficult task, more than he could possibly do. When the overseer discovered that the task was incomplete, he ordered Randall to strip off his shirt. To this demand Randall replied, "I have always tried to please you since you have been on the plantation, and I find you are determined not to be satisfied with my work, let me do as well as I may. No man has laid hands on me, to whip me, for the last ten years, and I have long since come to the conclusion not to be whipped by any man living." The overseer, realizing that the slave was determined, called three hands from their work, and ordered them to seize and tie him. Randall turned to the three and said, "Boys, you all know me; you know that I can handle any three of you, and the man that lays hands on me shall die. This white man can't whip me himself, and therefore he has called you to help him." Seeing that the slaves were frightened, the overseer ordered them all to go back to their work.[66]

The following day the overseer and three white companions attacked Randall from behind. Within a short time, Randall had laid them one after another prostrate on the ground from which position the overseer shot at him. As he fell to the ground they rushed up to him and beat him over the face and head with clubs. He was given one hundred lashes and left tied to the whipping post for the remainder of the day. The following day, he was taken to the blacksmith's shop to have a ball and chain attached to his leg. So adorned, he was forced

to work in the fields and perform the same amou.
as the other slaves. When his master returned, he v
pleased to find that Randall had been subdued i
sence." [67]

Josephine Brown noted that as the slave became m ...
lightened and consequently, often more militant, his value de-
preciated. A slave who defied punishment was usually shunned
by the slave buyer, for it was this slave who, by virtue of the
example he set, was deemed the most dangerous person on the
plantation.[68]

THE FUGITIVE

As previously noted, the narratives reveal that the fugitive
slave represented ultimate resistance to the system and to dehumanization.

In most cases, this was the slave who responded to the "cry
for freedom," or the slave whose basic human integrity rebelled against the thought of a life of subjugation.

There are, of course, reports of slaves who fled merely to
escape a beating, or to seek their families. Many ran away
with the intention of returning—but never did so—while
others escaped permanently, but never got any further than
the woods or swamps surrounding the plantation.

In any event, as demonstrated by the relative few who attempted to escape, it was surely an extraordinary slave who
became a fugitive. In this section, we shall discuss what the
slave narratives say about some of the reasons for running
away, how it was accomplished, success and failure, captured
fugitives and their treatment, and the attitude and reaction of
the nonfugitive slaves and whites toward the runaway.

Fugitives, claimed Austin Steward, were heard to say that
it was not so much the beating which induced them to leave
the slave states, as the thought of "dragging out a whole life
of unrequited toil to enrich their masters." [69]

Steward, who himself became a fugitive, denounced the
necessity that forced him to flee from his fellow man. He was
guilty of no crime, had committed no violence, had broken
no law, and "was not charged even with a fault, except of the
love of liberty and a desire to be *free!*" He claimed only the
right to possess his own person, and to remove it from oppression. Steward wrote:

Can the American people, who at this very hour are pouring out
their blood in defense of their country's liberty, offering up as a
sacrifice on the battle field their promising young men, to preserve
their land and hearthstones from English oppression [War of
1812]; can they, will they, continue to hunt the poor African slave
from their soil because he desires that same liberty, so dear to the
heart of every American citizen? Will they not blot out from
their fair escutcheon the foul stain which slavery has cast upon
it? Will they not remember the Southern bondman, in whom the
love of freedom is as inherent as in themselves; and will they
not, when contending for equal rights, use their mighty forces "to
break *every yoke*, and let the oppressed go free"? God grant
that it may be so! [70]

However, Moses Grandy suggested that before it *was* so,
the severe punishment to which the slave was constantly subjected, his inability to obtain redress, and the anxiety he endured at being separated from his family and companions
drove many a slave into the flight for freedom.[71]

This anxiety of the fugitive may be conceived from the
writings of William Wells Brown. As he traveled toward
the free states, Brown wrote, his "heart would at times leap for
joy," while at other times he felt as though he could go no
further. At such times, he would remember slavery, with its
"democratic whips, its republican chains, its evangelical blood
hounds, and its religious slaveholders," and when he "thought
of all this paraphernalia of American democracy and religion
behind" him, and the prospect of liberty before him, he was

buoyed; and his heart lightened as he forgot his hunger and fatigue.[72]

Because the fear of the slaves' escape was always with him, the master placed all manner of obstacles in the slaves' path and constantly exercised a most vigilant surveillance. Samuel Ward noted that the slave was not permitted to learn to read and write—for this could better prepare him to make his escape. He was not permitted to go out after ten o'clock at night without a written pass, or to be absent from the estate after nightfall. If he violated these rules, he was apprehended, imprisoned, and advertised as a fugitive. Whether he was actually seeking escape or not, a violation of one of these rules was tantamount to attempted escape and the slave received the severest possible punishment. Ward described the punishment as "more than ordinarily cruel for the fault—desire for freedom, in the freest country under the sun—both to cure him of any such desire or tendency in future, and to intimidate other slaves." [73]

The slave was aware of the possible consequences before he became a fugitive, whether or not he was successful. He had received lectures from his master on the poor climate and barbaric customs of the free states and Canada. Sometimes, however, the master went too far, and slaves were heard to say that they knew Canada was a good country for them, just because the master was so anxious for them *not* to go there.

Thus, wrote Ward, the slave learned to interpret his master's pretended solicitude and if the slave had the strength and stubbornness to go he then had to consider his plans. He told his secret to no one; not even his family or friends were to be trusted. Prior to the attempt he would appear satisfied with slavery, and least anxious for freedom. The slave harboring a plan of escape grew with it. If the plan was of his own design, claimed Ward,

He is more of a man for having conceived it. If it must be wrought out with his own unaided hands, it improves him to entertain the intention of doing it. If in the way of his resolution—and, still more, in the way of executing it—there stand many mighty obstacles of which he is well aware, but the extreme appals him not, he has in him all the elements of your moral or physical hero, or of both.[74]

The narratives describe some of the ways in which the fugitive made his escape, and how he got to his destination.

He generally traveled on foot, with scanty means. The runaway had everything going against him—the laws of the United States, big rewards offered for his capture, and no knowledge of the areas he was to pass through. He had no map or compass to guide him and was forced to hide from every face he encountered. He often despaired of reaching his destination, for there were few people along the way to help him until he reached areas further north. Isaac Williams wrote of the numerous times that "hypocrisy" did "clothe itself in the garments of benevolence, and self-interest be the governing motive, that he [the fugitive] would find too late that his confidence had been treacherously betrayed." [75]

If they were not betrayed, some of these fugitives headed for the free states and some managed to make the trip without creating suspicion. They often represented themselves as "turnpikers," who were going to a job north of the vicinity. This deception worked well for some, until they passed beyond familiar territory and had to ask directions. When they were compelled to make inquiries on the road, they were frequently interrupted with probing questions.

Fugitive slave Andrew Jackson was questioned as to his destination. He replied that he was a turnpiker, and, summoning all the courage at his command, that it was none of the questioner's business. He rummaged through his pockets, pretending to look for a pass, and finally the white man grew tired, concluded that everything was in order, and went on his way. Jackson noted that the slaveholders were more mindful of their neighbors' property and interests than any other group in the nation. He could not account for this as "any other supposition than the very peculiar *character of the property*. If slaves were like money, simply transferable by the will of the owner, I presume it would be quite different. But inasmuch as it often takes *legs* and *runs away*, it becomes a matter of mutual interest to protect his neighbor's 'rights' in order to render his own more secure." [76]

The narratives report other incidents of slaves who escaped, some almost humorous. Levi Coffin told of a male slave from Arkansas who had planned to make his escape. He managed to procure the free papers of a female and disguised himself in women's clothing. He put on a cap and provided himself with knitting. Thus equipped, he gained passage on a boat bound for Cincinnati. The captain examined his free papers, and finding them in order, he permitted him to travel on the boat.

On the boat trip, he only spoke when spoken to, imitating a woman's voice quite well. As the trip progressed he devoted himself to his knitting, and pretended to be in poor health. Some white females noticed him and felt it was unfortunate that a "sick old auntie" had to sleep on the deck, and one woman allowed "her" to sleep on the floor of her cabin. He arrived safely at Cincinnati and met a conductor of the Underground Railroad. He was advised that he could now dispense with his female apparel and assume his proper dress, but he said that this disguise had worked so well that he would wear it until he reached Canada.[77]

In a more serious vein, the narratives contain reports of many fugitives who escaped into the woods surrounding the plantation, but who were too ignorant and dispirited to try to go any further. According to Levi Coffin, some slaves fled to these swamps and took refuge among the thickets, "preferring the companionship of the deadly moccasin snake and the alligator, and the risk of death from starvation or exposure to the cruel treatment of their masters." Jamie Parker, however, alleged that hunger, fear, and ignorance often sent them back to the master "to seek a shelter beneath the lash that drove them forth." In one instance, reported to Ralph Roberts, two fugitives lived for over a year in a cave, about a mile from their master's estate. The slaves in the adjacent plantation supplied them with meat and bread.[78]

Such instances as the latter were not uncommon, for the fugitive often had family or close friends who met him at certain appointed places, and brought him the things he needed. The items that were most in demand were salt and corn flour, for the runaway lived principally on beef and hogs, taken from either his own master's or some other's stock.

The Georgia Narratives reported that some fugitives resorted to the most ridiculous sort of witchcraft to avoid discovery. One slave told the story of a fugitive

who visited a conjurer to obtain a "hand" for which he paid fifty dollars in gold. The symbol was a hickory stick which he used whenever he was being chased, and in this manner warded off his pursuers. The one difficulty in this procedure was having to "set up" the stick at a fork or cross-roads. Often the fugitive had to run quite a distance to reach a spot, but when the stick was so placed human beings and even bloodhounds, lost his trail. With this assistance, he was able to remain in the woods as long as he liked.[79]

Despite such efforts, however, fugitives *were* captured and when they were they were subjected to extreme punishment. Nevertheless, the Florida Narratives contain reports which allege that often after months of such treatment new attempts to escape were made.[80]

Sometimes, recaptured fugitives were killed and decapitated. Their heads were placed upon posts which lined the fields so that they could be seen by other slaves as a warning to them.[81]

Some men in the slave states made a business of raising and training dogs especially to hunt down and capture slaves for a fee of ten to twenty-five dollars per slave.

Occasionally, wrote Andrew Jackson, the slaves outsmarted the dogs by following the tactics of a fox, running back and forth, into streams, and in circles, to confuse the hounds. Jackson tried each tactic, running back and forth across a stream, and then along on the edge of the stream, successfully eluding the hounds.[82]

Not all fugitives were so fortunate. Kate Pickard wrote of many who were torn to pieces by the hounds as the slave-hunter watched passively. Slaves reported that runaways frequently bled to death after an attack by a trained slave-hound.[83]

James Watkins had been hunted by dogs, and when they caught up to him, they succeeded in tearing his clothes to rags. They then seized him by the throat and bit him about his body. When he was returned to his master an iron yoke with two bells was made for him to wear on his head. "This disgraceful badge," he said, "I wore day and night for three months." He was constantly taunted by his master about wearing the yoke, and was threatened that if he ever attempted to escape again he would wear it for life. The neighboring planters forbade him from associating with their slaves, for fear that he would contaminate them with the ideas of freedom.[84]

According to the narratives, fugitives were usually armed, and when attacked in the swamps or woods, would fight. Some had large knives made by their fellow slaves who were blacksmiths, others stole guns from the masters' houses. Fugitives who stole the guns were usually kept in shot and powder by other slaves on the estate, who would buy it from poor white men who kept country stores in the neighborhood.[85]

Groups of runaway slaves, so armed, often gathered together in the woods for mutual protection against capture. The narratives indicate that these runaways killed both hunters and dogs.[86]

The narratives contain reports of the treatment accorded to

captured fugitives. Charles Ball reported that his master called
all fugitives "Yankee niggers," because, although he constantly
lashed them, they never quit running away. He finally stopped
them by chaining two together with iron collars around their
necks. They were chained to spades, and made to do nothing
but dig ditches to drain rice swamps. They were kept this way
for two years and the master reported, "Better niggers I never
had." [87]

Linda Brent recalled that a runaway from her plantation
was captured and carried back to the estate. The master considered the usual forms of punishment too mild for this offense.
He decided to have the fugitive placed between the screws of
the cotton gin, to remain there as long as he had been in the
woods. Before this, however, the slave was whipped and then
washed with brine, to prevent his flesh from rotting. He was
then placed into the gin, his position permitting him to turn
only on his side when he could not lie on his back. Each
morning another slave was sent with a piece of bread and a
bowl of water to feed the captive. This slave was warned,
under penalty of punishment, not to speak to the runaway.

On the second morning, the bread was gone, but the water
remained. After four days the messenger slave informed the
master that the water had not been touched, and that there
was a stench coming from the gin house. The overseer was
sent to investigate the report, and when the press was un-
screwed, the dead body of the slave was found half-eaten by
rats and vermin. Linda mused that "perhaps the rats that de-
voured his bread had gnawed him before life was extinct,"
and then asked, "What did *he* [the master] care for the value
of a slave? He had hundreds of them." [88]

Toward the latter years of slavery, wrote Daniel H. Peterson, the fugitives more frequently made successful escapes to
Canada and the free states. Many settled among the Quakers.
These people, unlike most others in the United States, were
regarded by the fugitives as their friends. The peculiarity of

their religion, which they so devoutly practiced, impressed itself in the minds of the fugitives. To reach free territory, and to reside among Quakers, were among the highest aspirations of the fugitives. Thus, they obtained the best directions they could and set out for known Quaker areas. The Quakers afforded the fugitives "any and every protection consistent with their peculiar tenets." [89]

Henry Bruce reported there were slaves who did not have the courage to make their way to the north, and thus gain their freedom. Although such cases were rare, some chose to escape in order to be captured and sold to another master, feeling that they could do no worse and sometimes better.[90]

Some slaves, claimed Lewis Clarke, escaped to Canada and then returned to live with their masters, apparently seeking forgiveness for running away. In one such case the master was delighted with the slave, and thought he could now be trusted completely. He was sent around to the quarters of his and neighboring plantations to describe how bad Canada was. This slave, however, had one "sermon for the people;—the ear of the masters,—and another for the slaves." He encouraged the slaves to go and enlightened them on the route that they should take to Canada. After a while his master became so confident that he let him take his wife and children to Ohio, to a religious meeting. Clarke described how he "fitted out in good style, horse and wagon. They never stopped to hear any preaching, till they heard the waves of the lakes lift up their cheerful voices between them and the oppressor." The slave, who was described only as George, after reaching his destination, wrote an affectionate note inviting his master to visit him in Canada.[91]

The attitudes of whites and blacks toward fugitives were, as recorded in the narratives, usually predictable, sometimes strange.

The Alabama Narratives of the Federal Writers' Project contain stories of an interesting phenomenon. On almost every plantation there were some slaves who regularly hid themselves in the woods for months at a time. The master usually knew where a particular slave was hiding but made no effort to apprehend him. When he returned, not a word was said about his running away.[92]

Ralph Roberts recorded stories, reported by fugitives, of some whites residing in the slave states who felt such compassion for the fugitive, on the ground that he had been driven to escape, that they made no effort to capture him. One slave reported one such white man who suddenly came upon a fugitive asleep in the woods. He woke the slave, asked him a few questions, and after advising him to return to his master and to tell his master that he, the white, asked that the slave not be punished, left him.[93]

As reported in the section entitled "The Informer," some of the slaves who stayed on the plantation did betray runaways to the white man. Jacob Stroyer explained that if such a slave were exposed, and if the fugitive had the opportunity while in the woods, he would beat or kill him.[94]

However, in the opinion of most nonfugitive slaves, Samuel Ward claimed, the fugitive was superior to those he left behind. The fugitive had exercised patience, fortitude, and perseverance, "connected and fed by an ardent and unrestrained and resistless love of liberty, such as cause men admired to be everywhere—that is, *white men everywhere*, but in the United States." [95]

V

Attitudes, Relationships
and Customs

As might be expected, great portions of the narratives dwell upon the slaves' attitudes toward life on the plantation and life in general, their relationships with other slaves and whites, and their mores and modes of living. Much of this material is amorphous, extensive, and often unrelated to any specific and easily-defined topic. Nevertheless, the subject matter has been classified as narrowly as possible and an attempt has been made to maintain a certain thread of cohesiveness and continuity within the context outlined above.

SOCIAL STRATIFICATION AMONG SLAVES

Almost every slave spoke of the social distinctions extant in the slave quarters. According to William Wells Brown, the slave's status within the inner circle of the quarters was based upon the position he occupied in the plantation affairs. Brown also claimed that the same undefinable differences that existed in the white community existed among the black people.[1]

Robert Anderson confirmed what Brown said that those who were engaged as personal and house servants were on a higher social plane than the field slaves. In addition, one who associated with the "po' white trash" was held in contempt by his fellows. Those who belonged to a lower-class white owner were denigrated by those belonging to "quality folks." Slaves of the wealthier families bragged of their connections; many frequently spoke with pride of their value in the market, or on the plantation.[2]

From the plantations of "quality folks," said Benjamin Drew, came the better class of Negro. They lived better, held what were considered good positions, were educated, and had the confidence and respect of the master. Such slaves did not necessarily claim to be *better* than whites, but certainly that they were as good.[3]

According to Jane Blake, the "bought" slave was inferior to those born on the plantation. Those whose blood was mixed with Indian found it almost impossible to maintain a close relationship with the black community, and, she noted, the slave of unmixed breeding "held himself purer than the mongrel."[4]

Henry Bibb recalled that marriages between slaves of different castes were openly and strenuously opposed. Slave mothers yearned for their children to marry slaves belonging to wealthy owners, in the hope that such a master might gratuitously set the couple free, or give them an opportunity to buy their liberty. At the very least, said Bibb, the couple could have the advantages attendant upon belonging to a "proper family."[5]

The slave who felt strong class distinctions often found himself in difficulty when separated from the plantation. Without the protection of his former status, he faced a situation for which he was not prepared. For example, William Wells

Brown said that when his new owner discovered that he had only worked in the garden, driven horses, or worked around the house, his reply was, "Ay a gentleman nigger, are you? Well, you are gentleman nigger no longer." [6]

Brown reported that such a slave usually had to have his sense of status beaten out of him. The new overseer would soon discover this spirit and would seek a way to induce the slave to break the rules. If words alone were unsuccessful, the overseer would come into the fields and strike him, to provoke a fight which would eventually result in a whipping. So ingrained were the superiority feelings of some slaves, wrote Brown, that they would meet the provocation of the overseers with counterattack. Many actually killed the overseers and were forced to become fugitives. [7]

The Black Aristocracy

On the plantation, the house servants were, in the words of Austin Steward, "the stars of the party" and what may be termed the "black aristocracy." To the other slaves, they were the models of manner, style, and conduct; they were the better-class black. To the ordinary slave, observation of the house servants was often the only method of obtaining any knowledge of the manners of "genteel society." Hence, said Steward, on most plantations the house servants were regarded as a privileged class, and as such were greatly envied, and often bitterly hated. Jamie Parker, reflecting this feeling, observed that the house servant had

a carefully-written genealogy, kept after the most approved system of *slave*-heralding; the overseer himself being the *Herald*, or *King at Arms*. Aye, they have *pedegrie, title*, and *rank;* they have caste with the plantation stock; are classified with chairs and tables, stoves and kettles, beds and bedding; all goods and chattels under the immediate supervision of the overseer. [8]

Austin Steward noted that the house servant was sometimes the most despicable tale-bearer and mischief maker, who would, in consideration of a favor or a bribe, betray his fellow slave. Thus it was that potential escapes, insurrections, and thefts were detected quickly by the master, and sometimes, in such instances, it was necessary to send the house servant away to protect him from the vengeance of the betrayed slave.[9]

In turn, the house servant often acted as protection for the master. This was so, according to Steward, because the slave-holder was always aware that he stood "over a volcano, that might at any moment rock his foundation to the center, and with one mighty burst of its long, suppressed fire, sweep him and his family to destruction." [10]

The Arkansas Narratives reveal that just as the more apt and intelligent of the slaves were given special training for those places in which their talents indicated they would be most useful—i.e., girls were trained to do housework, cooking, and to care for children, while boys were taught blacksmithing and carpentry—so the more fortunate were trained as personal servants around the house.[11]

And, wrote Peter Randolph, the house servants were never treated as cruelly as the field slaves. They were better fed and clothed, "because the master and his family always expect to have strangers visit them, and they want their servants to look well." They would eat from the master's kitchen, wear broad-cloth, calico and sometimes ruffled shirts. Randolph said that the appearance and manner of the house servants caused many strangers to slavery to fall "in love with the peculiar institution." [12]

Randolph also noted that in many cases the house servant acted as the master's "model" slave, and that one of the reasons he was treated so well was that if he were required to accompany the master on a trip away from the plantation, and especially to a non-slave area, part of his duties would be to describe to others the nature of slavery and the treatment accorded slaves by the master.[13]

The importance of their positions caused many personal servants to deny their own families. Slaves claimed that although, in many instances, they were outraged by the sight of their wife or child being beaten, nevertheless they dared not venture out of the "great house." They simply returned to business as usual, as the need to prolong their affluence far outweighed their desire to protect their screaming relatives.[14]

Ralph Roberts claimed that some members of this "aristocratic" group looked with contempt not only upon members of their own race, but also upon most poor whites. Both the field slave and the poor white, he said, "had not a fair share of property or intelligence." [15]

One member of this privileged group was fugitive slave James Christian, who worked in the household of President John Tyler from 1841 to 1845. He had an intense dislike for Tyler because he was "a poor man." He disliked poor whites and took personal offense that Tyler married into a family which he considered "very far Tyler's superior." On the plantation, he said,

Tyler was a very cross man, and treated his servants very cruelly; but the house servants were treated much better owing to their having belonged to his wife, who protected them from persecution, as they had been favorite servants of her father's family.[16]

In analyzing the caste system and the black aristocracy, Henry Clay Bruce reported the presence of many in this class who were "high toned and high spirited." These slaves had as much self-respect as their masters, and were industrious, reliable, and truthful. According to Bruce, these individuals were acutely aware of their helpless condition and took advantage of every opportunity to improve upon it—even at the expense of the entire slave community. Such slaves, said Bruce, realized that they had no rights under the laws, and were, by those laws, no more than the chattels of their masters. Because they knew that they were obligated to give service for their natural lives, and because they recognized that the master alone could make their lives pleasant or miserable, "they did not give up in abject servility, but held up their heads and proceeded to do the next best thing under the circumstances, which was, to so live and act as to win the confidence of their masters, which could only be done by faithful service and an upright life." [17]

THE GREAT DECEPTION

The narratives indicate that, in order to survive, the slave lived a good portion of his life within a framework of deception.

Revealing his true feelings about the institution and/or his condition to the master would inevitably result in a beating. For whatever their reasons, slaveholders were intent upon convincing the non-slaveholding population, and, probably, themselves, that the slave was happy. As a consequence, they insisted upon smiling faces and the "right" answers to their inquiries.

Aaron reported that to prove this proposition masters often pointed to the fact that the "quarters" were constantly singing and dancing. Nevertheless Aaron felt that it was a shallow individual who did not understand the slaves' behavior. This mirth, he said, was often rather the effort of the mind to throw off and prevent troubles rather than the evidence of happiness.

[It] shows that a man wishes to be happy, and is trying for it, and is oftener the means of use to get it than the proof that it exists; and as to singing, why do prisoners sing in jails? We have all heard them. Does it prove solitary cells a paradise? Do jail walls, dingy light, and solitude make men so happy that they sing for joy? They sing to make pleasure for themselves, not to give vent to it. Their singing indicates a mind seeking amusement, rather than one content with what it has—a mind conscious of a want, and striving to satisfy it, rather than one rejoicing in a full supply.[18]

According to Aaron, the truth was that if a slave displayed any discontent he was treated worse and worked harder; every slave knew this. When the slave was alone in the privacy of his quarters, he constantly thought and spoke of freedom. James Bradley asserted that "he was never acquainted with a slave, however well he was treated, who did not long to be free." [19]

Frederick Douglass felt that the slave suppressed the truth rather than take the consequences of telling it, and in so doing he proved himself part of the "human family." [20]

The narratives are replete with reports of slave deception and the extent and areas in which it was employed.

George Johnson recalled one occasion upon which his master gave a fellow slave named Thomas a letter with instructions to carry it to a certain slave trader. Being somewhat suspicious, Thomas got a white man to read it to him. The white man told him that the letter indicated that he was to be sold. To avoid the sale Thomas induced a free Negro to carry the letter for him. Upon arrival, the slave trader handcuffed the freeman, and put him in his slave pen. When he saw them take away the free Negro, Thomas ran to the woods, received "passage" on the Underground Railroad and made his way to the free states. The freeman who had been jailed was ultimately released when the deception was discovered and both the master and the slave trader lost in the transaction. [21]

A similar situation was reported by William Wells Brown. He asked a sailor to read a note which he had been instructed to deliver. He was told that the note requested that Brown be whipped, and that he was carrying the dollar fee for the service. While meditating on the subject, he saw a Negro man about his size, and asked to whom he belonged. The Negro replied that he was a free man, and that he had been in the city for only a few days. Brown told the unsuspecting Negro that he had a note which would permit him to get into the jail in order to get a trunk to carry to one of the steamboats, but that he was so busy that he could not do it, although he had a dollar to pay for it. The free Negro asked for the job, and Brown handed him the note and the dollar and sent him on his way. Ultimately the free man received the whipping intended for Brown.

Brown alleged that such incidents demonstrated how slavery made its victims "lying and mean; for which vices it afterwards reproaches them, and uses them as arguments to prove that they deserve no better fate." Brown claimed that he deeply regretted the deception he practiced on this fellow and expressed his desire that at one time or other it might be in his power to make amends for this suffering in his behalf.[22]

Henry Bibb reported that some runaways took bridles with them, and when questioned by white men they would say there were searching for runaway horses.[23]

The Georgia Narratives relate that to avoid the beating which inevitably followed a failure to pick the required amount of cotton, slaves sprinkled the white sand of the fields on the dew-soaked cotton that they did pick, and, when it was weighed, they were credited with more pounds than they had actually picked. Another device was to dampen the cotton or conceal stones in the baskets, either of which would make the bag weigh more.[24]

Israel Campbell used a similar method of deceiving his master. He felt that his requirement of one hundred pounds of cotton per day was excessive, but rather than complain and be whipped or lose any of his privileges, he decided to slip a large watermelon into the bottom of his sack. The trick succeeded, and although he confessed that he was terribly afraid, he felt himself quite smart to play such a trick upon as "sharp a person as the master and the overseer." When the melon season was over, he used pumpkins, and finally filled his sack with dirt. Before the cotton season was over, every one of the delinquent slaves knew how to prevent a whipping, and they found it much easier to pick melons and pumpkins than to be beaten.[25]

Because he was a free man kidnapped into slavery, Solomon Northup's greatest desire was to conceive of a method of getting a letter secretly into the post office, directed to some friends or family in the free states who might be able to have him freed. He reported that the difficulty of such a task cannot be comprehended by one unacquainted with the severe restrictions imposed upon the slave. He was deprived of pen, ink, and paper; he could not leave the plantation without a pass, nor would a postmaster mail a letter for him, or any other slave, without written instructions from his owner. Nevertheless Northup managed to obtain a sheet of paper and made ink by boiling white maple bark, and, with a duck feather, he manufactured a pen. The letter was written to an acquaintance, stating his condition, and urging him to take measures to restore his freedom. He kept the letter for a long period of time, until an opportunity presented itself by which it could be safely deposited in the post office.

One day a stranger came to the plantation seeking a job as an overseer. His request was denied, yet he stayed on at a nearby farm working for his room and board. Northup considered him a worthless character, a gambler and an unprincipled man. Indeed, he eventually took a slave wife and became reduced to the position of laboring with the slaves—a rare and unusual spectacle in the slave states. Nevertheless Northup took every opportunity to cultivate his acquaintance and obtain his confidence so as to entrust the letter to his keeping. He finally decided to ask him simply if he would deposit the letter in the post office. Northup did not disclose the contents of the letter for fear that he might be betrayed, and he was assured that the letter would be deposited and that the secret would be kept. The very next day, his master confronted him with the story.

His ability to deceive was then put to the test. He denied the truth of the matter to his master. He claimed that the betrayer had been denied a job as overseer and was therefore merely attempting to instill in the master's mind the idea that all of his slaves were trying to run away, thus encouraging the master to hire him as overseer. Northup said that "he had just made that story out of whole cloth, 'cause he wants to get a situation. It's all a lie, master, you may depend on't." The master accepted the story as logical, the deception was once again successful, and the incident came to an end.[26]

THE MYTH OF THE CONTENTED SLAVE

Partially due to the self-preserving deception of the slaves themselves, but mostly because of gullible and uninformed non-slaveholding visitors to the plantation, a prevalent belief among many non-slaveholders was that, in general, slaves were basically content.

Benjamin Drew reported that occasionally one of these visitors was permitted to inquire of the slaves themselves how they were treated. The answer almost invariably was that they were treated well, had kind masters, were contented and happy and did not desire their freedom if it could be obtained only by leaving the family of their master, to which they claimed to be ardently attached. The inquirer would conclude, said Drew, that the abolitionists had greatly exaggerated the slaves' sufferings and that conditions were not nearly so bad as he had heard. What the visitor did not realize, claimed Drew, was that the slave had been taught how to answer this type of questioning, precisely to lead one to believe that he was well-treated and happy. Naturally, he said, these false representations, which the slave was forced to make for the sake of his own security, kept most of the non-slave-state population in ignorance of his true condition.[27]

Frederick Douglass, too, lashed out against those who went

into slave states, enjoyed the hospitality of slaveholders, and then reported on the favorable conditions of the slaves. Why was it, he asked, that the reports of contentment and happiness among the slaves came to the free states through the slaveholders or the slaveholders' friends? Why was it that the free states did not hear of this contentment directly from the slaves? The answer to these questions, said Douglass, "furnishes the darkest features in the American slave system." [28]

During the course of a lecture he was giving, Douglass asked that the reporter of the contentment of the slave be brought forward to answer a few "plain questions." Only then, he said, could it be determined if any importance should be attached to his testimony. When the man was brought to the stage, the following colloquy ensued:

Is he a minister? Yes. Were you ever in a slave state, sir? Yes. May I inquire the object of your mission South? To preach the gospel, sir. Of what denomination are you? A Presbyterian, sir. To whom are you introduced? To the Rev. Dr. Plummer. Is he a slaveholder, sir? Yes, sir. Has slaves about his house? Yes, sir. Were you then the guest of Dr. Plummer? Yes, sir. Waited on by slaves while there? Yes, sir. Did you preach for Dr. Plummer? Yes, sir. Did you spend your nights at the great house? or at the quarters among the slaves? At the great house. You had, then, no social intercourse with the slaves? No sir. You fraternized, then, wholly with the *white* portion of the population while there? Yes, sir. This is sufficient, sir; you can leave the platform. [29]

Douglass decried the fact that many non-slaveholders entertained vivid pictures of the slave's happiness. The masters claimed that their slaves often sang and danced; that time was allotted by the planter for his slaves to make merry and that this fact proved the contentment of the slave. Douglass felt, on the contrary, that it proved only that the slave possessed a strong spirit and that even slavery was not entirely able to kill the spirit of the bondmen. It proved further, said Douglass, that the slave could survive "despite of whips and chains, and extract from the cup of nature, occasional drops of joy and gladness. No thanks to the slaveholder, nor to slavery, that the vivacious captive may sometimes dance in his chains, his very mirth in such circumstances, stands before God, as an accusing angel against his enslaver." [30]

Douglass was astonished to find these people in the free states who pointed to the slaves' singing as evidence of their contentment and happiness. It was, he said, "impossible to conceive of a greater mistake." Slaves sang when they were unhappy, the song representing their sorrows; and they were "relieved by them, only as an aching heart is relieved by its tears." Slaves sang often to drown out their sorrows, but seldom to express happiness.[31]

Indeed, wrote Douglass, the songs that slaves sang told of their woes and bitter anguish. Every song was a diatribe against slavery and a prayer for liberty. To the person who equated song with contentment, Douglass responded,

the singing of a man cast away upon a desolate island might be as appropriately concluded as evidence of contentment and happiness, as the singing of a slave; the songs of the one and of the other are prompted by the same emotion.[32]

CRIME AMONG SLAVES

It was common knowledge among slaveholders as well as slaves that a great many slaves engaged in some form of petty pilfering. The narrators did not deny this, but explained that the allowance of food was usually inadequate, and therefore most of the thefts involved food. As a consequence, wrote Isaac Williams, chickens and hogs frequently disappeared. A mystery would hang over the disappearance and, said Williams, not a "trace was left to tell the sad tale; at least it would be sad to the thief if there was." According to Williams, when the week's rations were gone the slave became a self-appointed commissary department in quest of food. He sacrificed many hours of sleep to keep himself and his family from feeling the pangs of hunger.[33]

Williams claimed that most slaves believed in the Scriptures, and that in their view the taking of food from the master was not a violation of the commandment, "Thou shalt not steal" but rather an exercise of the gospel, "Where ye labor there shall ye reap." [34]

Frederick Douglass recalled that scarcely a day passed that a slave was not punished for stealing food. In order to prevent theft, masters employed several stratagems to keep the slaves out of the smokehouse, hog pens, and gardens. One of the most successful was placing tar on the fence protecting the food. If a slave was caught with tar on his clothes, it was proof positive that he had either been into the food supply or had made an attempt. This device worked very well and the slaves became as fearful of tar as of the lash. They realized the impossibility of touching tar without being beaten.[35]

Charles Ball reported that the slave who supplemented his "income" by stealing found many whites who were willing to buy the merchandise. These whites who ran the risk of dealing with slaves almost always took financial advantage of the slave, and the slave, knowing that he was in a dangerous situation, did not even attempt to bargain with his white "partner." [36]

Jacob Stroyer noted that slaves also stole from each other. Eventually, therefore, they developed several methods of detecting thieves in their midst. The most common involved the use of a Bible or sieve and graveyard dust.

For the first, four men were selected, one of whom had a Bible or sieve attached to a string. At night the slaves would begin at the first cabin and the one who held the Bible or sieve would shout, "John or Tom, you are accused of stealing a chicken from Sam." Another would reply, "John did not steal the chicken." The four would continue this repartee for several minutes, as the Bible or sieve dangled from the string. Finally one would ask, "Bible, in the name of the Father and of the Son of the Holy Ghost, if John stole that chicken, turn." If the Bible or sieve turned on the string it was proof of guilt.[37]

At times, said Stroyer, the Bible might turn when a slave who was beyond suspicion was named. When this happened the accuser would either charge the mistake to the slave who fixed the Bible or else the accused would reply that he had passed the coop from which the fowl was stolen on that very day. This explanation would be accepted by the others and one might respond, "Bro. John we see dis, how dat ting work, you pass by de chicken coop de same night de hen went away." However when the Bible turned upon the name of a known thief he would be forced to acknowledge his previously stolen goods or that he thought of taking the chicken at the time it was stolen, thus confirming the suspicions of the examining committee.[38]

According to Stroyer, another method of detecting thieves was with the use of graveyard dust. Slaves felt that no matter how untrue a man was during his life, on his deathbed he would tell the truth or risk going to hell. Thus, graveyard dust would be gathered from the grave of the last slave to be buried and placed in a bottle of water. The contents of the bottle was offered to the accused. He was told if he took the chicken and drank the water he would go straight to hell; if, however, he did not take the chicken he should have no fear of drinking the dust. Being usually superstitious, many would admit to being the thief rather than have anything further to do with the dust.

In each instance, said Stroyer, when the guilty party was found, he had to return four chickens for every one he had stolen. If he had none, he would promise never to steal again. If, perchance, all the men in the quarters passed the examination and thus no one was found guilty, the theft was blamed on outsiders.[39]

John Brown reported that many masters taught their slaves to steal from neighboring planters. If, thereafter, the neighbor came to inquire about the theft, the master would deny any knowledge of it, and would offer the slave part of the stolen merchandise or a pint of whiskey. When the actual theft was being perpetrated, the master made sure he was at home. If any of his slaves were caught, he would beat them in the presence of the neighbor, thus disclaiming all knowledge or compliance.[40]

The slave was often accused of crimes he did not commit. It was not unusual for a slave to be beaten to death or close to death for a just or unjust accusation of theft. This is illustrated by the following incident related by Israel Campbell. A slaveholder claimed that a missing hog was traced to his neighbor's slave quarter. The master of the accused slave, seeking to avoid trouble with his neighbor, offered to pay for the animal. The neighbor was dissatisfied with such a disposition and insisted that the only way in which he could be repaid was to "take it out of their backs." The master would not consent to this, but his neighbor was determined either to settle it in this manner or to have the slave imprisoned and publicly punished. The matter was ultimately settled by giving the unjustly accused slave fifty lashes.[41]

Lewis Clarke claimed that if the slave took from a non-slaveholder, he considered himself guilty of doing wrong; however, with regard to his master's property, he was a slave, and he could not stop to inquire whether his master would approve of him helping himself to what he needed.[42]

Some slaves, said Clarke, even rationalized that if the slave was property, how could he steal from his master? How could a piece of property steal another piece of property? If both a slave and a horse were missing from a plantation, who was to say the horse did not steal the slave?[43]

SLAVE MORALITY

In addition to the ways of deception and crime among slaves, the narratives also contain discussion of the broad philosophical concept of the morality, the right and wrong of their actions.

John Brown claimed that many slaves did not think it wrong to deceive, for that example was set everywhere around them. Indeed, Brown reported that the slave felt that he was living under a system of cheating, lying, and deceit, and having been taught no better, did not see the wrong in it as long as he did not act against his fellow slave. As a rule, said Brown, a slave thought nothing of stealing from the master, but "would have allowed himself to be cut to pieces rather than betray the confidence of his fellow-slave." [44]

Lewis Clarke said that the slave who stole from another slave was called "mean as master" or "just as mean as white folks." This, he claimed, was the lowest comparison used by the slave. They had, according to Clarke, "No right for to complain of white folkes, who steal us all de days of our life, nigger dat what steal from nigger, be meaner nor all." [46]

Linda Brent told of one fugitive who was able to circumvent in his own mind the immorality of stealing money from his master, in the following manner: His master had died, and he felt "dis nigger had a right to money nuff to bring him to de Free States. So I tuk some of his bills, and put 'em in de pocket of his ole trousers. An wen he was burried, dis nigger ask fur dem ole trousers, and dey gub 'em to me. You see I didn't *steal* it; dey gub it to me." [46]

Thus, asked Andrew Jackson, was the slave, with limited and confused concepts, with whom the strongest argument was punishment, susceptible of morals? Jackson answered that "there must be some ideas of order to understand goodness, to feel the charm of virtue; there must be a will of one's own, and that will must be exercised to contradiction before it can courageously battle with vice." The slave, said Jackson, in his destitution of light, and his prostration of will, could not have a character for morality. Right and wrong to the chattel, was what he was commanded and what he was forbidden. His will was not free, for it was only what other people dictated, and his whole energy tended to destroy in him "the conservative principle of every being, for the sake of putting in its place the capricious *self* of somebody else." [47]

On the other hand, Linda Brent related that some slaves were scrupulous about taking anything from their masters on false pretenses. Jupiter Hammon was one who fell into this category. He felt that it was wrong for the slave to steal from his master and just as wicked not to take care of the master's goods. If the slave stole because he would not be found out, it was, said Hammon, "very wicked and provoking to God." Although some slaves rationalized their action by claiming that the master was unjust, Hammon felt that there was no excuse for taking anything that belonged to the master, because it was the slave's duty to be faithful. Furthermore, he said, "all the time spent idly, is spent wickedly, and is unfaithfulness to our masters." [48]

Hammond preached to his congregation, "God will certainly punish you for stealing and for being unfaithful. All that we have to mind is our own duty. If God has put us in bad circumstances, that is not our fault, and he will not punish us for it. If any are wicked in keeping us so, we cannot help it, they must answer to God for it. Nothing will serve as an excuse to us for not doing our duty." [49]

Josiah Henson recognized the concept of right and wrong in a moment of violent passion. He had planned to escape, which he felt necessitated the killing of the master. As he approached the sleeping slaveholder he hesitated as the thought occurred to him that a Christian should not commit murder. Although he knew of slaves killing whites before, he recognized that in those instances it was self-defense, to prevent others from killing slaves. He saw in his actions a crime, the killing of a person who in his particular case had not injured him. He reported that this incident filled him with much shame and remorse and led him to believe that "it was better to die a Christian death, and to have a quiet conscience, than to live with the incessant recollection of a crime that would destroy the value of life, and under the weight of a secret that would crush out the satisfaction that might be expected from freedom and every other blessing." [50]

According to Lewis Clarke, one of the most common moral issues discussed among slaves was whether it was right for a slave to run away, and not pay for himself. Some said they would be willing to pay, if they knew to whom to pay the money. Others felt that the only person they could think of paying was themselves. Clarke recalled one slave who went so far as to state that he would like to sue his former master for wages and interest, for the years he had spent in bondage. [51]

Henry Clay Bruce felt that there was no other group in modern history that had been held in subjugation and ignorance as long as had the American slaves, and reduced to such a state of immorality that they had not the slightest conception of the moral law. Bruce found it unnecessary to inquire who was responsible for this shame, whether it was the fault of the black people.

In his opinion it was the sin of the American people, who had gone to Africa, stolen children from their homes and parents from their families, and brought them to America to be reared as cattle; and regardless of the rights of humanity and the laws of morality, had reduced them to slavery "and robbed them of all conceptions of chastity and virtue." [52]

SUPERSTITION

The narratives reveal that the morality of many slaves found its basis in their superstition. This is not unusual in view of the further revelation of the narratives that the slaves were, in various degrees, almost universally superstitious.

Charles Ball reported that slaves believed in ghosts, witches, conjuration, voodoo, fortune-telling, and the existence of numerous other supernatural agents. No tale of a miraculous character was too absurd to be given credit with them, and the devil himself was well known to all.[53]

William Wells Brown claimed that to the slave and the poor white "the devil was a real being, sporting a club-foot, horns, tail, and a bump on his back." [54]

Furthermore, said Brown, the influence of the devil was sometimes greater than that of God. For example, if a slave had stolen something, and the fear of God came over him, he would likely ask the Lord to forgive him, but he would still keep the stolen item. However, if the fear of the devil came upon him, he would drop what he had stolen and run from the scene.[55]

Brown reported that a large number of slaves had implicit faith in voodooism. Some slaves who were comparatively intelligent, refused to touch a pin, needle, or other such object dropped by a fellow slave, because if the person who dropped the article had "spite against them, to touch anything they dropped would voudou them, and make them seriously ill." [56]

Brown attended one meeting of slaves in which he witnessed this "art" performed. A group of slaves gathered around the fire; they were of both sexes and of all ages. The conversation stopped when the slave who held the title of "queen" entered the meeting. She was accompanied by two assistants carrying a cauldron and a box.

The cauldron was placed over the fire. As the queen drew a wand from her dress, the crowd of slaves formed a ring about her. Her "first act was to throw some substance on the fire, the flame shot up with a lurid glare—now it withered in serpent coils, now it darted upward in forked tongues, and then it gradually transformed itself into a veil of dusty vapors. At this stage, after a certain amount of gibberish and wild gesticulation from the queen, the box was opened, and frogs, liz-

ards, snakes, dog liver, and beef hearts drawn forth and thrown
into the cauldron. Then followed more gibberish and gesticulation, when the congregation joined hands, and began the
wildest dance imaginable, keeping it up until the men and
women sank to the ground from mere exhaustion." [57]

Referring to another aspect of slave superstition, Brown
reported that nearly every large estate had at least one slave
who claimed to be a fortune-teller. This slave was often treated
with more than ordinary respect by the others. Brown told of
the slave Dinkie, who was deeply immersed in voodooism and
fortune-telling. He wore a snake's skin around his neck, and
carried a petrified frog in one pocket and a dried lizard in the
other. He had been on the plantation for many years, yet no
one could remember any time when he was called upon to
work. He was held in such esteem, said Brown, that even the
whites, "throughout the neighborhood, tipped their hats to the
old one-eyed negro, while the policemen, or patrollers, permitted him to pass without challenge." Moreover, the slaves
stood in mortal fear of him and were always upon their best
behavior in his presence. It was literally true, according to
Brown, that "this man was his own master." [58]

Jacob Stroyer reported that many slaves believed that
witches frequented the plantation. They were called "old
hags" or "jack lanterns," and, according to Stroyer, "both
men and women, who, when they grew old, looked old, were
supposed to be witches." Slaves would gather in the cabin
that overlooked vast open areas of the plantation and if they
saw a flickering light in the distance they would consider it
the appearance of a witch.[59] When the light was gone, the
witch was supposedly on the plantation in the form of a person who would assimilate into the quarters.

Stroyer reported it was sometimes said that witches went
into some of the cabins and hid themselves until the family
went to sleep. If a slave saw the witch enter the cabin, he
would use the Bible to force it out by placing the Bible on

the spot where the witch was seen. If a Bible was not available, red pepper and salt were mixed and spread throughout the cabin, but, said Stroyer, "in this case they generally felt the effects of it more than the witch, for when they went to bed it made them cough all night." [60]

According to Henry Bibb, many slaves believed in conjuration, a mystical invocation of the supernatural by the use of various powders prepared by the slave. Some said that it could prevent their master from exercising his will over the slaves, and was often used by the slaves to give them power to prevent their masters from flogging them. The substance most frequently used was some bitterroot, chewed and spit toward the master when he became angry with the slave. Other powders were prepared to be spread around the great house to achieve the same result.

Bibb himself had once had great faith in conjuration. He was led to believe that with its assistance he could do almost anything without being punished. His own procedure was to go to a cow pen, get fresh cow manure, mix it with red pepper and white people's hair, and then place the ingredients in a pot over a fire. The mixture was scorched until it could be made into a powder, which he sprinkled about his master's bedroom, and in his hats and boots. Bibb recalled that the smallest "pinch of it scattered over a room was enough to make a horse sneeze from the strength of it." [61]

The Georgia Narratives of the Federal Writers' Project contain numerous methods and purposes of conjuration. One method was to take a lizard and parch it. The remains were put into something that the victim was to eat, and when the food was eaten the individual would be conjured. Others believed that an old person could punish anyone by taking a chip of wood, spitting on it and then throwing it at the victim. It was said that thereafter, "in two weeks time maggots would be in 'em." [62]

Several of the Georgia Narratives reported that salt was

used quite frequently in the practice of conjuration. According to these slaves, salt was used to make a gambler lose his money. To do this, all that was required was to stand behind the gambler and sprinkle some salt on his back. From that moment on he would lose his money. Some females slaves used these ingredients to force a husband to stay at home. They take "some salt an' pepper an' sprinkled it up an' down de steps, . . . an' den she taken a plan eatin' fork and stuck it under de door an' de man stayed right in de house until she moved de fork." [63]

Another slave reported that if one wanted to destroy someone, he sprinkled some salt and pepper around him "an' it'll make 'em bus' dere brains out." Or, if one wanted someone to move away, he went out to a grave yard, stuck his hand down into the middle of a grave, "an' git a handful of dat red graveyard dirt an' den you comes back an' sprinkles it 'roun dere door an' dey's gone, dey can't stay dere." [64]

Finally, one slave offered a method for the victim to use to determine if he had been "conjured": If the slave was feeling ill, and he wanted to determine whether or not someone had been trying to conjure him, he would take a silver coin and place it in his mouth. If the coin turned black, that was a sure sign that someone was working a conjure on him. [65]

ILLNESS, INJURY AND TREATMENT

The narratives indicate that apparently because of a lack of proper medical care, sick or injured slaves were treated, to a great extent, by each other in accordance with their superstitious beliefs.

Although Francis Fedric reported that some slaveholders took precautions against disease and epidemics by giving their slaves medicine in the form of tonics or salts at the beginning of spring, the majority of the narratives deny that such practices existed. [66]

For example, Henry Bibb wrote that when slaves were ill

they received little or no medical attention, and consequently, although they possessed little or no medical knowledge, they were the sole judges of their illnesses. Bibb recalled that because many did feign sickness to avoid work, all were presumed to be lying when they complained. The master would conclude that "there was nothing the matter, and that he only wanted to keep from work." [67]

James L. Smith related the following illustrative incident of the master's attitude toward the sick or injured slave: A tree had fallen and crushed the knee of a young slave. In the absence of medical attention, his knee began to shrink and contract. When his mother went to the great house to tell of her son's illness, the master responded that he had enough "niggers" and that this slave was not "worth much anyhow, and he did not care if he died." [68]

According to William Still, slaves complained that their health was too poor for field work and begged to be assigned to less difficult duties. Still reported that intolerant masters answered that work was the best medicine and that they would cure their slaves by returning them to the fields. Furthermore, the overseer would be ordered to whip the complaining slave every day, to "make her work or kill her." Josiah Henson confirmed this and claimed that the fixed principle on the plantation was that "a nigger will get well anyway." [69]

Charles Ball reported that, in August, slaves working in warm climates and swampy areas often contracted a malarial-type fever called ague. On some plantations this fever was not regarded as a disease, and if the slave had no other ailment he was not withdrawn from the fields. Ball saw slaves "compelled to pick cotton, when their frames were shaken so violently, by the ague, that they were unable to get hold of the cotton in the burrs, without difficulty." Ague, which induced dropsy and consumption, caused the death of many, yet Ball contended that it could have been prevented by arresting it at its inception.[70]

The Georgia Narratives indicate that treatment of illness varied from plantation to plantation and that because some slaves were regarded as valuable property, masters *did* engage physicians for serious illnesses. Doctors, however, often refused to go to the cabins to treat the patients, and slaves had to be carried from their beds to the great house for medical treatment. If the doctor refused to attend to the slave at all, as some did, the older slaves would care for him. Some masters treated their slaves themselves in order to save the money that would have to be spent on a physician. If the slave did not quickly recover, he would be ordered to work, and if he refused he would be beaten. Sometimes, however, the punishment was ineffectual, for the slave could not muster enough strength to go to the fields.[71]

Louis Hughes recalled that one member of the "quarters" was instructed in the use of home remedies. He was told the properties of each medicine, how it was used, for what purpose it was given and how much constituted a dose. Two of the more common remedies were boiled red peppers and "cow foot oil." If these did not effect a cure the slave was forced to drink a quart of boiled chimney soot, which was supposed to act on the body's system as salts or castor oil. Hughes reported that most slaves chose to work rather than take this medicine.[72]

INFORMATION AND COMMUNICATION—
THE SLAVE GRAPEVINE

The narratives indicate that, in general, the slaves were isolated, both physically and directly by the master, and indirectly by reason of their lack of education, from the flow of ideas and information concerning local and national topics. Nevertheless, it is apparent from many of the slave narratives that there was a great desire for such information and that because of this desire, reports of local, national, and even international events circulated rapidly among the slaves.

Henry Clay Bruce reported that every plantation had a

"grapevine," or "spy" network, that supplied information from the great house or other plantations. All important decisions or problems of the master's family were known by the "quarters" and discussed in some detail. According to Bruce, slaves would listen carefully to slaveholders' conversations "on political matters, or about the fault of another slave and as soon as opportunity would admit, go to the quarters and warn the slave of his danger, and tell what they heard master say about the politics of the country." [73]

Booker T. Washington wrote that the "grapevine telegraph" was kept busy night and day. News of local and national events was carried swiftly from plantation to plantation as information was received from the slave who accompanied the master to the free states. Washington said that free Negroes were a valuable source of information, but generally the slave learned of news by overhearing the master, his family, or a neighbor. Lewis Clarke reported that as far west as Kentucky, the "quarters" discussed the emancipation in the West Indies a very short time after it took place. The reaction was one of great joy, he said, for they expected they would be set free next and they lived in hopeful anticipation for many years. [74]

Usually, asserted Sam Aleckson, the house servants were the first link in the slaves' "grapevine." Arrangements would be made for these slaves to go to the quarters and report any news they might gather during mealtime. Information came easily to the house servants because masters would rarely notice them around the house or garden. They were described to be "as dense as a block of stone," and this alleged density constituted their concealment. [75]

Henry Clay Bruce recalled that one issue rarely discussed in the presence of slaves was the politics of the slave question. Nevertheless, by various means the slaves learned of news in this area as well, and in the secrecy of the night, would meet in a central cabin and discuss it. Bruce noted that the slave—

or the free Negro—who could read was an important figure in the "grapevine." He acquired bits of information and newspapers to read in the cabins. He might purchase newspapers from white merchants by passing as a freeman or messenger of the master, while the quarters anxiously awaited his return.[76]

Harriet Tubman reported that some of the "grapevine" news was relayed in song. This was usually when a slave was about to escape to the free states. As one intended fugitive passed the doors of the cabin, he bid farewell by singing "When dat ar ole chariot comes, I'm gwine to lebe you, I'm boun' for de promised land, Frien's, I'm gwine to lebe you. But I'll meet you in de mornin', . . . on de oder side of Jorden, for I'm boun' for de promised land."[77]

The narratives indicate that the grapevine reached into the quarters and great house of other plantations. Even if the master did not permit any association with the slaves of another plantation, his people knew of the conditions of others. Many plantations used mills which were not located on their grounds, and slaves of several planters would meet, and, while conducting business, exchange information—information which enabled the slave to make comparisons and interpretations of his life, the lives and conditions of other slaves, and, generally, of the institution.

According to Anthony Burns, grapevine sessions would often end in a discussion of "the good land far away to the North where no slaves were, and where all of the negro race were as free as their white brethren." Such conversation, wrote Burns, would kindle the fire of freedom in the hearts of many.[78]

Linda Brent reported that, on occasion, slaves took political sides. For example, the grapevine supplied the slaves with enough information about Massachusetts to lead them to the conclusion that prior to the passage of the Fugitive Slave Law, "slave holders did not consider it a comfortable place to go to in search of a runaway."[79]

During Lincoln's campaign for the presidency, said Linda Brent, slaves miles from any railroad, large city, or newspaper discussed the issues. And, according to Booker T. Washington, when the Civil War began, every slave felt that though other issues were involved, "the primal one was that of slavery." Even the most ignorant slave on a plantation felt that freedom would be the one great result of the war. Every success of the Union forces was watched with intense interest and sometimes the "quarters" received the results of the battles before the master did. Such information was gotten by the slave who was sent to the post office and who would stay there long enough after performing his task to hear the conversations of the people who congregated there.[80]

Washington said that masters could not understand how the "quarters" were able to keep themselves accurately informed about national questions. He claimed that from the time "Garrison, Lovejoy, and others began to agitate for freedom, the slaves throughout the South kept in close touch with the progress of the movement," and that their discussions proved that they understood their nation's political situation, and that they "kept themselves informed of events." [81]

RELATIONSHIP OF THE SLAVE TO OTHERS

In addition to reports of the slaves' own interpersonal activities, the narratives are rife with discussion of their relationships with nonslaves. This section deals with some of the more common and most often mentioned of these contacts.

The Overseer

In a previous chapter, the black driver was discussed as part of a method of control exercised over the slaves in operating the master's business. This section deals with the black driver's white counterpart, the overseer. Both performed the same function; but the slaves' relationships with the white overseer was somewhat different than with the black driver, who was, after all, a fellow slave.

Robert Anderson reported that not all of the overseers seemed human. Some of them would whip, club, and otherwise punish and torture the slaves from morning to night, never satisfied, and keep the slaves constantly on the grind and their nerves stretched to the breaking-point. On the other hand, others would treat the slaves with some consideration, using firmness but not cruelty, pushing the slaves when they felt the need for it, and when leisure time came, letting them relax. Anderson claimed that the more humane overseers would usually get more work done in the long run than the drivers who treated slaves with contempt. He said that the slaves were willing to put their best into their tasks when they were treated humanely, and that when they were treated otherwise, they used their wits to escape from all the work they could, and would lag behind or shirk when the overseers were not looking.[82]

Solomon Northup wrote that the small planter who did not have a large number of slaves did not require the services of an overseer, but acted in that capacity himself. On larger estates, however, employing fifty or a hundred slaves, overseers were deemed indispensable. On such plantations, overseers would ride into the fields on horseback, armed with pistols, knives, whips, and several dogs. They would follow behind the slaves, keeping a lookout on the gang. In a description of overseers in general, Northup listed what he considered to be the requisite qualifications: "utter heartlessness, brutality and cruelty." It was, said Northup, his function to produce large crops, and this was accomplished no matter what the cost in suffering.[83]

Slaves who reported in the Georgia Narratives agreed that "the lowest down whites of slavery days were the average overseers. A few were gentlemen, one must admit; but the regular run of them were trash—commoner than the 'poor white trash'—and, if possible, their children were worse than their daddies." To many of these slaves, the term overseer was synonymous with slave driver, with cruelty and brutishness.[84]

Frederick Douglass suggested that the traits necessary to the overseer were pride, ambition, and perseverance. In addition, he recalled that his overseer was artful, cruel, and obdurate. The plantation was the ideal setting for the full exercise of all of these traits, and most overseers were very much at home in this atmosphere. Douglass asserted that the overseer would interpret the slightest look, word, or gesture of the slave as impudence, and would treat it accordingly. There was to be no answering back to him; no explanations were permitted, even if the slave had irrefutable evidence that he had been wrongfully accused. His overseer acted fully under the maxim established by the slaveholder: "it is better that a dozen slaves suffer under the lash, than that the overseer should be convicted in the presence of the slaves, of having been at fault." To be accused by the overseer was to be convicted, and to be convicted was to be punished; "the one always following the other with immutable certainty." To escape accusation was the only way to escape punishment and few slaves had the ability to do either under the direction of the overseer.[85]

According to Douglass, many overseers were motivated by the fact that they themselves had to crouch at the feet of the master, and consequently demanded this debasing homage of the slave. They were, he said, "cruel enough to inflict the severest punishment, artful enough to descend to the lowest trickery, and obdurate enough to be insensible to the voice of a reproving conscience." The overseer, summarized Douglass,

spoke but to command, and commanded but to be obeyed; he dealt sparingly with his words, and bountifully with his whip, never using the former when the latter would answer as well. When he whipped, he seemed to do so from a sense of duty, and feared no consequences . . . Always at his post, never inconsistent. He never promised but to fulfil. He was, in a word, a man of the most inflexible firmness and stone-like coolness.[86]

The unknown slave who dictated his story to Ralph Roberts described overseers as "those dreaded and despised obstacles between slaves and their owners, who commonly have no bowels of compassion for the slave, and little care for the interests of the master." This same slave claimed that because they felt that the right to discipline belonged properly only to the master, most slaves submitted at once to the most unjust treatment from the master, but shrank with terror from the overseer's hands. They contended that the overseer cared nothing for them, and that they never expected his justice to be tempered with mercy. Indeed, although the severity of the overseer's treatment was usually in line with the master's wishes, it was sometimes necessary for the master to overrule the overseer to protect his slaves. A master, it was reported, might become so enraged at an overseer's brutality that he would threaten to whip him if he did not change his ways. For the most part, however, the narratives indicate that the master did not interfere with the overseer's treatment of slaves but placed them completely in his hands.[87]

Henry Box Brown reported that his overseer used to rise early in the morning, not to further the legitimate interests of his master, but in order to rob his master and the slaves that were under his control. Nevertheless, his early rising was looked upon by the master as a token of great devotion to his business, and as he was a very pious member of the Episcopalian Church, the master placed great confidence in him. As a consequence, it was no use for the slaves to complain to the master of anything the overseer did, for he would not listen to a word they said, but gave full sanction to his overseer's conduct "no matter how tyrannical or unjust that conduct, or how cruel the punishments which he inflicted; so that that demon of an overseer was in reality our master." [88]

Other narratives indicate that instances such as this occasionally produced resistance from the slave. Goaded into uncontrollable madness, the slave turned violent, despite his awareness that the gallows awaited anyone who killed his overseer. In one instance reported by Solomon Northup, a slave was given the task of splitting rails. In the course of the day, the overseer sent him on an errand which occupied so much of his time that it was not possible to complete the task. The following day he was reprimanded by the overseer for not finishing the job. He was told that the loss of time occasioned by the errand was no excuse, and was ordered to kneel and bare his back for the lash. The slave submitted until he lost control and, insane with pain, sprang to his feet, seized an axe, and chopped the overseer into pieces. So complete was his satisfaction with what he had done that he made no attempt whatever to escape and related the entire affair to his master. The slave declared himself ready to expiate the wrong by the sacrifice of his life. As he was led to the scaffold, wrote Northup, "and while the rope was around his neck, he maintained an undismayed and fearless bearing, and with his last words, justified the act." [89]

William Still wrote that even far less violent resistance by the slave was regarded by the overseer as an unpardonable offense. For the most trivial act the slave could be whipped to death. Even in such cases, the overseer was indifferent to the protests of the master—for he knew his master could not use the word of his slaves against him, and sometimes the master himself would not acknowledge such testimony. Thus, wrote Still, there was often nothing to restrain the overseer from using the most unnatural and inhumane cruelty on the slave. Because of such treatment, asserted Henry Watson, the overseer was regarded by the "quarters" with detestation and fear, as a being to whose rage and cruelty there were no limits. Yet, James Williams recalled that overseers were constantly telling the slaves that they were the kindest of overseers; that, if anything, they were too indulgent. [90]

According to the Georgia Narratives, on plantations where slaves knew that the overseer was on trial, and that the master would fire him if he saw that he could not handle his gang, slaves often took advantage of him by refusing to follow directions and even fighting with him. This would cause a reduction in productivity and a laxity in the quarters. Sometimes their efforts were so successful that the overseer found himself embarrassingly trying to explain the situation to his employer or even looking for another job.[91]

Jacob Stroyer reported that many an overseer did not like the idea of a slave working at a trade of his own choosing. He would say to the master that this was the worst thing a slave could do, because if the slave had things his own way, he might consider himself as important as the driver. Besides this, said the overseer, that particular slave's influence could spread to other plantations and eventually there would be no servants left in the slave states. Jamie Parker asserted that the overseer felt this way because he himself was inadequately trained and educated. The overseer had his "own good reasons for insisting that 'the people' should not be instructed," for he might be illiterate, and could not accept the fact that a particular slave was better skilled or educated.[92]

The Poor White

According to Charles Ball, poor whites were scattered throughout the slave states, and generally they served the same purpose as the slaves, i.e., servants to the slaveholders. The most abject poverty had, throughout their lives, been the companion of these poor people, "of which their clayey complexions, haggard figures, and tattered garments, gave the strongest proof." Henry Clay Bruce claimed that even coffee was too expensive for the poor whites, and that the only opportunity these people had to get a cup was when they were invited by the master. It was, said Bruce, always a "godsend to them, not only the good meal, but the honor of dining with the big boss." [93]

Bruce reported that, since they were illiterate, their conversation did not exceed what they had seen and heard. Bruce asserted that the slaves considered it an objectionable weakness in the master if he associated in any way with a poor white, although such a relationship was the exception, and not the rule. [94]

Bruce reported that these poor whites seemed to live for no higher purpose than to spy on the slaves, and even to lie about them to their masters. They would, he claimed, watch the slaves and report every violation of the rules. Their highest ambitions were gratified if they became overseers, slave drivers, or patrollers. This class was, in Bruce's words, "conceived and born of poor blood, whose inferiority linked its members for all time to things mean and low." Bruce asserted that the presence of a large number of typical poor whites, held in what most slaves considered a degree of slavery, was a contradiction to the assertion that white blood was superior to black. If the poor whites had any superior blood in their veins, would they have remained in the slave states, generation after generation, filling menial positions, with no perceptible degree of advancement? The slave answered in the negative because "the truth is, that they had inferior blood; nothing more." [95]

Henry Bibb noted that the poor whites were considered by the masters on a par, in point of morals, with the slaves. They were generally ignorant, intemperate, licentious, and profane. Some would associate socially with the slaves, and were often found gambling together with them and encouraging them to steal from their owners. Poor whites were often the recipients of slave-stolen corn, wheat, sheep, chickens, or anything else which they could conceal easily. Indeed, according to the North Carolina Narratives, there were many poor whites in the slave states who wanted to see slavery abolished in self-defense. They despised the institution because it had impoverished and degraded them. They mixed with the slaves and, with them, envied their masters. In almost every respect they looked upon the masters as the slave did.[96]

Henry Clay Bruce went so far as to state that the Emancipation Proclamation not only freed the slaves, but the poor whites as well, for they occupied a condition nearly approaching that of slavery. They were nominally free, but that freedom was greatly restricted due to the prejudice against them. They were often employed by the ruling class to do menial jobs, but even while so engaged, were not allowed to eat with them at the same table.[97]

Henry Bibb reported that a master who was rich, aristocratic, and overbearing looked upon the poor white man with utter contempt because he was a laboring man who earned "his bread by the 'sweat of his brow,'" whether he be moral or immoral, honest or dishonest." Whether the man was black or white, said Bibb, if he performed manual labor for a livelihood, he was looked upon as inferior to the slaveholder and but little better off than the slave. Although both slaveholder and poor white lived under the same laws, one was rich and the other poor; one was educated and the other was uneducated; one had a home, land, and influence, and the other had none. Under such circumstances, many members of that particular class of non-slaveholders were actually anxious to see slavery abolished, but few dared say it in public.[98]

Henry Clay Bruce asserted that the poor whites had little or no honor, no high sense of duty, little or no appreciation of the domestic virtues, and were content to "grovel in the mire of degradation." He felt that the poor whites were held in slavery just as real as the blacks', and that their degradation was, to most slaves, more condemnable—because, since they were white, all the world was open to them, yet by choice they remained in the slave states in a position of quasi-slavery.[99]

Joseph Vance Lewis expressed a similar view and claimed that this freedom of the poor whites was a fact that often filled the slaves with indignation. There were many poor whites, he claimed, who were as poor in personal effects as the slaves, and yet they did not have to be controlled by a master, to come and go at his command, to be sold for his debts or whenever he wanted extra pocket money. The preachers of the slaveholding gospel told the slaves in their sermons that they should be "good boys" and not destroy the master's property nor steal his food; but they never told this to the poor white people, although it was well known that they encouraged the slaves to steal, trafficked in stolen goods, and stole themselves. Lewis asked, why the difference? He felt that most slaves were the equal of these poor whites, and that this fact made slavery an even greater wrong.[100]

What was worse, in the opinion of William Wells Brown, was that these poor whites were almost inevitably the leaders of the anti-Negro disorders, lynchings, and the like. If slavery were abolished, he said, the south would be the cradle of liberty, the haven of America, only "when the typical poor whites of that section have died off, removed, or become educated, and not 'till then." [101]

The Free Negro

William Wells Brown asserted that no class of supposedly free people in the world were more oppressed than the free Negroes of the slave states. Each state had its code of "black laws," which were rigorously enforced, and the freemen were constantly degraded. Brown enumerated some of the restrictions placed upon free Negroes. In some slave states, free black women were not permitted to wear veils about their faces in the street, or in any public places. A violation

of this law meant "thirty-nine lashes upon the bare back."
The same punishment was inflicted upon any free black man
who was seen in the streets with a cigar in his mouth, or a
walking stick in his hand. When walking the streets, free
blacks were forbidden to take the inside of the pavement.
Punishment of fine and imprisonment was meted out to any
found out of doors after the hour of nine at night. In many
states, an extra tax was imposed upon every member of a free
colored family.[102]

Jermain Loguen noted that free Negroes had no rights or
privileges beyond a permitted residence in the slave state,
which, he claimed, gave them nothing that deserved the name
of protection from the wrongs of white men. Thus, some
slaves, and most slaveholders, regarded slavery as a better
condition that that of the free Negro. Loguen was not the
only slave who said, from experience, "If I must live in a
slave state, let me be a slave."[103]

According to Henry Clay Bruce, a slave who was freed by
his master had only a few more privileges than he had had in
bondage. If he remained in the area, he had to choose a
guardian to transact all his business, even to the extent of
writing a pass for him to go from one township to another
in the same county. He could not own real estate in his own
right, except through his guardian, nor could he sell his crops
without his written consent. The guardian charged the free
Negro for everything he did for him, which was usually a
drain upon his resources. In many cases, said Benjamin Drew,
slaves reported that free Negroes were prohibited from visiting among the slaves. This prevented them from having any
contact with slaves, except when hired to work for the master.[104]

Adding to the difficult plight of the free Negro was the
1857 *Dred Scott* decision, which, said William Craft, was
"the crowning act of infamous Yankee legislation." Craft interpreted the opinion of the Supreme Court, which was com-

posed of judges from both free and slave states, as having held that "no coloured person, or persons of African extraction, can ever become a citizen of the United States, or have any rights which white men are bound to respect. That is to say, in the opinion of the court, robbery, rape, and murders, are not crimes when committed by a white upon a coloured person." Craft felt that these judges had descended from their "high and honorable position down into the lowest depths of human depravity," and "are wholly unworthy of the confidence of any people." [105]

Bethany Veney reported that the feeling against free Negroes could not be ascribed solely to whites. Free Negroes were often described by slaves as a "rude set" and a group despised by everybody. They were despised by the slaveholder because he could not subject them to his will as he could the slaves, and despised by the slaves, because they envied the possession of this nominal freedom, which they were denied. Thus, the slaveholder's contempt and the slaves' envy were closely allied. [106]

Jermain Loguen said that the free blacks and poor whites were the lowest grade of society in the slave state and if either had an advantage over the other, "it is so trifling, and the grade of both so contemptible, as to be unworthy of notice." So, too, a slave whose story was recorded in the Arkansas Narratives compared the free black with the slave as follows:

With de "free niggers" it was just de same as it was wid dem dat was in bondage. You know there was some few "free niggers" in dat time even' 'fore de slaves taken outen bondage. It was really worse on dem dan it was with dem what wasn't free. De slave owners, dey just despised dem "free niggers" an' make it as hard on dem as dey can. Dey couldn't get no work from nobody. Wouldn't any man hire 'em or give 'em any work at all. So because dey was up against it an' never had any money or nothin', de white folks make dese "free niggers" sess [assess] de taxes.

An' 'cause dey never had no money for to pay de tax wid, dey was put up on de block by de court man or de shriff an' sold out to somebody for enough to pay de tax what dey say dey owe. So dey keep these "free niggers" hired out all de time most workin' for to pay de taxes. . . . Yas suh, Boss, it was heap more better to be a slave nigger dan er free un.[107]

According to the Florida Narratives of the Federal Writers' Project, some free Negroes risked their lives by spreading information which they thought would aid the enslaved Negroes to become free; others actively participated in the escape of slaves. Free Negroes were often suspected of being the authors of conspiracies. Often their homes were searched and if any weapons were found they were put in jail or hung. As late as 1858, reported William Wells Brown, a movement was made in several slave states to impose exorbitant taxes upon free Negroes, in failure of the payment of which they were to be sold into slavery. Maryland introduced a bill levying a tax of two dollars per annum for all colored male inhabitants of the state over twenty-one years of age and under fifty-five; and one dollar for every female over eighteen and under forty-five. If a property-holder refused to pay, his or her goods were seized and sold. If the freeman had no property to seize, his body was taken and hired out to the highest bidder who agreed to pay the tax. If they were unable to rent the Negro at all, he was to be sold to any person who would pay the amount of tax and costs for the shortest period of service.[108]

Benjamin Drew reported that some free Negroes were denounced by the slaves as betrayers. Slaveholders would offer rewards to the free Negro population to expose fugitives or plots of rebellion. Occasionally a fugitive was caught or a plot was broken up before it got under way. Free Negroes were at times used for patrol work. These men were likewise branded as betrayers and slave-hunters. Sometimes the free Negro who was engaged in this activity had white blood in

VI

The Slave's Interpretation
of the Institution

The narratives contain much analysis of the institution of slavery itself as well as of the world at large.

The analysis is sometimes profound, sometimes simplistic, often angry, and almost always moving.

For the sake of convenience the chapter is divided into sections and subsections bearing titles which announce the general topic of discussion. However, it should be borne in mind that, on occasion, the subject matter may somewhat transcend the section heading.

THE SLAVE'S REACTION TO HIS STATUS

Intellectual Aggression and Protest

James Pennington claimed that he was induced to write his narrative out of a desire to counteract what he considered to be a general disposition on the part of non-slaveholding whites to overlook the fact that "the sin of slavery lies in the chattel principle, or relation." He was outraged when he heard someone speak of "kind masters," "Christian masters," "the mild form of slavery," or "well-clothed and fed slaves" as extenuations of the institution. Pennington felt that such a person either had deliberately distorted the truth, or was unaware of the true nature of the system. Furthermore, he vigorously denied the often-expressed opinion that the Negro, who toiled to enrich white society, who had helped to establish the foundations of white institutions, but who had nevertheless been lowered into slavery, needed only a second-class civilization, and a "lower standard of civil and religious privileges than the whites claim for themselves." [1]

The very nature of slavery, he continued, lived and moved on the chattel principle, or, in his words, "the bill of sale principle." The lash, starvation, and nakedness, to a great extent, were the inevitable consequences of the institution which was in constant conflict with the natural disposition of man. The relationship between slave and slaveholder was so delicate that it was liable to become violently entangled at any moment.[2]

To the individual who claimed that most of the slave's troubles were brought on by disobedience to the master, and that if the slave behaved he would be well treated, another ex-slave, Isaac Williams, answered that it was simply not human nature always to "behave," and that it was impossible to spend one's life subject to another will without becoming rebellious, either vocally or physically.[3]

Benjamin Drew reported that the slave often heard people say, "Why don't you accomplish something?" To such a question the slave replied by asking the inquirer to look at the black man—his manliness crushed out of him and kept in gross ignorance. To ask the slave to accomplish something under such circumstances was "like tying a man or weakening him by medicine, and then saying, 'why don't you go and do that piece of work, or plant that field with wheat and corn?' " [4]

In replying to the charge that the slave could not take care of himself, that he would starve to death on his own, Andrew

Jackson demanded that those who expressed this thought cite a case "where anything like a fair opportunity has been given, of a self-emancipated slave, who has not secured a comfortable subsistence by his own exertions." He had known of numerous whites, he wrote, whose advantages were better than his own, yet who never managed as well as he did and who often came to him for aid. These same men, he reported, would later make the false claim that "the niggers cannot take care of themselves." [5]

If, asserted Jermain Loguen, every slave, or even a considerable number of them, had manifested a spirit of protest, the masters might have succumbed and given them freedom, or at least treated them more justly. Slavery, said Loguen, could endure only so long as its victims were submissive and servile. [6]

Charles Ball reported that the nature of the slave's protest was sometimes aimed inward and the slave sought self-destruction. When the slave did destroy himself, wrote Ball, the master was sometimes unwilling to acknowledge this occurrence to his neighbors, for he did not want this act to be attributed to his own cruelty. The same master who witnessed the severe flogging of his slave, and manifested no pity, often expressed profound regret if the slave took his life. Peter Bruner added that some slaves, realizing that the master could be "embarrassed," would mutilate themselves, forcing the master to call for medical aid. [7]

David West, reporting to Benjamin Drew, looked upon slavery as a disgrace, asserting that no man could keep the "laws of God and hold to slavery." To the remark that the master had the right to hold slaves because they were given to him by his father, he asked, would this theory excuse them for stealing if their fathers had been thieves? [8]

Peter Randolph asked the people of the United States:

Will you defend slavery? Will you cast your vote for a slaveholder? Think before you speak; consider well before you act.

Could you have that fair young being you one day hope to call your wife torn from you, and publicly sold to the service of a debaucher? Would you think it too much to call on the laws of the land for redress? Would you think it asking too much to call out the whole military force of the country to the rescue? Oh, no! And could you restrain yourselves, and behold the loved forms of your aged parents reeking with their own blood, drawn forth by one who calls himself their master? Indeed, no! no dungeon deep and loathsome enough for such a one; no gibbet too high to swing him on, as an example to all his kind. And what better are your loved ones than those millions of colored suffering brothers and sisters? Ask no more, "why meddle with slavery?" As you would receive assistance, give it to others.[9]

In discussing the slave's lack of a heritage, James Pennington asked:

Suppose insult, reproach, or slander should render it necessary for him to appeal to the history of his family in vindication of his character, where will he find that history? He goes to his native state, to his native country, to his native town; but nowhere does he find any record of himself as a *man*. On looking at the family of his old, kind, Christian master, there he finds his name on a catalogue with the horses, cows, hogs, and dogs. However humiliating and degrading it may be to his feelings to find his name written down among the beasts of the field, *that* is just the place, and the only *place* assigned to it by the chattel relation. I beg our Anglo-Saxon brethren to accustom themselves to think that we need something more than mere kindness. We ask for justice, truth and honour, as other men do.[10]

Zamba protested the enslavement of his people by attacking such American symbols of freedom as the flag and the immortal George Washington. The flag, he suggested sarcastically, should be improved in the following manner: the stars should be replaced by the famed eagle with a whip in its beak, a bunch of cigars for the arrows in one claw, and a gray bottle in the other. These three symbols, in conjunction with the stripes, more truly represented the propensities and tendencies of a nation of slaves and slaveholders. While discussing the flag, he asked what the heroes of the nation had ever effected for the "cause of true and rational freedom." He said that the Declaration of Independence stated that men were born free and equal; and that freedom is the birthright of every man. Thus, unless the defenders of slavery could prove that slaves were brutes, lacking minds and souls, the masters must plead guilty to the inconsistency of "bursting asunder with one hand the chains and fetters of King George the Third—which weighed so heavily upon their own limbs—whilst with the other hand they were firmly and cruelly riveting chains and fetters, ten times more weighty and galling, around the limbs of their colored fellow men—their brethren: thousands and tens of thousands of them born in the same land." [11]

Some slaves reported to Benjamin Drew that they had received such harsh treatment that they had contemplated, and often carried out, arson and murder. John Little was so bruised and wounded that his frustration grew to open aggression. His patience having been exhausted, he could no longer cope with the mental and physical torture of the system. He reported that he was fully determined to kill, even if he were to be hanged, and "if it pleased God, sent to hell: I could bear no more." He prayed that if anyone defended this institution, that person should be abused as much as he was, should experience the agony of irons and whips, then should be sold a thousand miles away and live it all over again. "I think," said Little, "he would be tired of it too." Slavery was a curse because it led to color hatred, it led to the white man's abuse of "a 'nigger' because he is a 'nigger,' and the black to hate the white because he abuses him." [12]

James Roberts likewise attacked the institution in forceful language. He hoped that in some way he would be able to contribute his might to the destruction of the institution. His unceasing wish was to have an outside force strike a blow at human bondage, which the combined forces of the earth could not resist. This, he reported, was his "unceasing prayer while life lasts." [13]

Slave Insurrection—Physical Aggression and Protest

The previous section dealt primarily with what may be termed the intellectual or vocal manifestation of the slave's protest against their status. There is also discussion in the narratives of the physical manifestation of this protest, including insurrection, rebellion, the master's fear of such aggression and the slave's attitude toward it.

The most famous slave revolt was the Nat Turner Rebellion. It took place over a period of a few days in 1831 near Richmond, Virginia. Nat Turner, a lay preacher and the slave leader of the revolt, armed approximately fifteen to twenty-five slaves and free Negroes who during those few days allegedly killed about sixty whites.

Henry Clay Bruce reported that the Rebellion, the most serious and successful attempt ever made, created "no little sensation amongst the slaveholders." [14]

Henry Box Brown reported that during that time the city of Richmond was in a chaotic state. He recalled that he did not know precisely the cause of the excitement, for he could get no satisfactory information from his master, and that the only thing that he and the other slaves knew was that some blacks had plotted to kill their owners. He then learned through the grapevine that it was Turner's Insurrection. During those few days, according to his report, the entire city was in wild agitation, and the whites appeared to be terrified beyond measure. Large numbers of slaves were whipped, placed in irons and "half hung, as it was termed—that is, they were suspended from some tree with a rope about their necks, so adjusted as not quite to strangle them—and then they were pelted by men and boys with rotten eggs." [15]

The Turner Insurrection was the reason for the enactment

of a law forbidding more than five slaves to congregate unless they were at work, as well as of another law calling for the silencing of all Negro preachers.[16]

James L. Smith confirmed that when the insurrection broke out, the slaves were forbidden to hold meetings. Nevertheless, he reported, they would meet secretly in the quarters. As an example of the reaction of a slaveholder to the insurrection, he related that on his plantation, a slave child died and the slaves wanted to make arrangements to bury it. They went to the great house to seek permission from the master to have a funeral. He sent back word for the slaves to bury the child without any funeral services. Despite this order, the child was buried and that night about fifty to seventy slaves met to hold a service for the dead child. Shortly after it began the master was awakened by the noise, and broke into the cabin.[17]

He demanded to know what the slaves were doing there, and told them it was "against the law for niggers to hold meetings." The slaves replied that they were holding a funeral service for the child and the master accepted the explanation and left. Smith claimed that the object of his interrupting them was to find out whether they were plotting some scheme of insurrection among the people. Such, he claimed, was the fear that was spread by Nat Turner.[18]

Jamie Parker asserted that after the Turner Rebellion, the question of whether slaves should be granted any privileges became the subject of great concern. Parker reported that it was finally decided that there would be less cause for insurrections if more privileges were taken away.[19]

Linda Brent noted that many non-slaveholders sought out Negroes to kill and that, in order to avoid the wholesale slaughter of the blacks, some more rational masters put their slaves in jail to protect them. It was common practice, according to Miss Brent, for slaveholders to search the slave quarters and the homes of free Negroes looking for guns and ammunition. She recalled that when the Rebellion broke out, the news threw her town into a great commotion. She said it was strange that the slaveholders should be alarmed "when their slaves were so 'contented and happy'! But it was so." [20]

Miss Brent described some of the consequences of the insurrection and the fear caused by it. She reported that it was the custom every year in her town to have a military muster. On this occasion every white man shouldered his musket and the so-called country gentlemen wore military uniforms. The poor whites, of course, took their places in the ranks in civilian dress, some without shoes or hats. In 1831, this affair had taken place before the news of the Turner Rebellion and when the slaves were told that there was to be another muster (after the Rebellion), they were surprised and joyful; they thought it was going to be another holiday. When Miss Brent was informed of the true reason for the muster, she imparted the information to the few slaves she could trust. She asserted that she would gladly have proclaimed it to every slave, but she dared not. "All could not be relied on. Mighty is the power of the torturing lash." [21]

By morning, whites had come from everywhere within twenty miles of the town. She expected the quarters of slaves and free Negroes to be searched, and knew it would be done by country bullies and poor whites. She asserted that nothing annoyed these people so much as to see colored people living in comfort and respectability; so she made arrangements for their arrival with special care. She arranged everything in her home as neatly as possible. She saw the crowd of soldiers; drums and fifes were playing martial music. The soldiers were divided into companies of sixteen, each headed by a captain. Orders were given and the soldiers went in every direction, wherever a black face was seen.

Miss Brent claimed that this was considered an opportunity for the poor whites, who had no slaves of their own, to scourge, and they exulted in every chance to exercise a little brief authority. Little did they realize, she said, that the power that trampled on the Negro people also kept them, the poor whites, in poverty, ignorance, and moral degradation. In any event, brutality was inflicted upon innocent men, women, and children, against whom there was not the slightest ground for suspicion. In a few cases "the searchers scattered powder and shot among their [the slaves'] clothes, and then sent other parties to find them, and bring them forward as proof that they were plotting insurrection." In every part of town, men, women, and children were whipped in order to extract confessions from them. The homes of free Negroes, unless they were protected by some influential white, were robbed of clothing and everything else that the patrol could carry away. Women hid themselves in woods and swamps, to keep from being punished. If any husbands or fathers complained of this treatment, they were tied to the public whipping post and beaten for telling lies about white men. No two people, said Miss Brent, that had the "slightest tinge of color in their faces dared to be seen talking together." [22]

Toward evening the violence increased. The patrols, stimulated by drink, committed still harsher brutalities:

Shrieks and shouts continually rent the air. Not daring to go to the door, I peeked under the window curtain. I saw a mob dragging along a number of colored people, each white man, with his musket upraised, threatening instant death if they did not stop their shrieks. Among the prisoners was a respectable old colored minister. They had found a few parcels of shot in his house, which his wife had for years used to balance her scales. For this they were going to shoot him on Court House Green. What a spectacle was that for a civilized country! A rabble, staggering under intoxication, assuming to be the administrators of justice! [23]

She also reported that the "better class" of the community exerted their influence to save innocent people, and succeeded in a few cases by keeping them locked in jail until the excitement was abated. The white citizens found that their own property was not safe from the patrols they had summoned to protect them and, consequently, they were disbanded and sent back to the country.

The next day, the town patrols were commissioned to search the quarters of Negroes living out of the city. More outrages were committed with impunity. For days horsemen were seen with Negroes at the ends of ropes, compelled by the whip to keep up with the speed of the horse, until they arrived at the jail. Those who had been beaten and were unable to walk were washed with brine and thrown into wagons and carried to jail. One slave who had not the strength to endure the beating, promised to give information about the conspiracy. It was later discovered that he knew nothing and had never even heard of Nat Turner. According to Miss Brent, the "poor fellow had, however, made up a story, which augmented his own sufferings and those of the colored people." [24]

Finally the wrath of the slaveholders was somewhat appeased by the capture of Nat Turner, and, as nothing was proved against the blacks, those who were imprisoned were released. The slaves were sent to their masters, and the free Negroes were permitted to return home. For some time, visiting between quarters was forbidden on her plantation, all requests for funerals were denied, and Negro churches were demolished.[25]

The Turner Rebellion reinforced the fear created by the Santo Domingo massacres of the late eighteenth century, in which every white man, woman, and child was put to death at the hands of revolting black slaves. This fear was ever-present in the slaveholding states. Although the rebellion on Santo Domingo was rarely mentioned by the slaves, references are made to the fear of the white community caused by this upheaval and the fact that because of this fear, slaveholders insisted that America must not free the slaves if it were to avoid a recurrence of the Santo Domingo massacre. Nevertheless, slaves like Mrs. Ellis, a fugitive in Canada, remarked that "if the whites were to free the slaves, they would incur no danger." She insisted that another Santo Domingo would not occur, and that the black people would go to work without any trouble. David West also felt that if the slaves were freed they would not revolt as the blacks did in Santo Domingo. He believed that if the slaveholders were to say, "Here boys, you are free; you may go to work for me at so much a day, —if 't was done all over the South, there would be no trouble." [26]

Some slaves felt that the rapidly increasing number of Negroes in America would eventually lead to an insurrection of gigantic proportions. Zamba, for example, claimed that there existed a large group of able-bodied blacks—men who, with a "little discipline and with proper arms, would be found no contemptible soldiers." If aroused in the cause of freedom, they would, he said, lay down their arms only with their lives.[27]

Zamba asserted that revenge was one of the strongest human passions, "especially in the mind of a man who has received no education, and who is daily subjected to degradation, insult, and tyranny." He declared that the slaveholder did not have the privilege of trampling upon the black man. He recalled that fires were started almost every night in the city, and sometimes four or five times in a night. He stated that not only were firemen ready to respond to calls, but that the militia was placed at every street corner as well, "ready to vomit death and destruction on that portion of the community who are by law and custom so cruelly oppressed, that no faith or trust can be placed in them." He claimed that if the Negroes had been granted their rights as men and reasonable beings, they would have been the first to try their utmost to put down fire or rebellion. But as the situation stood, the majority of Negroes actually seemed to enjoy the extensive fires, "delighted that they can give their white masters so much trouble and vexation." [28]

Frederick Douglass issued a warning to the American people regarding the potential power of the slave community. He asserted that America could not always sit in peace and repose; "that prouder and stronger governments than this have been shattered by the bolts of a just God; that the time *may* come when those they now despise and hate [the slaves] may be needed; when those whom they now compel, by oppression, to be enemies, may be wanted as friends; what *has* been *may* be again." Douglass warned that those who, for two centuries, had been engaged in cultivating the fields of America may "yet become the instruments of terror, desolation, and death throughout our borders." If the United States should become engaged in a war, he asked, what would be the position of the slaves? How are you to sustain an assault from England or France, "with this cancer in your vitals?" Douglass felt as Zamba did, referring to the tremendous increase in the number of slaves, that the American people should recognize that this was a fearful multitude to be in chains.[29]

The Slave's Awareness of Social Prejudice against the Negro

For many slaves, freedom brought with it an awareness of social prejudice against the Negro. Moses Grandy reported that in the free states, black men were not permitted to sit in the same seats in church as the whites, nor to enter public conveyances. The fugitive slave, he wrote, "had to be content with the decks of steamboats in all weathers, night and day, not even our wives or children being allowed to go below, however it might rain, or snow, or freeze; in various other ways, we were treated as though we were a race of men below the whites." [30]

According to Grandy, the Negro who was fortunate enough to attain some education often suffered more than the uneducated. The more refined his feelings, the more he felt the hate and prejudice. This natural feeling was, said Grandy, aggravated by the fact that "an educated Negro, as a rule, is treated no better than one uneducated." The educated Negro was made the object of particularly offensive treatment because of his superior attainments, and was considered to be "out of his place; he is thought to be 'assuming the place of a white man.' " [31]

One slave who dictated his story to C. G. Parsons said that many whites entertained so deep a prejudice against the Negro that they could not associate anything beautiful, industrious or intelligent with a black complexion. John Little asserted that while in bondage he was abused *not* because he did anything wrong, but simply because he was "a nigger." Numerous other slaves confirmed Little's statement and said that masters hated them for no particular reason other than their color. They asserted that masters whipped them to reinforce the awareness that they were black, and that these masters operated on the theory that "niggers always should be whipped some, no matter how good they are, else they'll forget that they are niggers." [32]

Andrew Jackson witnessed racial prejudice in the free as well as the slave states. He concluded that the reason for it was something other than color—that it was actually recognition of caste. For example, most of the talk he heard was directed against social association between the races. He said that while it may be that man had a right *not* to associate if he wished, nevertheless many whites in the slave states failed to practice what they advocated. He had often been to dances held by Negroes on the plantation. While engaged in their amusement the slaves would often be interrupted by whites who would come in and crowd the slaves off the floor and make the black women dance with them. If any slaves showed the slightest resistance or anger, they were "knocked down, and if we laid a hand upon the *gentlemen*, the law punished us severely." [33]

Jackson reasoned that if there was so much "natural repugnance" to color, why did these men take so much pleasure in crowding into black society, in such unmanly ways, and trampling upon all laws of honor and decency? Why were there so many Negro children in the slave states whose skin was almost white? And why did the white population prefer Negro servants and waiters? Jackson felt that it was neither reason nor judgment which condemned him, for when these virtues were present he was treated as an equal human being. But, he said "when pride and prejudice speak, it is in language of haughtiness." Thus, if people were blind the Negro would be as good as anyone, "for their *mind* and *heart* would be put in the scale and not the *color of the skin*." [34]

Benjamin Drew reported that even in Canada the prejudice against the black man was strong. In one community with many fugitives, Drew reported a complete white withdrawal from the public school when Negroes were admitted. As the black students sat down, the white children left their benches. In a day or two, the whites had withdrawn completely, leaving the school to the teacher and his Negro students. The matter was ultimately settled by the posting of a notice—"select school"—on the schoolhouse; and, as Drew reported, "the white children were selected *in*, and the black were selected *out*." [35]

Austin Steward observed the gradual improvement of the Negro in the free states and asserted that as prejudice diminished, the black race would advance. He felt that prejudice was the sole impediment to a higher state of improvement for the Negro. However, he also noted that prejudice against color was not being destroyed quickly enough and that its effects on the downcast and discouraged Negro were severe. He observed it existing

in many of our hotels: some of them would as soon admit the dog from his kennel, at table, as the colored man; nevertheless, he is sought as a waiter; allowed to prepare their choicest dishes, and permitted to serve the white man, who would sneer and scorn to eat beside him. Prejudice is found also, in many of our schools,—even in those to which colored children are admitted; there is so much distinction made by prejudice, that the poor, timid colored children might about as well stay at home, as go to a school where they feel that they are looked upon as inferior, however much they may try to excel.[36]

Steward also condemned the church, for he saw that the hateful prejudice, so injurious to the Negro and his soul, was not excluded from the "professed church of Christ." He often heard mention of the "hated Negro" in the houses of worship in America, and asked, "How long, O Lord, must these things be?" Thus, he concluded, because of slavery and the presence of deep racial hatred, the Negro was being driven from his native land; unprotected by the government under which he was born, and for which he would gladly have died. He claimed that the Negro was so frustrated with the policy and attitude of the American people that he would most likely take up arms against his birthplace in the event of a rupture of relations between the United States and Canada or Great Britain. England, he claimed, could very easily "collect a regiment of stalwart colored men, who, having felt the oppression of our laws, would fight with a will not inferior to that which activated our revolutionary forefathers." [37]

Levi Coffin asserted that intermarriage received the most severe criticism from whites as well as many Negroes, and sometimes resulted in violence. In one case, a mulatto former slave was employed by a family from Massachusetts that was living in Missouri. The ex-slave was almost white and possessed none of the Negro features. After a while the mother of the family gave her permission to the ex-slave to marry one of her daughters. While the wedding was taking place, the news spread throughout the community that a Negro had married a white woman. An infuriated mob stormed the home and proceeded to search for the bridegroom—"several shades lighter than some of themselves—who dared to marry a white woman." The bridegroom escaped as though he were a fugitive slave and the mob became so frustrated that they seized the bride and dragged her through the streets as a demonstration of their indignation.[38]

The indignant citizens searched every Negro home for this "terrible criminal who had committed so great a sin as to marry a woman a shade lighter than himself, and that with the full approbation of her mother." The news of this marriage spread throughout the state and the public sentiment became more aroused. The "dreadful prospect of amalgamation loomed before the people like an impending curse." The state legislature was forced to take action to ban such infringements on white society and a law was passed levying a fine upon any clergyman or magistrate who performed a marriage ceremony between a white and a person who had "a drop of colored blood." Finally, several state officials visited the home of the offending family and urged the bride to apply for a divorce. The girl, alarmed by threats from the mob, yielded and signed a petition for a divorce. The legislature granted the petition, divorced the couple, and, said Coffin, "the young lady was declared free from the disgraceful alliance." [39]

RACE MIXTURE

The sexual liberties taken by the master with his female slaves were mentioned often in the narratives and have been referred to previously. Many of the narratives discuss the consequences of these relationships which quite naturally resulted in a mixture of the races.

Louisa Picquet mentioned the telltale mulatto, quadroon, and octoroon faces which stood out, unimpeachable symbols of the deep moral pollution of the slave state. These terms were used, said Henry Clay Bruce, "because we would have been pure black, were it not that immoral white men, by force, injected their blood into our veins, to such an extent, that we now represent all colors, from pure black to pure white, and almost entirely as the result of the licentiousness of white men, and not of marriage or by the cohabitation of colored men with white women." [40]

James Roberts noted that as time passed the mixed race in the slave states constantly increased, that there were thousands of slaves who did not differ in complexion from the whitest slaveholders. Nevertheless, wrote Frederick Douglass, the fact that the master was his father was of little consequence to the child. For it was ordained, and established by law, that the children of slave women followed the condition of their mother. Douglass said that this was so "obviously to administer to their own lusts and make a gratification of their wicked desires profitable as well as pleasurable; for by this cunning arrangement, the slaveholder, in cases not a few, sustains to his slaves the double relation of master and father." [41]

Slavery was bad enough for the black, said Douglass, but it was worse for the mulatto or quadroon. These slaves suffered the additional hardship of being subjected to the degradation and misery of slavery and while frequently being aware that their own fathers were treating them as property. This was especially so when they contrasted their condition with the pampered luxury of lawful children, who were not whiter and very often not so good-looking as they. It was not uncommon to see a quadroon with a lacerated back caused by a father's flogging. Some slaves in this condition often swore to kill their fathers if they attempted to flog them. Such children, who became hostile to their fathers and masters, were usually sold as uncontrollable servants. [42]

Douglass noted that children of mixed blood were a constant offense to the mistress and she was continuously disposed to find fault with them; especially when she suspected her husband of showing to his mulatto children favors which he withheld from his black slaves. The master was frequently compelled to sell these slaves, out of deference to the feelings of his white wife. Douglass said that as "cruel as the deed may strike any one to be, for a man to sell his own children to human-flesh mongers, it is often the dictate of humanity for him to do so; for unless he does this, he must not only whip them himself, but must stand by and see the white son tie up his brother, of but few shades darker complexion than himself, and ply the gory lash to his naked back; and if he lisp one word of disapproval, it is set down to his parental partiality, and only makes a bad matter worse, both for himself and the slave whom he would protect and defend." [43]

Lewis Clarke reported that there were no slaves that were as badly abused as those of mixed blood. He recalled one instance of a female slave who had been mistaken for a planter's daughter. Under this misapprehension, a young man addressed some conversation to her. The mistake was discussed in the quarters with some amusement until the mistress heard of it and went into a rage. She took her vengeance for this innocent mistake upon her husband's child, in order to make sure that "no body thought she was white." Accordingly, on one hot day, she forced the girl to undress and work in the garden in order to burn her back. While she was working the mistress threw water on her back to make it blister, and then she beat her on the blistered back. Clarke also wrote of mistresses who would force a husband to sell his black mistress and child, then see to it that the mother and child were separated when the trader resold them.[44]

Because thousands of slaves resembled their white fathers, the narratives contain some novel and bizarre pictures of plantation scenes. James Roberts reported that his master could be seen riding in the family carriage on the seat beside his slave child, who was driving. Five white children and the white wife would sit in the rear; and in the next carriage might be two servants, both the children of the master by a black woman, and two other children inside, by the same black woman and master. Thus, there were ten in all, five free, five slaves, all children by the same father.[45]

Roberts stated that these children grew up with a common desire for freedom. The one refused to be enslaved by the other; for both, feeling a common parentage, felt an equal right to liberty. Whichever attempted to oppress the other caused conflict. The mulatto child, feeling degraded and outraged by his own brother, would, said Roberts, resist "unto death, and wade in blood to obtain that liberty which, reason tells him, is as much his right to enjoy as others of his own blood-kind." Roberts recalled another illustration of this strange situation when two half-brothers were arguing. The white child contended that the mulatto should submit to him, that he was nothing but a Negro and a slave; and the mulatto maintained that he was as good as the other, because his master was the father of them both. A fight ensued, and the two mothers came and took sides with their respective sons. If it were not for the intercession of the father, wrote Roberts, terrible would have been the results. The master parted the four and sent them to their respective houses.[46]

William Craft asserted that, in endeavoring to reconcile a girl to the consequences of a relationship with him, the master would sometimes "marry" her. Although it was unlawful in the slave states for anyone of purely European descent to intermarry with a person of African extraction, and thus the union was not legally a marriage, nevertheless, a white man could live with a Negro woman without materially damaging his reputation in society. Sometimes, however, he actually considered her to be his wife, and treated her as such. She, too, might regard him as her lawful husband. If there were any issue of this union, they were often freed and given a proper education. More often than not, however, the great majority of such masters cared nothing for the happiness of the women with whom they lived, nor for the children whom they fathered. In any event, as the woman and her children were legally the property of the man, who stood in the anomalous relation to them of husband and father, as well as master, they were liable to be seized and sold for his debts, either with or without his approval, should it become necessary.[47]

Thus, William Mitchell reported the case of a slaveholder in Georgia, whose slave wife died when their child was quite young. Although a slaveholder, the father was not a trader in slaves. The mother had been a quadroon and the father a white man, therefore there was no appearance of African blood in the child. He maintained this double relationship to this child, both as father and master, and, said Mitchell, "but for this the child would have been a precious jewel in social society." As she grew, the thought of being a slave never entered her mind, and despite the prohibition of law, she was educated in her father's house. The master's violations of these and other laws were tolerated because of the influential position he held in the community.[48]

At the proper age, she became the mistress of the house, which to some extent obviated the necessity for his marrying, which, had he done, would have revealed the child's condition to herself and the world. Eventually, he failed in business, and his property was taken to satisfy his creditors. Falling short a thousand dollars, his creditors asked for his housemaid. He had been unaware that his creditors knew anything of his relationship to her as a master, and he replied that she was his daughter. "True, but she is also your slave as well," said the creditors. His daughter was in the power of the law and he in the power of his creditors, and, despondent, he submitted to the will of his creditors and sold his own child.[49]

Levi Coffin related a similar occurrence. A slaveholder owned a beautiful slave woman, who was almost white. She soon became the mother of a child, in whose veins ran the blood of the master, and whose African ancestry was undetectable by even the closest observer. The boy grew to the age of three when the master, for family reasons, decided to send him away. He was properly educated, and grew up as a free man, accepted into the white community. He had not the slightest knowledge of his mother's background, and no one knew he was the son of an octoroon slave woman. He made a comfortable living, was a good citizen, a member of the Methodist Church, and was well respected by all who knew him. In the course of time his father died, and when time came to settle the estate, the little child was remembered. It was decided that he belonged to the estate and, as a valuable piece of property, his father's creditors resolved to gain possession of him. Without his knowledge, the son was sold to a trader who was given a bill of sale, for the family preferred to have a sum of money instead of a servant who might indeed prove very valuable, but who could, without doubt, give them a great deal of trouble. He had been free all his life, and it was thought that he would not readily yield to enslavement.

One evening the slave dealer came with several men, burst into the young man's home and seized him as he lay asleep. When he demanded the reason for his seizure, they showed him the bill of sale, and informed him that he was a slave. The dealer hurried him out of his home, and took him to the slave market. To get him black enough to sell without question, they washed his face in tan ooze, tied him in the sun, and, to complete the transformation, cut his hair short and burnt it with a hot iron to make it curly, whereupon he was sold into bondage.[50]

Thus, wrote Austin Steward, as time passed, the African was not the only slave in America. Eventually, he said, there was as much European blood in the veins of the enslaved as there was African; and the increase was constant. Frederick Douglass claimed that this fact was a constant, ever-present reminder to the slaveholder of the fearful retribution which might eventually overtake him. Every year, said Douglass, brought with it multitudes of these slaves; a new group of people was springing up in the slave states, held in slavery and looking different from those originally brought to America from Africa. Thousands were ushered into the slave society annually, owing their existence to white fathers, who were, in many instances, also their masters.[51]

THE EFFECT OF SLAVERY ON THE MASTER

Passing references have been made to the effects of the institution on nonslaves. This section will deal in more detail with what some of the narratives describe as the effects of slavery on the master.

I have divided it into two parts—a discussion of the social, economic, and psychological effects of slavery on the master and his family, and a discussion of the extensive and detailed material dealing with one specific effect, the master's fear of slave rebellion.

The Social, Economic, and Psychological Effects of the Institution on the Master

Charles Ball reported that it almost seemed to be a law of nature that slavery was as destructive to the master as to the slave; for while it stupefied the slave with fear, and relegated him to a position beneath the condition of other men, it also brutalized the slaveholder by its continual tyranny, and made him the "prey of all the vices which render human nature loathsome." The brutalization of the slaveholder was by no means unnatural, said Ball, for the nature of the "peculiar institution" was such as to brutalize anyone in the position of master. Many slaveholders, he insisted, were coarse and vulgar, unprincipled, cruel in their conduct, and addicted to licentiousness. Josiah Henson gave a similar description, and charged that the institution itself turned the slaveholder "into a tyrant, and the slave into the cringing, treacherous, false, and thieving victim of tyranny." [52]

"Everywhere that slavery exists," wrote Austin Steward, "it is nothing but *slavery*." Referring to an early period of American history, he said the slave found it just as brutal to be beaten "with a piece of iron in New York as it was in Virginia." Brutality was necessary, he said, to degrade and reduce the slave to the abject and humble state which slavery required, and the effect of this brutality was as disastrous to the man who held supreme control as to the victim.[53]

Andrew Jackson interpreted the bitterness between slaveholding families as a habit they developed because of their constant abuse of other people. Jackson believed that if the masters had treated the slave in a humane manner, they would not have had such a bitter feeling toward one another.[54]

With respect to the brutality of the institution, Solomon Northup asserted that it tended to make every white in the slave areas a militant. Every man, he claimed, carried a weapon, and was prepared to use it without hesitation. To Northup, the slaveholder was more nearly a savage than he was a civilized and enlightened being, because he witnessed immense human suffering and listened to the agonizing screeches of the slave as he was beaten and bitten by dogs, and so it could not "otherwise be expected, than that they should become brutified and reckless of human life." [55]

Northup felt that this was not the fault of the man so much as it was the fault of the institution. The master could not withstand the influence of the atmosphere, habits, and associations that surrounded him. Thus, taught from childhood that fear and punishment alone would control the slave, he was not prepared to change his outlook in his adult years.[56]

Jane Blake went so far as to state that since slavery was unmitigated evil, more harmful to the slaveholders and their families than to the slaves, if it were banished from the nation, even the most brutal owners would say "it is good riddance." [57]

Booker T. Washington elucidated and confirmed what Miss Blake said by asserting that the slave system destroyed the spirit of self-reliance and self-help. He claimed that the institution itself was so organized as to make physical labor the sign of degradation and inferiority. Physical work was some-

thing to be avoided by a white man. Washington's master had
done little to teach his sons a trade or anything of productive
industry. Not much more was done for the white female, for
all work was taken care of by the slaves. Thus, he concluded,
the system had imbued the white community with the feeling
that physical labor was not a proper vocation for a slaveholder
or any other white man.[58]

John Brown asserted that because of this feeling, the poor
white was in a worse condition in the slave state than in the
free, because labor was made a shameful occupation, "and a
man does not like to go to work in his own fields for fear that
folks should look down upon him." Thus, said Brown, because
the poor white refused to resort to an honest living, he would
induce slaves to steal and would act as the thieves' agent.[59]

According to Brown, an additional consequence of the institution was that it made the master jealous of every man who
worked with *free* labor. If such an individual lived in a slaveholding community, the masters attempted to force him to
leave. Brown described an incident illustrating this point. An
individual named John Morgan came to his community. Although he was against slavery, he was not an abolitionist, and he
was resolved to employ many free men, both white and black.
After a short while, his financial success was observed by the
slaveholding community. In Brown's words, his "cotton was
much better, and fetched a higher price in the market. The reason was that his men were not forced to pick the cotton in the
wet, so the fiber came out cleaner." Soon the masters became
jealous of him and alleged that he would "spoil all their 'niggers,' injure the settlement, and damage the system of slavery,
so he must be got rid of." Indeed, Morgan was eventually de-
frauded out of his land, and his resort to the courts brought
him no satisfaction. Brown asserted that the slaveholders
bribed his lawyers and turned the court against him by "saying
that he was a friend of the niggers; so he could not get his case
fairly heard." Nevertheless, the lawsuit was continued until

Morgan's finances were exhausted, and he was forced out of court, financially unable to continue the legal battles. Thus, said Brown, this independent free farmer now had nothing with which to live, and was compelled to do as the other poor whites did, "that is, to depend chiefly upon the colored people." [60]

William Wells Brown noted that the slaveholder who sent his child to a free state for an education often found it difficult finding a place to board him. This, claimed Brown, was due to the fact that the slaveholder's children spread their "vices among the children with whom they associated in the free state, to such an extent that parents have often taken their children out of school on the introduction of the children of slaveholders." Although he reported that a deep prejudice existed in the free states against Negroes, there were many who preferred a black to the son of a slaveholder as friend for their children. [61]

Brown, paraphrasing an old proverb, wrote that "no man can bind a chain around the limb of his neighbor, without inevitable fate fastening the other end around his own body." While the master degraded the slave, he himself became degraded; by preventing education from reaching the slave, the master kept his own children in complete ignorance. Hence, Brown said,

the immoralities which have been found to follow in the train of slavery in all countries and all ages, are to be seen in their worst forms in the Slave States of America. This is attributable to the degree of ignorance which is deemed necessary to keep the enslaved in his chains. It is a fact admitted by the American slaveholders themselves, that their slaves are in a worse state of heathenism than any other heathen in the civilized world. There is a constant action and reaction—the immoralities of the slave contaminate the master, the immoralities of the master contaminate the slave. The effects of the system are evident in the demeanor of the slaveholders. [62]

The Fear of Rebellion

Most of the slave narratives indicated that the slaveowners had persuaded themselves that their slaves were a dangerous class. The precautions they took and their evident apprehensions proved that they were in earnest. Thus, one reporter stated that special laws, cruel punishment, and patrols were required—"in the opinion of the slaveholders—to keep them [the slaves] from murder and rapine." [63]

Isaac D. Williams asserted that slaveholders were so fearful of insurrection that if three or four Negroes met together and entered into a conversation, they were subject to a flogging. This, he said, was to assure that they would be "very brief in their future conversation with each other." [64]

In their own minds, wrote Austin Steward, whites often turned the most innocent gatherings of slaves into conspiracies for insurrection. Steward reports one such incident in which the slaves on a particular plantation held a social gathering without the consent or knowledge of the master. In the midst of the party, the music suddenly stopped and every slave assumed a listening attitude. The slave who was kept on the lookout shouted to the listeners the single word "patrol!" which was followed by tumult. Many, said Steward,

screamed in afright, as if they already felt the lash and heard the crack of the overseer's whip, others clenched their hands, and assumed an attitude of bold defiance, while a savage form contracted the brow of all. Their unrestrained merriment and delicious fare, seemed to arouse in them the natural feelings of self-defense and defiance of their oppressors.[65]

When the patrol entered the quarters the lights went out. In the darkness they fought and struggled with each other, amid the explosion of firearms. Two members of the patrol were killed; others were beaten and lay helpless beside the slaves who had given their lives in the fight. The fight finally ended and the remaining slaves escaped to the various plantations from whence they had come. The word of this occurrence was carried from one plantation to another, exaggerated accounts were given, and, said Steward, "prophecies of the probable result made, until the excitement became truly fearful." Every white in the community was now discussing the fact that the "insurrection" among the slaves had commenced and how the patrol had been brutally ambushed. The following day armed whites flocked from every area of the community, swearing vengeance on the ruthless slaves. "Nothing can teach plainer than this," asserted Steward, "the constant and tormenting fear in which the slaveholder lives." The master of the plantation on which the incident had occurred was beset and harassed by his neighbors to give up his slaves to be tried for insurrection. He resisted, contending that slaves had the natural right to act in their own self-defense, especially when on their own plantation and in their own quarters. The officials of the community contended, however, that as his slaves had "got up a dance," and had invited those of the adjoining plantation, the patrol was only discharging its duty in looking for them. Thus, despite the master's protests, the slaves were punished and the incident was recorded as an insurrection that was destroyed before it could do a great deal of damage.[66]

Although the rules and regulations of the various plantations were often dissimilar, Jamie Parker stated that one rule was almost ubiquitous: in order to avoid free assemblage and an opportunity to plot insurrection, the slaves must, to the greatest possible extent, be kept within the bounds of the plantation to which they belonged. As a consequence, they could not even leave to visit a relative on an adjoining plantation without a written pass from the master.[67]

James Williams claimed that many slave owners who heard sermons by slave preachers felt that they were the instruments which would lead to insurrection among the slaves, and, after the Nat Turner Rebellion, many were not allowed to preach at all. Often, he said, slaves were flogged if they were even found singing or praying at home.[68]

Moses Grandy said that although they were allowed to go to the places of worship used by the whites, many slaves wanted to hold their own religious meetings, and would meet privately in the woods for this purpose. When they were discovered they were beaten and forced to reveal who else was there. Many were shot and killed, Grandy said, depending on how severe the fear of rebellion was.[69]

Charles Ball reported that the overseer who permitted the slaves under him to go about without a pass soon lost the confidence of his master, lost his job, and found reemployment impossible. His reputation certainly suffered less if he did not grant passes at all, except for the most urgent occasion. Ball said that because of the fear that prevailed, the planter would have "no more of permitting his slaves to go at will, about the neighborhood on Sunday, than a farmer in Pennsylvania has of letting his horses out of his field on that day. Nor would the neighbors be less inclined to complain of the annoyance, in the former, than in the latter case." [70]

Many fugitives reported to Benjamin Drew that white men in the free states worked days, and slept nights, without fear, but that in the slave states the masters did not have this comfort. The overseer watched during the day, and the master was on the lookout at night. They reported that masters would often be seen at the great house window with a gun and that "sometimes the window would fly up—'Who's that?' —then the man must give an account of himself." [71]

John Little asked, "How can men, who know they are abusing others all day, lie down and sleep quietly at night, with big barns of corn, and gin-houses full of cotton, when they know that men feel revengeful, and might burn their property, or even kill them?" And, he added, the slaves *did* feel the stirrings of revenge, and the slaveholders knew it.

The slaveholder, said Little, was simply "afraid of his slaves: it cannot be otherwise." [72]

Isaac D. Williams felt that it was unfortunate that slaves were not armed, for then they could fight their way to freedom. But weapons in the hands of the slaves were not to be tolerated. Any incident in which a slave was found with arms would have started newspapers and telegrams calling for the suppression of an insurrection of the entire slave population. The intended fugitive knew, said Williams, that if this happened it would have been next to impossible to escape. Williams reported that many slaves received as many as five hundred lashes or even the death penalty because a revolver was found on them and they refused to reveal the source. Whites who sold weapons to blacks, free or bond, were sentenced to the penitentiary for long terms, or suffered in some other way equally bad. Williams claimed that slaves were not even permitted to buy a jackknife without special permission from the master. [73]

Samuel Ward asserted that the master's deceitful promise of freedom often was the cause of his own fear. The following example was reported by Ward and confirmed by James Roberts. During the War of 1812, said Ward, slaves were called out to fight for their country. General Andrew Jackson was alleged to have said that any slave who fought for him at New Orleans would thereafter be given his freedom. Both slaves who reported this incident asserted that their masters had agreed to Jackson's terms and permitted their slaves to fight. When the battle was over, however, the slaves who had fought asked that the General live up to his promise. Ward and Roberts both claim that Jackson replied, "You are not my property, and I cannot take another man's property and set it free." The masters then denied any knowledge of such an agreement with Jackson, and all slaves who had fought at New Orleans were returned to their plantations. The slaves, said Ward, were denied the slightest share in the liberties for which they had fought and bled. Incidents such as this, he said, caused guilt and fear on the part of the masters, and frustration and anger among the slaves.[74]

William Greenleaf Eliot's report of the narrative of Archer Alexander revealed that freedom was the most talked-about subject when the slaves did assemble. According to Eliot, at one religious meeting, Alexander went so far as to say that "by the 'Claration of 'Dependence all men was ekal, and that to trade in men and women, jess like hogs and horses, wasn't 'cording to gospel nohow." The report of this incident spread to the slaves of other plantations, and the whites began to hear of it. The white community held a meeting and informed the slave's master of the episode. They demanded that "as a Christian man it was required that he should send Aleck South"; and that to keep such a mischief-maker there was dangerous, for a slave insurrection would surely follow.[75]

The Alabama Narratives of the Federal Writers' Project indicate that many of the threatened insurrections feared by the slaveholders were created in their own minds and that the slaves were the last to hear about it. A typical case was reported by Peter Still. In the summer of 1840, when the political excitement of "Tippecanoe and Tyler too," spread throughout one slave area, a convention was held, and men from both parties were loud in their defense of the liberties of the nation. Speeches were made, songs were sung, and, said Still, "each busy patriot seemed to imagine himself destined to save the nation from misrule and consequent destruction." [76]

The slaves did not remain indifferent listeners to these conversations concerning liberty. They interpreted the conversations literally, and imagined that the dawn of liberty had come. To the slave, wrote Still, it meant that *they* were to be the recipients of this freedom. The whites, they said, were already free, and if liberty was to become universal—

and both political parties declared it would become so—"then the 'black folks' too, would soon enjoy its blessings." [77]

The talk of liberty spread from the town slaves to the plantation slaves; the news was communicated in whispers at first—but, said Still, "as they became more certain that their hopes were well grounded, they gradually grew bolder, till at length they dared to discuss the subject in their religious meetings." The slaveholders of the community learned of these discussions, and established a system of espionage, to discover the identity of the plotters of the insurrection. The black preachers were silenced; all meetings of slaves forbidden, and patrols were established throughout the area. Every Negro, free and bond, who encountered the patrols was whipped; even the pass, he said, "often lost its magic, if the bearer chanced to have the reputation of being a man of spirit." [78]

Panic pervaded the entire community. "The negroes intend to rise!" was

whispered with white lips by timid ladies in their morning visits; and every sigh of the night-wind through the lofty trees was interpreted by the fearful into the rush of the black assassins. Old stories of Negro insurrections were revived, and the most faithful and attached servants became objects of suspicion.[79]

Eventually, of course, the fear subsided and a few old privileges were restored to the slaves. However, according to Still, this incident proved to the slaves that the slaveholders' confidence was always imperfect, and easily shaken.[80]

Israel Campbell reported that when the fear of insurrection was occasionally revived, the whites would make up elaborate stories about the so-called "plots." Patrols would then go around to the slave quarters and frighten the slaves with guns and whips. The slaves became so frightened that they would tell almost any kind of lie which they thought the patrol wanted to hear. When the whites thought they had succeeded in quelling the alleged insurrection, they would begin punishing those that had been "betrayed." Some they hung, others they burned, and some of those "they thought not so guilty, they merely pulled cats backwards on their bare bodies." One such imagined plot, known as "*Murrell's* Insurrection," took place in 1836 and was described by Israel Campbell. After the plot had been "exposed" the slaveholders felt confident they had saved the lives of their wives and children and preserved their property from destruction. Campbell described the subsequent slaughter thus: Two large forked poles were inserted in the ground and a pole laid from one to the other, to serve as a mass gallows. The whites arrested every black preacher and free Negro they could find. All were hung. The heads of the preachers were cut off and put on the poles, which were then placed along the roads, where they remained until they were bleached. This demonstration was to serve as a warning to slaves who had any thoughts of joining any further insurrection.[81]

Some of the narratives in the Fisk University collection reported that "poor whites" sometimes falsely told the slaveholders that they had information indicating that the slaves were going to revolt. The slaves thought this was done because the poor white often felt that the slave had more in life than he had. One slave even asserted that for this same reason one poor white had claimed that he wanted to see all slaves dead.[82]

J. C. Brown confirmed this and related the following example: It had been reported that many Negroes had joined in a conspiracy allegedly extending over a three-hundred-mile area. A free Negro, a blacksmith, was suspected of being the leader of this conspiracy. When the patrols searched his shop and found some old guns, butcher-knives, and other such implements, he was swiftly jailed and then hung. Twenty years later, a poor white in the area was convicted of murder. Under the gallows, he confessed that twenty years earlier he had been employed to place the incriminating implements under the blacksmith's floor.[83]

Zamba explained that this fear of rebellion and the alleged part that free Negroes played in them was the reason for the reluctance of the states to permit emancipation of slaves. Laws were passed to prevent humane masters from emancipating their slaves or slaves from purchasing their freedom. In some states emancipation could not be granted without express permission from the legislators. Zamba said that the difficulty of this procedure operated very nearly as a total prohibition of individual emancipation. This procedure, he said, was "somewhat akin to, but even more difficult to obtain than, procuring an act of Parliament in Britain for any important matter." [84]

According to Jane Brown, most slaves claimed that if they were set free there would be no rebellion; that only if the slave were kept in bondage would there be insurrection. Nevertheless, she said, some did report that discontent pervaded the entire black population, bond and free, in all slave states, and that human bondage was ever fruitful of insurrection, wherever it existed, and under whatever circumstances. William Wells Brown confirmed, as we have read, that every slave community felt that it lived on a volcano that was "liable to burst out at any moment." [85]

THE SLAVE AND THE RIGHTS OF MAN

In those portions of the narratives in which the slaves interpreted the institution, there is a good deal of discussion and analysis of the rights of slaves as individuals in comparison with, and as related to, free men. Some of this expression is prophetic, profound, and even, at times, thrilling.

The Cry for Freedom

Aaron asserted that the desire for freedom was uppermost in the minds and thoughts of all slaves, and not even imminent death destroyed this desire. He wrote of slaves on their death-bed, begging their master to give them their liberty before they died. Aaron described the following illustrative collo-quy between master and slave:

"I want to die free, massa." His master replied, "you are going to die soon, what good will your liberty do?" "O master, I want to die free." He said to the slave, "you are free." "But do write it master, I want to see it on paper." At his earnest request he wrote that he was free, the slave took it in his trembling hand, looked at it with a smile and exclaimed, "O how beautiful! O how beauti-ful!" and soon fell asleep in the arms of death.[86]

Andrew Jackson also wrote that the slave's love of liberty was as deep in his thinking as it was in any other man's, and that the slave was as sensitive of wrongs and sufferings, not-withstanding his obvious submission. He claimed that white men, under similar oppressions, would be as submissive as the slaves were, for when men of any color find they must submit to wrong and injury, and that there is no escape, the color of the skin does not create any difference.[87]

Jackson also reported that although some slaves were not so severely treated as others, this did not make them less im-patient to be free. The sense of wrong done to them in keeping them as slaves, he said, was nevertheless keen, if only because of their constant reflection that they were both morally and legally entitled to freedom. Jackson proclaimed that if "the 'Declaration of Independence,' as it is called, which states that all men are endowed by their creator with the inalienable right to life, liberty and the pursuit of happiness," is correct, there was not a slave in the world who would not be justified in fighting his way to fredom.[88]

When he witnessed an Independence Day celebration, Jack-son felt a disgust within him that could not be repressed, for he thought that such celebration was a farce. The orators quoting the language of the American Revolution, such as, "give me liberty or give me death! and to hear them talk of the 'triumphs of liberty' and of this 'free and happy nation,' while the clanking of the chains of 3,000,000 of American citizens is ringing in their ears, is enough to make *one who has worn these chains*, feel like calling fire from heaven to consume such mockery of the sacred Genius of Liberty." [89]

The narratives of Benjamin Drew confirm that other slaves, too, had this view of liberty; that it was a matter of liberty for the mind; that there was a certain freedom of thought, which could not be enjoyed unless they were free—that is to say, for example, if one dreamed of something beneficial to oneself, one should have the liberty to execute it. Thus, Alexander Hemsly did not escape because of any sudden impulse or fear of punishment, but from a natural desire to be free. He stated that had it not been for family and friends, he would not have remained in slavery as long as he did. He claimed that there was a spirit within the fugitive, a feeling for victory or death; and, as a consequence, the desire for freedom was so intense that some determined never to be taken alive. [90]

To Henry Bibb, a Kentucky slave, the Ohio River formed the boundary of his existence. And to him it was an impossible gulf. He wrote:

I had no rod wherewith to smite the stream, and thereby divide the waters. I had no Moses to go before me and lead the way from bondage to a promised land. Yet I was in a far worse state than Egyptian bondage; for they had houses and land, I had none; they had oxen and sheep, I had none; they had a wise counsel to tell them what to do, and where to go, and even to go with them, I had none.

Sometimes standing on the Ohio River bluff, looking over on a free state, and as far north as my eyes could see, I have eagerly gazed upon the blue sky of the free North, which at times constrained me to cry out from the depths of my soul, oh! Canada, sweet land of rest—oh! when shall I get there? Oh, that I had the wings of a dove, that I might soar away to where there is no slavery; no clanking of chains, no captives, no lacerating backs, no parting of husbands and wives, and where man ceases to be the property of his fellow man. These thoughts have revolved in my mind a thousand times. I have stood upon the lofty banks of the river Ohio, gazing upon the splendid steamboats, wafted with all their magnificence up and down the river, and I thought of the fishes of the water, the fowls of the air, the wild beast of the forests, all appeared to be free, to go just where they pleased, and I was an unhappy slave! [91]

As a child Frederick Douglass felt that there was a better day coming, that it could not be that he should live and die in bondage. Douglass said that he felt then that he would as soon be "killed running as die standing." If there was a God, he said, "let me be free! Is there any God? Why am I a slave?" His desire for liberty came early in life and he firmly resolved that all he could lose by attempting to escape was his life.[92]

Naturally, not all slaves felt the intense desire for immediate freedom. Jupiter Hammon, for example, acknowledged that liberty was a great thing, and worth seeking, but only if it could be gotten honestly and in good conduct, by prevailing upon the master to set the slave free. He himself did not desire freedom, yet he wanted other slaves, especially the young, to be free. He felt that those slaves who had grown up under the system had always had masters to care for them, and that such slaves would hardly know how to take care of themselves, if they were emancipated. Although he agreed that liberty was uppermost in the slave's mind, as it was in the master's, he realized, he said, how much money had been spent, and how many lives lost, defending their own liberty (in the American Revolution). He expressed a wish that the slaveholder would have opened his eyes, when he was fighting for his liberty, "to think of the state of the poor blacks, and to pity us." But, he felt, this was by no means his most important concern, for attaining freedom in "this world, is nothing to having the liberty of the children of God." [93]

Hammon preached that the slaves had little time on earth, and that it did not matter what condition they were in if it prepared them for heaven. "What is forty, fifty, or sixty years," he said, "when compared to eternity?" He felt the slave owed a great deal to the white man for bringing him to a land where he had been taught the gospel, and that should the slave ever get to heaven, he would find none to reproach him for being black, or for being a slave. He concluded that the slaves should not think of their bondage, for if God wished, he would see them free, in his own time and way.[94]

The narratives reveal, however, that Hammon's sentiments did not reflect those of a majority, or even a large segment of the slave population. More often they indicate that the slave who attained freedom found this moment to be one of the most exciting he had ever experienced. As Frederick Douglass stated, "I felt as one may imagine the unarmed mariner to feel when he is rescued by a friendly man-of-war from the pursuit of a pirate." [95]

William Wells Brown wrote angrily of the institution and white society. Brown claimed that slavery had penetrated into all segments of society; that it had taken root in the free as well as the slave states. Leaving the question of the influence of slavery on the slaveholder, Brown turned his attention to the free state, and asked, "What is the contaminating influence over the great mass of the people of the North?" He felt that the people of the free states—being connected with the slave states—must *by necessity* have become contaminated. He asserted that few benevolent associations, formed for the purpose of carrying out Christian principles, had sought to apply those principles truly to slaves and slavery, and none even said anything to condemn slavery.[96]

For example, the American Bible Society, according to

Brown, sent Bibles throughout the world, yet three million slaves never received a single Bible from this organization. When the American Anti-Slavery Society offered a donation of five thousand dollars to this group to send Bibles to the slaves, the Society refused even to attempt the venture.[97]

Brown also condemned the American Tract Society for never publishing a tract against slaveholding. He claimed that this agency published works attacking licentiousness, intemperance, gambling, sabbath-breaking, and dancing, and almost "every sin that you can think of, but not a single syllable has ever been published by the American Tract Society against the sin of slaveholding." Brown concluded that from the actions, and lack of action, he witnessed, slavery had destroyed the sense of morality of both slave and non-slave society.[98]

To the entire nation, he said, "But for the blighting influence of slavery, the United States of America would have a character, would have a reputation, that would outshine the reputation of any other government that is to be found upon God's green earth." [99]

He asked the American people to look at the struggle of its forefathers for liberty. "What did they struggle for? What did they go upon the battle-field for, in 1776?" They went, he asserted, for the purpose of obtaining freedom and democracy, for the purpose of instituting a democratic government. Nevertheless, he said, America now claimed that slavery was the cornerstone of the nation, that two hundred years had sanctioned and sanctified American slavery.[100]

Brown examined further the struggle for liberty in 1776. The men of the nation, he said,

went forth upon the battle-field and laid down their bones, and moistened the soil with their blood, that their children might enjoy liberty. What was it for? Because a three-penny tax upon a tea, a tax upon paper, or something else had been imposed upon them? We are not talking against such taxes upon the slave. The slave has no tea, he has no paper, he has not even himself, he has nothing at all.[101]

To call the United States a land of liberty, while men were held in bondage, was hypocrisy. Some men, said Brown, have called the United States the "asylum of the oppressed; and some have been foolish enough to call it the 'cradle of liberty.' If it is the 'cradle of liberty' they have rocked the child to death." [102]

With the coming of emancipation, the expression of the slave's desire for freedom became more vocal. Booker T. Washington reported that there was more singing in the quarters than usual. It was bolder in tone, and openly expressed the desire for freedom. Previously most of the songs of the quarters had referred to freedom, but the slave had been careful to explain that the freedom in their songs referred to life after death, and had no tie with their present world. With emancipation they threw off the masks and were not afraid to let it be known that the " 'freedom' in their songs meant freedom of the body in this world." [103]

Some slaves, said Washington, when they were finally in possession of freedom, found it a more serious thing than they had expected. The older ones, whose best days were gone, were especially worried. These men, who had spent a half-century in bondage, found the abolition of the institution a difficult thing to understand. Nonetheless, he wrote, the vast majority of the slave population, if not the entire body of Negro slaves, willingly and enthusiastically accepted freedom.[104]

Awareness of the Fallacy of Negro Inferiority

Slavery was obviously not an institution designed for the training and production of superior talents. Samuel Ward noted this fact and explained further that most slaves were forever marked by the institution in some way, either physically or psychologically. It was almost impossible, said Ward, to spend the greater part of one's life in a condition such as slavery and to escape, entirely or even to any significant extent, the influences of the institution upon one's character. Ward claimed that this was as true of slaveholders as it was of slaves. The slaveholder, he said, never lost "the overbearing insolence, the reckless morals, the peculiarly inelegant manners and the profligate habits, which distinguish too many of them." Thus, he asked, should the slave be expected to be better than the institution or the slaveholder made him? Should the slave be expected to be any better than his master? [105]

Even Ward, who escaped the institution at an early age, reported that he was never able to lose completely the influence of his slave origin. Ward stated that this influence showed itself in his thoughts, his superstitions, his narrow views, and his awkwardness of manners. He said, "The infernal impress is upon me, and I fear I shall transmit it to my children, and they to theirs! How deeply seated, how far reaching, a curse it is! " [106]

Ward claimed that the Negro was, whether as slave, fugitive, or freeman, equal to other poor immigrants, and superior to many. Take him as a whole, said Ward, and he was "a lover of freedom, a loyal subject, and an industrious man." Ward felt the Negro slave had been censured unfairly, "as if he and his ancestors had been civilized, evangelized, highly educated, and especially favored, for the past fifty generations." He concluded that he considered himself, and Negroes as a race, equal to any race of men, including other races which had never been slaves. He asked that the Negro be judged by the same fair standard of character which was applied to other peoples, and by which they were estimated. [107]

Austin Steward echoed Ward and reported that the alleged inferiority of the Negro was used by some as a justification for enslavement. Others apologized for the institution by using the same argument and saying that the African was inferior to the Anglo-Saxon in every respect. Steward denied this and asserted that the Bible informed mankind that "God hath created of one blood all the nations of the earth; and that even if it were otherwise, he still did not understand why the more favored class should enslave the other." Although the African had a darker complexion, the Negro had the same desires and aspirations as the white man. Steward analyzed that "food required for the sustenance of one, is equally necessary for the other. Physically, they alike required to be warmed by the cheerful fire when chilled by our Northern winter's breath; and alike they welcome the cool spring to the delightful shade of summer." [108]

Steward also contended that if it were true that the black man was inferior, it appeared strange that he should be held responsible for the violation of laws which he had been declared too ignorant to help in establishing, or even to understand. It was also strange, he remarked, to see the black man in bondage and forced to work to maintain his master and himself, having been declared incapable of maintaining either. Thus, asked Steward, if the white man's analysis of the Negro be true, why was he not freed? What was the concern of the master to hold so "miserable and useless a piece of property? Is it benevolence that binds him with his master's chain?" [109]

Steward concluded that the white man who considered the Negroes to be "an indolent, improvident and vicious class of persons" should consider the obstacles in the black man's way. In the face of these obstacles in the United States, he said, and the oppressive power of prejudice, it was almost impossible for the Negro to attain the most of his natural abilities.[110]

Nevertheless, Steward asserted that in North America the black man would one day equal the Anglo-Saxon in all things. Africa, he noted, had been powerful as a nation before the white man invaded her shores and purchased her conquered captives with worthless trinkets. He wrote that he had every

reason to believe that though Africa was no longer a great nation, her captive people would one day be acknowledged as free men by the people of America. Despite the prejudice that existed in America, he said, there were men of talent among the blacks inferior to none. He advised that the black man should cease looking to the whites for examples or imitation; that he should look to his own characteristics, and his own perseverance and industry, and learn from them that he is of no inferior quality. The great failing of the Negro, he said, was lack of unity of action perpetuated by limited advantages; but he called on his race to gain their rights or die in the struggle. He asked them to come together in an indissoluble tie of brotherhood, to stand together in the coming conflict for freedom and the elevation of their race throughout the United States, to speak out for their ignorant and enslaved countrymen regardless of the reactions of the "haughty tyrants, who may dare lift their puny arm, to frustrate" their attempt.[111]

Linda Brent wondered about the reaction of the white man, if he were placed in the situation of being brought up as a slave with generations of slaves as ancestors. Although she admitted that the slave was in an inferior position, she claimed that he was held there by the ignorance in which the white man compelled him to live, by the master's torturing his manhood out of him, and by the inhuman treatment that forced him to remain as a brute.[112]

Jane Blake recalled that the process of instilling feelings of inferiority in the Negro was sometimes subtle, sometimes quite overt. As an example of the subtlety, she related that one day, in the presence of her master's son, she kissed the cheek of a young northern visitor. The little visitor was terrified. He immediately wiped off the kiss, and exclaimed that he did not want to be made black like her. The master's son resented this indignity to his "dear old mammy," and threw his arms around her neck, kissing her fondly, and ex-

claiming, "My old mammy will never make anybody black." Although there was a positive response from the son, the incident symbolized the nature of the subtle degradation to which the slave was constantly subject.[113]

William Wells Brown admitted that the condition of the black man, considered from a mental, intellectual, or moral point of view, could not compare favorably with the white's. But this fact, he said, did not elevate the whites, when in truth it was they who were responsible for the intense degradation of the Negro. He asserted that the Negro had not always been an inferior race and denied the charge of natural inferiority. He cited the times when the black man "stood at the head of science and literature." For example, he said, the Ethiopians were black, and in their earliest periods of history they had attained a high degree of civilization, and the knowledge of science gained by them was adopted by Egyptian civilization. He also noted that the black man was engraved on Egyptian monuments, not as a slave, but as a master. Brown claimed further that Minerva, the goddess of wisdom, was an African princess. Atlas and Jupiter were located by the mythologists in Africa. Though these were fabled beings, he said, they indicated "who were then considered the nobles of the human race." Brown continued and cited Tertullian, St. Augustine, and Terence, a refined and accomplished scholar, as black men from Ethiopia; moreover, he added, "Hanno, the father of Hamilcar, and grandfather of Hanibal, was a negro." [114]

Brown was proud of his antecedents, and asserted that no amount of hate and prejudice could destroy this background. He felt that the Negro had an intellectual genius, as did all men, which only needed cultivation to develop, but that "the mind left to itself from infancy, without culture remains a blank. Knowledge is not innate. Development makes the man." [115]

No nation, said Brown, had ever developed by its own,

unaided efforts, or by an inward impulse which took it from barbarianism to civilization; and there was nothing in race or color that imparted susceptibility of improvement to one race over another.[116]

Finally, Brown concluded that

as the Greeks, and Romans, and Jews drew knowledge from the Egyptians three thousand years ago, and the Europeans received it from the Romans, so must the blacks of this land rise in the same way. As one man learns from another, so nation learns from nation. Civilization is handed from one people to another. Already the blacks on this continent, though kept under the heel of the white man, are fast rising in the scale of intellectual development, and proving their equality with the brotherhood of man.[117]

Ideas Regarding Manumission

In addition to decrying the institution and calling for its abolition, the narratives also contain some actual proposals regarding the manner in which emancipation could be accomplished, including reasons therefor and the possible or probable consequences thereof. Some of these proposals appear to be logical and reasonable, while others are so bizarre that they reflect only the desperation of their source.

Peter Randolph addressed himself to the argument of the master that he was not to blame for slavery, but that he inherited it from his father. Randolph said, "Would it be sensible to suppose that generation after generation were justified in becoming drunkards, because some ancester had been? Certainly not; any person who reasoned thus would be considered insane." Randolph also reported that the master further defended his position by stating that he had bought and paid for his slaves, that perhaps his whole property was in them, and why should he give them up and thus lose his whole fortune? To this Randolph responded that if in fact the master's entire property consisted of human beings, "surely he should give it up, though he starved in conse-

quence." And finally, in response to the assertion that the master could not prosper without the slave, Randolph said:

Let them grant to men their rights; make them free citizens; pay them justly for their honest toil and see the consequences. All would be better and happier. Slavery enriches not the mind, heart or soul, where it abides; it curses and blights everything it comes in contact with.[118]

Samuel Ward spoke of one of the reasons for the delay in the slave's march toward freedom. In an apparent contradiction of the statements of William Wells Brown, Ward claimed that every group in America had a history to stir their manhood, except the Negro. The Greek, he said, had a heritage of the "Golden Age," and the Jew was proud of his ancestry as he hoped for "the restoration of Israel." All groups had something to encourage and stimulate them, but the American Negro had no such encouragement. What was "there for him in past history? Slavery. What is the condition of the majority of his class? Slavery. What are the signs of the times, as far as the disposition of their oppression is concerned? Continual slavery."[119]

Nevertheless, wrote James Roberts, the question was often asked, "Will slavery ever cease in this country?" The only way Roberts could give a rational and satisfactory answer was to judge the future by the past. Roberts asserted:

about two hundred years ago slavery was introduced to this country, and in progress of time was found to exist in nearly all of the states which are now free. If we look at the causes which led to emancipation in those states which did emancipate, we shall find these causes to be two in number, and that these same causes are still in operation in the present slave states; and like causes will produce like effects.[120]

Roberts argued that the first of these causes was morality. Since its beginning, he said, individuals in private life, in the church, and in the state, had strong feelings that the system

of human bondage was a great moral wrong opposed to every social, civil, political, and religious interest of the United States. Those in private life who were activated by a high sense of moral duty had instructed their households regarding what they conceived to be harmful to the highest interests of the American citizen. As a consequence, their children grew up and entered into the various stations and relations of life with sentiments adverse to slavery and in turn widened the bounds of antislavery views in the country. Some of these people entered the church as lay members and ministers and, hence, certain churches and families were the first to bring the evils of slavery to the attention of legislators.[121]

The second catalyst of emancipation, according to Roberts, was political expediency. Thousands of men in government supported measures favoring abolition, not from moral impulses, but from political interest. These people, he said, were convinced that free labor would be more conducive to the various interests of the states than slave labor, and therefore they favored emancipation.[122]

These two causes, said Roberts, had been operating conjointly, and it was to the influence of morality and political expediency that the emancipation of the free states was to be attributed. Roberts cited Missouri and Delaware as his cases in point. He said that Missouri was brought to the verge of emancipation by

the powerful operation of the combined force of the moral and expediency principles, working upon the public mind, increased by surrounding influences coming from the adjacent free states (where everything that pertains to the glory and honor of states so far excels the slaveholding states), and the moral sense of the surrounding civilized world, which is strongly against the system of slavery, and increasingly so. Missouri, under these influences will soon be a free state. She is now free soil in her political principles, and will soon be so in her constitution and government. The state of Delaware also, which is nominally free, is free soil, having been driven up to this point by the force of the principles

referred to. She will soon emancipate all her slaves, and she and Missouri be added to the present constellation of free states; and thus the process will go forward til every state in the union shall be free.[123]

William Anderson also had a plan for abolishing slavery. He felt that Congress should set aside a territory somewhere in the United States for the Negro people, to which free and slave could emigrate. Congress, he said, should then appropriate several millions of dollars in lands or otherwise, upon receipt of which the slaveholders should give the slaves their liberty. Thereupon as slave labor would still be needed, their present masters, or others, could hire them as they chose, for a small compensation, while in the meantime, the slaves should be given the advantages of an education. Anderson felt that by this arrangement the masters would eventually get three times the work done, and on the whole the master and the slave would ultimately prove a blessing to each other.[124]

By this plan, said Anderson, the Negro would be encouraged to work hard to maintain and educate his family because he would be sharing in the opportunities which the nation had to offer. Every Negro would work to support himself; the overseer's wages would be saved, and there would be no need for the warlike atmosphere of the slave states. Meanwhile, all those that were so disposed could immigrate to the free territory and "many would go with their families and wealth —and there would soon be a large colony established." [125]

Zamba felt, notwithstanding the urgency of the abolitionists, that emancipation should be gradual, for the sake of both master and slave. Although Britain had granted freedom to the slaves all at once in her colonies, it must be borne in mind, he said, that many of these slaves had had the benefit of education for many years previously, and further, that the few years of apprenticeship preceding emancipation served as a kind of modification between slavery and freedom. In

some measure this prevented many negative consequences which might have resulted from too sudden a change in the condition of the slaves.[126]

Zamba, aware that the Congress did not have the power to emancipate the slaves all at once, suggested a plan which would gradually accomplish that end. His plan was, basically, to have the slaveholders compensated for freeing the slaves. Congress, he said, could pass a law imposing an annual tax of three dollars upon every black in America. This tax would be paid by or for free Negroes as well as slaves, and that at this rate slavery would be abolished in thirty years.[127]

Zamba asserted that the sum which would be paid out as tax, in thirty years, for each Negro, would only amount to ninety dollars, and for this, at the end of the thirty years, the planter would receive two hundred and fifty-three dollars, on condition that he emancipated his slaves. It might be, he said, that the number of Negroes would, in thirty years, have increased. So, he also suggested, would the annual tax increase, and consequently the capital and interest; thus, the one would go to balance the other.[128]

Zamba felt that "there is no planter who owns one hundred negroes, but can easily manage to pay a tax of three hundred dollars per annum; especially if he reflects what a boon it will confer on millions of oppressed fellow-creatures; and finally that it will all *revert to him threefold*." As for the free Negroes in the country, few could not afford the tax; and those who were indigent could have the emancipation tax paid by some charitable person. Zamba was convinced that there were thousands of abolitionists who would contribute to see the tax forthcoming from the poorest Negro in the country, and if an appeal were made to the Negro's friends in other countries, he felt there would be thousands of dollars sent annually from the abolitionists of England, to assist in the emancipation scheme. Zamba calculated that three dollars per person

per annum, would, in the first year yield about ten millions of dollars, at 6 percent; and compound interest on this sum, and on ten millions additional every year, for thirty years, would at the end of that period amount altogether to eight hundred and forty five millions of dollars; or two hundred and fifty three dollars per head, *compensation* money, for each Negro slave—man, woman and child,—in the whole United States of America. This would be *more* than *double* the amount of compensation money paid to the planters in the British colonies, for emancipating their slaves: the average paid them for 800,000 slaves was twenty five pounds, or one hundred and ten dollars per head.[129]

Elizabeth Keckley argued that the slaveholders were not as responsible for slavery as the men who framed the constitution. She said that the law of slavery descended to the slaveholders and that it was only natural that they recognized it since it was manifestly in their interest to do so. Yet a wrong was inflicted on the Negroes; it was a custom which deprived them of their liberty. Her solution to this problem of human destiny was a gradual emancipation, so that there would be no social convulsion. But first, she said, the immorality of slavery had to be recognized as a truth by those who gave force to the moral law. She asserted that an act may be wrong, but unless the ruling power recognized the wrong, conviction was hopeless. Principles may be right but they cannot be established immediately. She concluded that the great mass of people were slow to reason to this principle or to establish moral force. When the American Revolution established the United States, an evil was perpetuated! Slavery was more firmly established; and since the evil had been planted, it must pass through gradual change before it could be eradicated.[130]

William Wells Brown, in pursuing his plan of emancipation, used the British counterpart as evidence that it could be successful. To the assertion that "general ruin followed the black man's liberation," Brown claimed that in the British

colonies, long before Parliament had passed the act of emancipation, the fact was well established that slavery had impoverished the soil, demoralized the people, and brought the planters to a state of bankruptcy and all the islands to ruin. He pointed out that the free blacks were the least embarrassed financially, and that they appeared to be in more comfortable circumstances than the whites. He explained that there had been a large number of free blacks in the British colonies, Jamaica alone having fifty-five thousand before emancipation. Most of the plantations, however, were owned by persons residing in Europe who had never even seen the colonies, and operated by agents, overseers, and clerks, whose mismanagement, together with the blighting influence which slavery took with it wherever it went, brought the islands to impending ruin. The European owners, despairing of getting any return from the West Indies, pocketed their share of the twenty million pounds sterling which the Parliament gave them, and abandoned their plantations. Other planters, living in the colonies, formed combinations to make the emancipated people labor for scarcely enough to purchase food. If they were found idle, the tread-wheel, the chain gang, the dungeon, and other modes of legalized torture were inflicted upon them. Through the determined and combined efforts of the landowners, the condition of the free Negro was as bad, if not worse, for the first three years after emancipation, as it had been under slavery.[131]

Nevertheless, Brown argued, the slaves were eventually emancipated without a drop of blood being shed by the enfranchised blacks. The colonies rose from the blight under which they labored during the time of slavery, and the land increased in value. Above all, "that which is more valuable than cotton, sugar or rice—the moral and intellectual condition of both blacks and whites" was better than ever before. Thus, he concluded, all parties had benefited by the abolition of Negro slavery in the British possessions.[132]

Other slaves also looked to England for help. Austin Steward reported that whenever they heard of the English people doing something for black men, they were delighted. When news of the emancipation of slaves in the West Indies was made known, it was a day of rejoicing by the American slave. In response to the charge that England was originally to blame for tolerating slavery, Steward asserted that she had repented for the evil, speedily broke the yoke of the institution, and let the oppressed go free. To the claim that the poor of England were slaves to the aristocracy, Steward replied that "oppressed they may be, and doubtless are, as the poor are apt to be in any and every country, but they are not sold in the market, to the highest bidder, like beasts of burden, as are the American slaves." No Englishman, added Steward, however poor, destitute, or degraded he might be, did not own himself, his wife, and children; nor did he fear that they would be sold from his home.[133]

To William Wells Brown, among the many obstacles which had been imposed against emancipation in the United States, the most formidable was the series of objections concerning the slaves' alleged lack of appreciation of liberty, and lack of ability to provide for himself. Brown felt that it had been clearly demonstrated that the enslaved people were as capable of self-support as any other class of people in the country. It was well known, said Brown, that throughout the slave states a large group of slaves had been for years hired out and that many whites paid a very high price for their labor. Some mechanics had been known to pay as much as six hundred dollars annually, in addition to providing food and clothing. This group of slaves, by their industry, had taken care of themselves so well and their appearance had been so respectable that many of the states had passed laws prohibiting masters from letting their slaves out because it made the other slaves dissatisfied to see so many of their

brethren well provided for, and accumulating something for themselves in the way of luxuries.[134]

In addition, according to Brown, one of the clearest demonstrations of the ability of the slave to provide for himself in a state of freedom was to be seen in the prosperous condition of the large free Negro population. Those who had been slaves, or who were descended from slaves, had acquired material wealth despite public sentiment, law, and prejudice. They had acquired large tracts of property and it was because of this industry, this sobriety, this intelligence, and this wealth, that there existed so much prejudice on the part of slaveholders against them.[135]

As for the proposition that the slave lacked appreciation of freedom, Brown asserted that this thought was folly. The slaveholder, it was claimed, asserted that the slaves would rise to defend the slave states. Robert Toombs, said Brown, had, in fact, threatened to arm his slaves, for they could be trusted to defend their homeland, and it was based upon such stories that many people in the free states felt that the slave was satisfied in his situation, that he would not want his freedom even if it was offered, "and that the slave population was a very dangerous element against the north." Brown rejected this theory and asked, why should anyone have supposed for a moment that because a man's color differs he was content to remain a slave, or that he had no inclination or desire "to escape from the thralldom that holds him so tight? What is it that does not wish to be free." [136]

Thus, said Brown, "What shall be done with the slaves if they are free? You had better ask, What shall we do with the slaveholders if the slaves are freed?" Brown claimed that the slave had shown himself better fitted to take care of his own needs than the slaveholder. The slave was the bone and sinew of the plantation; he was the producer, while the master was nothing but the consumer. The slave had the strength, the determination, and the will; and if the free Negro was taken

as a sample of what the black man was capable of doing, everyone must be satisfied that the slaves could take care of themselves.[137]

In response to the claim that if the slaves were emancipated they would not be received with equality, Brown stated, "every man must make equality for himself." He asserted that no society or government could make a man equal. He did not expect the slave to become equal overnight, but asked only for the opportunity to let him make equality for himself. For example, he said,

I have some white neighbors around me in Cambridge; they are not very intellectual; they don't associate with my family; but whenever they shall improve themselves, and bring themselves up by their own intellectual and moral worth, I shall not object to their coming into my society—all things being equal.[138]

Brown felt that the issue of the lack of acceptance of the Negro as an equal was idle talk, for he did not demand that the black man be accepted any more than the uncultivated and uncouth white man. What he did demand for the slave was that white society should "take their heels off his neck, and let him have a chance to rise by his own efforts." [139]

He asserted that the receipt of equality by the Negro, the securing of personal, political, social, and religious rights, did not make it incumbent upon the white man to take the slave into his house or social circles, beyond what was accorded total strangers. Such a fear should not exist among the whites, he said, for "no advocate of Negro equality ever demanded for the race that they should be made pets." To protect for the Negro his natural, lawful, and acquired rights, was all that he asked.[140]

Brown said that the fear of Negro equality emanated from the uneducated class of whites, who were more afraid of the Negro's ability "than of his color rubbing off against them; men whose claim to equality is so frail that they must be

fenced about, and protected by every possible guard." This class, said Brown, conscious of its own inferiority, recognized that to aid the black man was to create an unwanted competition, and that consequently, the Negro was looked upon by them with a sense of jealousy which required that every means, fair and unfair, be used to keep them in an inferior state.[141]

Brown concluded,

as with the eagle, so with man. He loves to look upon the bright day and the stormy night; to gaze upon the broad, free ocean, its eternal surging tides, its mountain bellows, and its foam-crested waves; to tread the steep mountain side; to sail upon the placid river; to wander along the gurgling stream; to trace the sunny slope, the beautiful landscape, the majestic forest, the flowering meadow; to listen to the howling of the winds and the music of the birds. These are the aspirations of man, without regard to country, clime or color.[142]

VII

Slavery in
a Civilized Society

The narratives indicate that slaves were at least *aware* of the nationwide conflict over the issues of slavery. Few slaves, however, wrote or dictated a great deal by way of analyzing these issues. Nevertheless, those who did were obviously well informed and showed insight and acuity.

This chapter will deal with some of the general thoughts about slavery expressed in the narratives, and some of the thoughts of slaves or ex-slaves regarding certain specific issues.

SOME THOUGHTS ABOUT THE NATIONAL ISSUE OF SLAVERY

Austin Steward reported that during the life of the institution, the antislavery truth had been spreading. The slaveholder and his sympathizers argued that it was the abolitionist who was guilty of tightening the bonds of the slave, who increased the slave's hardships, and blighted his prospect for freedom by his

alleged kindness in mistakenly showing the slave the enormity
of this sin. Steward denied this argument, asserting that the
abolitionist had no direct influence over the individual slave,
that it was the master who was responsible, by his unwilling-
ness to shed sufficient light on the institution to display its
moral corruption, and by his avarice and idleness, which induced him to hold fast that which he considered his source of
wealth. To support his position, Steward examined the intolerant spirit of the slave states and argued against the assertions
of the slaveholders that this institution of slavery was without
wealth and instituted by God. Why, asked Steward, were the
mails so closely examined, and fines imposed on prohibited
antislavery literature? Was it beyond the slaveholders' power
to refute the arguments presented or were they fearful that
the slave would become enlightened? What "but this same
fearful and intolerant spirit,—this overbearing, boasting, spirit,
was it, that cowardly attacked a Christian Senator [Charles
Sumner], while seated unsuspectingly at his desk, and felled
him to the floor, bleeding and senseless?" [1]

Steward reported that the slave states were under attack by
the abolitionists and free-state supporters. They said that the
slaveholders had no right to hold men in bondage or to extend
slave territory. Steward asserted that the slave interests had no
right to "usurp Kansas,—no right to murder 'Free State men,'
and no right to sustain there a set of 'ruffians' to make Kansas
a slave state." Furthermore, wrote Steward, the slaveholders
had no right to live on the unrequited toil of the slaves; to
sell them to the highest bidder, and to spend the proceeds of
the sale in idle extravagance. Nevertheless, Steward felt that
the slave states had held the balance of power in Congress too
long to yield it, and that whatever they asked of the government, they expected to obtain without objection. When the
master turned his blood hounds loose on fugitive slaves, the
antislavery population would be expected to, and would, aid

in the recapture of runaways. And, claimed Steward, should too much dissent be heard they (slave states) would certainly do what they "have threatened for the last quarter of a century,—'Dissolve the Union.' " [2]

Other narratives confirm that Steward was not alone in his reaction to the antislavery crusade.

In 1830, John Thompson obtained a newspaper containing the speech of John Quincy Adams, regarding a "petition of the ladies of Massachusetts, praying for the abolition of slavery in the District of Columbia." Thompson read and reread this speech to himself and to the quarters "until it was so worn that he could scarcely make out the printing." Thompson reported that this group of slaves spent many hours meditating upon this speech and that by receiving it the group discovered that there were places where the Negro was regarded as a man, and not as a brute, where "he might enjoy the 'inalienable right of life, liberty, and the pursuit of happiness.' " Little did Mr. Adams know, said Thompson, when he was uttering that speech, that he was "opening the eyes of the blind; that he was breaking the iron bands from the limbs of the poor slave, and setting the captive free." [3]

Archer Alexander was a Missouri slave whose narrative was dictated by him to William Greenleaf Eliot. Alexander asserted that in 1863 the political and social conditions of Missouri were rapidly changing. He felt that the free-soil doctrines of Thomas H. Benton were taking possession of the public's mind, and he praised Francis P. Blair, Jr., to whom, he felt, "the whole nation owes a debt of gratitude which has never been adequately acknowledged." He echoed Blair's feelings that the best interests of Missouri demanded the extinction of slavery, and that even if it could be defended as right and profitable in the slave states, it was a blight and a curse in Missouri. [4]

Alexander predicted that the more intelligent slaves were be-

ginning to feel that there were new conditions affecting their relationship with their masters, and "that in some way or other it might soon be changed altogether." According to Alexander, the slaves felt this change as much as their masters.[5]

One such slave, Aaron, analyzed the Liberty Party. He stated that this party was organized on the principles of '76, and "founded on the truth that 'honesty is the best policy.'" The members of this party held that there was one burning question in the politics of the nation which must be settled before any other. Until slavery was settled right, they said, the American Revolution was incomplete, and the history of the United States was unfit to be written. The Liberty Party, asserted Aaron, was not the enemy of the slaveholder but exactly the reverse, because the establishment of justice was, or should have been, the intent and objective of all parties.[6]

Neither, said Aaron, was the Liberty Party the enemy of the Constitution. If the Constitution were construed as enforcing the restoration of fugitives who escaped from slavery, then that document was an inconsistency and a contradiction, being

made to stab that very liberty which it was designed to shield. It becomes a reproach, a piece of hypocrisy, an abomination. Men will not so construe it, or so obey it; they hold to it, and are ready to spend their treasure and their blood for it, as an instrument ordained to establish justice; to secure the blessing of liberty. They fearlessly put it to every honest man, can you commit what you know to be a most base and despisable crime, to wit, assist in delivering a poor hunted fugitive slave, to the human hyenas, who claim property in his sinews, and then in the broad daylight of 1843, justify yourself by pleading obedience to a constitution which bears on its forehead the inscription, 'to establish justice, to secure the blessing of Liberty?' No you can't. That would be violating the spirit for the sake of obeying what is really not in the letter, but what the slaveholders persuaded the framers that a compromise was a treachery to liberty.[7]

THE AMERICAN COLONIZATION SOCIETY

A specific issue of great concern to the slaves was the American Colonization Society. The narratives indicate that the slaves were aware that the Society had originated and supported attempts to have laws passed empowering the states to send free Negroes and slaves to Liberia, Africa. According to many thoughtful slaves, including James Watkins, these measures were founded not upon love or pity for the Negroes, but rather upon deep-seated hatred, and fear of black insurrection. Watkins claimed that despite its faults, most Negroes, including the slaves, loved their native United States and deplored only "the hatred of the American to the race they have so deeply injured [which] seems to pervade their institutions." [8]

Moses Grandy confirmed that most slaves considered America their home, and although their forefathers came from Africa, they themselves knew nothing of that country.[9]

An example of the average slave's reaction to colonization was given by James Williams. While in slavery, Williams was asked if he wished to be free and to go to his own country. Williams looked at the questioner with surprise, and inquired, "What country?" When he was told that the questioner was referring to Africa, he replied that he was born in Virginia. He was then told that his father was African and that many free blacks were going to Liberia. He was again asked to answer honestly whether he would prefer to remain a slave or to be set free on condition that he go to Africa. He replied that he would rather remain as he was.[10]

Other slaves considered the idea of colonization outside the United States the height of folly. They considered themselves as important as the mineral wealth of the nation, or the producing capabilities of the soil, for neither of the two could be made available without the laborer. William Wells Brown asserted that four million workers could not be spared from

the slave states, and that all time "has shown that the negro is the best laborer in the tropics." [11]

The slaves, said Brown, once emancipated and left on the lands, would produce four million new consumers.

The cost of keeping a slave was only about nineteen dollars per annum, including food, clothing, and doctors' bills. Negro cloth, negro shoes, and negro whips were all that were sent south by northern manufacturers. Let slavery be abolished, and stores will be opened and a new trade take place with the blacks south. Northern manufacturers will have to run on extra time till this new demand will have been supplied. The slave owner, having no longer an inducement to be idle, will go to work, and will not have time to concoct treason against the *stars and stripes*.[12]

On the lighter side, and again referring to the American Colonization Society, Brown noted sarcastically that "none but an American slaveholder could have discovered that a man born in a country was not a citizen of it." [13]

With respect to the idea of sending only free colored people to Africa, some slaves, including James Wilkerson, felt that this was merely a design to rid the United States of its free blacks and to enable the slaveholder to import thousands of people from the shores of Africa to the slave market. Wilkerson claimed that this would eliminate the threat of potential insurrection of the free blacks and make room for additional slaves, who could be kept under much stricter control.[14]

In this regard, Austin Steward stated that if the American people entertained the idea of ridding themselves of the hated Negroes by colonizing them on the soil of Liberia, they were surely mistaken. The black men, he felt, "are Americans; allied with this country by birth and by misfortune; and here will they remain,—not always as now, oppressed and degraded,—for all who have any interest in the matter, will know that the free colored people are rapidly advancing in intelligence, and improving their condition in every respect." [15]

Steward reported that the colonizationists talked of the duty they owed Africa, and how intelligent and prosperous everything was in Liberia. But, said Steward, when "that delightful country asked to be taken into fellowship with the United States, and to have her independence recognized—oh, then he [the white man] lifts his hands in horror and begs to be excused from so close a relation." Steward asked,

would they refuse to acknowledge the independence of Liberia, if their interest in the colored people was genuine, especially when several other nations had done so? Oh no. But that is not "*the rub.*" How could one of our lordly nabobs of the south, sit in Congress with perhaps one of his own manumitted slaves as a representative from Liberia or Hayti! He would die of mortification. Very well then; but let him talk no more of sending colored men to that country to make them freemen.[16]

There were, according to Steward, some blacks who, from a sense of duty or a longing for freedom, might have been induced to go. Some of these slaves did, on occasion, express the desire to be freed even on the colonizationists' terms.[17]

Daniel H. Peterson also reported that several slaves felt that there was no part of the known world to which they could go in which they would not be subjected to disadvantages, with the sole exception of Liberia. They admired the Liberian laws which were encouraged by the United States. They felt that America was bound to protect and raise up Liberia to a level with herself, and were encouraged by the purported good lands, large fields of employment, and the opportunity to develop their talents.[18]

Peterson asserted that in Africa there were no doors shut to the black man, and that all was "as free as the air of heaven." Peterson thus urged, "go forth without delay, and claim your rights as a freeman and freewoman and you will have great causes to rejoice." He claimed that in a few years they would be a great nation, respected by the rest of mankind, that the

agriculture and industry of Africa could some day influence the world, and that her ships would visit all nations and her flag wave in every area.[19]

THE FUGITIVE SLAVE LAW

An analysis of the narratives indicates that perhaps the single most significant issue of the mid-nineteenth century was the enactment, interpretation, enforcement, and effect of the Fugitive Slave Law of 1850. So great was their concern about this matter, and so thorough was their analysis of it, that the gamut of their emotional responses to it ranged from anger and fear to relief and gratitude.

William Green, for example, felt that although the law caused a great deal of misery, it also did a great deal of good, in that it caused many hitherto docile fugitives to seek the sanctuary of Canada and it aroused the abolitionist sentiments of many previously apathetic free whites.[20]

Green asserted that with the passage of this law, Negroes, both free and bond, recognized that in the land of their birth and of their fathers they could no longer find repose under the Constitution. Many realized that they must now flee from the land of republicanism to a monarchial one, in order to enjoy freedom.[21] By this law, passed in Congress in 1850, all slaves who had escaped from bondage and had taken refuge in the free states were subject to recapture at any subsequent time. James Watkins said, "so cruel and relentless it is, that it makes punishable with fine and imprisonment any parties who may be convicted of giving even a cup of cold water to one of these sons of sorrow and wretchedness." [22]

According to Watkins, the sixth section of the law alone, which stated, "In no trial or hearing under this act shall the testimony of such alleged fugitive be admitted in evidence," was enough to condemn the whole act, for it was a clear violation of the Fifth Amendment's due process guarantee. It was,

said Watkins, also a violation of the Constitution of each free state, which guaranteed personal liberty to all, unless deprived of it by "due process of law," and maintained that the right of trial by jury shall be inviolate.[23]

As interpreted by the courts, the bare testimony of the slaveholder was sufficient evidence of his right to the return of the fugitive, and the alleged fugitive was not permitted to procure or produce evidence to establish his freedom. Watkins reported a case in Detroit, where a Negro was brought before the court as a fugitive. Counsel for the defendant presented an affidavit of the slave which averred that he was manumitted by deed of his claimants for seven hundred dollars, which they had received, and that the deed was in the possession of the defendant's friends in Cincinnati. Based upon this affidavit, counsel moved that the case be continued until the deeds of emancipation could be procured and brought to court. The court denied the motion on the ground that a continuance was unnecessary as the deed would be inadmissible even if produced; that the court had no power to inquire into any defense the Negro might have against the claim; and that its jurisdiction was limited to a determination of whether the case presented on the part of the claimants was sufficient to entitle them to a certificate of removal for the Negro. This being the decision of the court, Watkins claimed that "no coloured man North can be safe for a single day." [24]

According to Watkins, the worst part of the law to the non-slaveholders was that, by its seventh section, this "atrocious and abominable law made it a crime, punishable with heavy fines and imprisonment, to be either directly or indirectly a party to the escape of a slave." In addition, the slave hunters were empowered to call for the aid of free citizens in carrying out these provisions, and any one who refused was also exposed to a heavy penalty. What was most astounding to Watkins was that this law had "the patronage and support of the ministers of religions in the slaveholding states." [25]

Harriet Tubman asserted that she could "trust Uncle Sam wid my people no longer," and that the law had "brought 'em all clear off to Canada." She claimed that while the free states sustained the law which hurled the fugitives back into slavery, it was impossible for the Negro to become a man.[26]

Austin Steward felt that with the passage of this law, the free states had no right to feel that they owned no slaves or were not connected with the system. It might have been true that the law of the free states prohibited the holding of slaves, but

is the poor, flying fugitive from the house of bondage, safe one moment within your borders? Will he be welcome to your homes, tables, your firesides? Will your clergyman bid you clothe and feed him, or give him a cup of cold water. . . . Or will your own miserable Fugitive Slave Law close the mouth of your clergy, crush down the rising benevolence of your heart; and convert you into a human blood hound, to hunt down the panting fugitive, and return him to the hell of slavery? [27]

Steward recognized, of course, that there were some in the free states who would violate the law. A few did remain who "in defiance of iniquitous laws, throw open wide their doors to the trembling, fleeing bondman." These people, he claimed, did help the fugitive on his way to Canada, but it was done at night and quietly, making no noise, "lest an United States' marshall wrest from you the object of your Christian sympathy, and impose on you a heavy fine, for your daring to do to another as you would he should do to you." [28]

Slave hunting in the free states was, according to Linda Brent, "the beginning of a reign of terror to the colored population." Many families who had lived in freedom for years fled from it now. A slave discovered that his husband or wife was formerly a fugitive and had to escape to insure his own safety. Even worse, because a child followed the condition of its mother, the Negro discovered that the children of a

family with even one slave parent were liable to be seized and carried into slavery. In every free state there was consternation and anguish, but, asked Miss Brent, "what cared the legislators of the 'dominant race' for the blood they were crushing out of trampled hearts?" [29]

Miss Brent described some of the miseries brought on by the passage of this law. Few Negroes ventured into the streets; only when necessary did they leave their homes, and when they did, they traveled as much as possible through back streets. They considered it a disgrace for a city to call itself free, when "inhabitants, guiltless of offense, and seeking to perform their duties conscientiously, should be condemned to live in such incessant fear, and have nowhere to turn for protection!" Impromptu vigilance committees were formed. Every black person and every friend of the Negro was on constant watch, and evening newspapers were examined carefully "to see what Southerners had put up at the hotels." [30]

William Parker confirmed the reports of Linda Brent, and stated that in the free cities, both whites and blacks were fully resolved to leave no means untried to thwart "the barbarous and inhuman monsters who crawled in the gloom of midnight, like the ferocious tiger, and, stealthily springing on their unsuspecting victims, seized, bound, and hurled them into the ever open jaws of slavery." Parker reported that the antislavery people united together, regardless of all personal considerations, to save the fugitive from capture. They thoroughly examined all matters connected with the law, and were cognizant of the plans adopted to carry it out. This was generally accomplished through correspondence with reliable persons in various sections of the slave states, and thus the vigilance committees knew the slave hunters, their agents, spies and betrayers. Parker asserted that the business of slave hunting was conducted by only a few men "willing to degrade themselves by doing the dirty work of four-legged blood hounds." According to Parker, the slave hunters consorted

with constables, police officers, aldermen, and even with mentors of the legal professions "who disgraced their respectable calling by low, contemptible acts, and were willing to clasp hands with the lowest ruffian in order to pocket the reward that was the price of blood." Every official facility was offered the slave hunter, and

whether it was night or day, it was only necessary to whisper in a certain circle that a negro was to be caught, and horses and wagons, men and officers, spies and betrayers, were ready, at the shortest notice, armed and equipped, and eager for the chase.[31]

The Fugitive Slave Law, asserted Samuel R. Ward, stripped the Negro of all manner of protection, of the writ of *habeas corpus*, of trial by jury, or of any other law of civilized nations. There were no longer any legal safeguards of personal liberty, and the fugitive was thrown back upon only the natural rights of self-defense and self-protection. The law solemnly referred to each Negro, fugitive and free, the question of whether he would submit to being enslaved or whether he would protect himself, even if in so doing he risked his life. It gave the fugitive the alternative of dying free or living as a slave. Thus, Ward warned,

Let the men who would execute this bill beware. Let them know that the business of catching slaves, or kidnapping freemen, is an open warfare upon the rights and liberties of the black men of the North. Let them know that to enlist in that warfare is present, certain, inevitable death and damnation. Let us teach them, that none should engage in this business, but those who are ready to be offered up on the polluted altar of accursed slavery . . . let all the black men of America say, and we shall teach Southern slave-crats, and Northern dough-faces, that to perpetuate the union, they must beware how they expose *us* to slavery, and themselves to death and destruction. present and future, temporal and eternal![32]

THE UNDERGROUND RAILROAD

An issue of the mid-nineteenth century which has received great historical coverage throughout the years, but which the narratives mention only rarely, was the Underground Railroad.

This mode of escape was neither a railroad nor was it usually underground. What it was, basically, was a network of escape routes for slaves who were encouraged and aided by abolitionists who had established these routes and arranged for various stations along the way to the free states.

The stations were usually the homes of other abolitionists, whites, or free Negroes, where the fugitive could "lay over" on his way north. The stations were manned and operated by managers or "station masters," whom John Brown described as "noble heroes" who worked "for suffering and oppressed humanity and for no other reward than the satisfaction of their conscience." [33]

Brown explained that the railroad was for the exclusive use of slaves who were running for freedom, and that its managers, stations, and plans were usually well-kept secrets. Even prior to the Fugitive Slave Law, detection brought with it fines, imprisonment, and in some cases, death, yet the operators of the railroad received no financial rewards from what was termed the "forwarding business." [34]

Brown claimed that station masters belonged to almost every class of society, and were dispersed in all of the regions through which the railroad passed. Its branches were numerous, and required extensive and constant supervision, not only to prevent accidents (the catching of a fugitive), but also to gather information. Frequently the train would be kept waiting several days, or as much as a month, if the danger signal was flashed, which meant that the slave hunters were in the

vicinity of the station. The situation during these times was most critical, "for though the cunning and daring of the reckless and experienced slave-hunter may be baffled, it is a far more difficult feat to delude the sagacity of the four-footed colleagues that frequently accompany him [bloodhounds], and who can 'snuff a nigger an eternal distance off, and nose him out anywhere,' so admirably are they trained to their cruel work." [35]

Frederick Douglass saw the railroad in a different light. He did not approve of the term "Underground Railroad," and, due to the open declarations of the abolitionists that they were engaged in these activities, considered it the "Upperground Railroad." Although he praised the station masters for their daring, and applauded them for voluntarily subjecting themselves to persecution and danger by openly avowing their participation in aiding fugitives, he nevertheless saw little good resulting from the activities of the railroad for the slave or the abolitionist. He felt that the declarations of the abolitionists were a "positive evil to the slaves remaining, who are seeking to escape"; and that they would stimulate the master to greater watchfulness and increase his ability to capture his slave. [36]

Douglass nevertheless felt that a debt of gratitude was owed to the slave in the slave states as well as to those in the free states, for aiding the fugitives on their way to freedom. Nothing, said Douglass, should be said or done to hinder the slave in bondage from attempting to escape. He suggested that the master be kept in profound ignorance of the escape routes; to leave him to "imagine himself surrounded by myriads of invisible tormentors, ever ready to snatch from his infernal grasp his trembling prey. Let him be left to feel his way in the dark; let darkness commensurate with his crime hover over him; and let him feel that at every step he takes, in pursuit of the flying bondman, he is running the frightful risk of having his hot brains dashed out by an invisible agency." [37]

ABOLITION AND THE ANTISLAVERY CRUSADE

Surprisingly, the narratives contain only rare and usually only passing comment about the abolitionists and the antislavery movement in general.

According to Frederick Douglass, slaves were, for the most part, aware of the existence of the abolitionists, but if their information came from the slaveholders, their feelings about them were usually negative.[38]

James Williams explained this situation as being the result of the fact that if a slave ran away, or set fire to a barn, or killed an overseer, the motivation for his act was blamed, by the master, on the abolitionists.[39]

The narratives collected by Benjamin Drew reveal that a good many slaves were actually terrified of them and were convinced that if they escaped and fell into the hands of the abolitionists they would either be imprisoned, tortured or re-sold into slavery by them.[40]

Levi Coffin reported that the abolitionists were often accused by slaveholders of obtaining the labor of fugitives on false pretenses. The slaveholders claimed that the abolitionists would employ them for several months on the promise of good wages and then tell them that the former master was in their pursuit, hustling the fugitive off to Canada without paying the wages due.[41]

The Anti-Slavery Bugle's collection of slave documents indictates slaves were so often warned about the alleged crimes of the abolitionists that when slaves were told "that abolitionists are in the habit of skinning the black man for leather, and of regaling their cannibalism on his flesh, even such enormities seemed to us possible." [42]

Henry Clay Bruce reported that he and a group of other slaves were being transported from Brunswick, Missouri, to Virginia via Cincinnati. Just before reaching Cincinnati, some

poor whites on deck told his group of slaves that when they reached that city the abolitionists would come to their quarters and "even against their will take them away." The group did not even know what the word abolitionist meant, but they concluded that abolitionists must be "some wild beast or Negro-trader, for they feared both and were greatly frightened," so much so that they went to their master and informed him of what they had been told. The master informed his coffle that the story had a great deal of truth in it, and the entire group was put ashore until the boat finished its business in Cincinnati and then came to pick them up again. Bruce felt that his ignorance of the true mission of the abolitionists and his consequent failure to join them at that time, caused him to work as a slave for "seventeen years afterwards." [43]

Despite the warnings of the slaveholders, Peter Still reported, slaves who had the opportunity to visit and return from the free states almost always modified their ideas of these "desperate characters," the abolitionists. Nevertheless when they returned and were questioned by whites about the abolitionists, they would usually have sense enough to answer as they knew the whites wanted them to. For example, one such slave returned and reported that he was "skeered, all the time he was in Cincinnati; and did not dare to go out after night." One night he "reckoned he heard the abolitionists fightin' in the streets"; but "he was away up stairs, and too badly skeered to come down." He knew, said Still, that the moment he spoke a word in favor of the abolitionists and the free states, he would be accused of poisoning the minds of the surrounding slaves. Therefore he "represented the black people of Cincinnati as being wretchedly poor; and the contrast which he drew between the laborers of that city, and the *happier slaves* by whom he was surrounded, would have delighted the author of the 'South Side View' " (a term used to describe the pro-slavery attitude). [44]

Frederick Douglass, too, when advised by what appeared to

be sympathetic whites to escape to the free states and seek out the abolitionists, pretended not to be interested and treated their talk as if he did not understand. Many white men had been known to encourage slaves to escape, and then, to get the reward, catch them and return them to their masters.[45]

The narratives indicate, of course, that even among those who were *not* directly exposed to the abolitionists, not all slaves were ignorant of their true motives, and that therefore many did not fear, but rather welcomed them. Isaac Williams reported that as a consequence abolitionists were rarely permitted to visit the slave quarters, and in order to do so had to elude the master's vigilance and see them at night. At such meetings they would enlighten the slaves with the ideas of the value of liberty and describe it as the natural inheritance of every man.[46]

When rare visits to the plantation were permitted, the abolitionists would often express a desire to purchase the freedom of "house servants whose clean complexion rivaled their own beauty and who, by long association with educated and refined people, acquired something of their air of good breeding and were very different from other slaves." Most slaveholders refused to sell their slaves to free-state abolitionists to be freed by them. They felt that it had a bad effect on the other slaves, who would "sigh in vain for that freedom which would be pictured to their eager minds in such a glowing and vivid manner." [47]

Frederick Douglass noted that the most common arguments made by the so-called free-state "neutrals" against abolitionists were: let the slaveholders alone, and they would emancipate their slaves; abolitionists, agitation only retarded the progress of the slaves' freedom; the slaveholders were induced to retain more firmly what the abolitionists attempted to wrest from then. Maintaining this position, he felt, made the neutrals of the free states as guilty as the pro-slavery people everywhere. These people of the free states, and their sympathizers, said Douglass, were linked "to a decaying corpse, which has de-

stroyed the moral health" of the nation. This connection, he said, came about due to a union of government, a union of political parties, and a union in the religious organizations, all of which had served to destroy the moral sense of the free-state people and to impregnate them with sentiments and ideas in conflict with the basic democratic American institutions. In a moral sense the entire American nation was responsible for slavery, and shared the guilt with every slaveholder. While the United States permitted slavery to exist, every American citizen had to "bear the chagrin of hearing his country branded before the world, as a nation of liars and hypocrites; and behold his cherished national flag pointed at with the utmost scorn and derision." Douglass said that this institution was the shame of the entire American people, a blot upon the American name, and the "only national reproach which need make an American hang his head in shame in, the presence of monarchical governments." [48]

According to Douglass, the existence of slavery here blunted the rebukes of the United States against all tyranny abroad. America could make no criticism of other nations, because to do so would bring, in return, only ridicule, contempt, and scorn. America, said Douglass, was made a byword to a mocking world, and this would continue to be so, so long as slavery existed on the nation's soil. Douglass invoked the spirit of American patriotism, not in a narrow and restricted sense, but

with a broad and manly signification; *not* to cover up our national sins, but to inspire us with sincere repentance; *not* to hide our shame from the world's gaze, but utterly to abolish the cause of that shame; *not* to explain away our gross inconsistencies as a nation, but to remove the hateful, jarring and incongruous elements from the land; *not* to sustain an egregious wrong, but to unite all our energies in the grand effort to remedy that wrong.[49]

On the other hand, slaves asserted that slaveholders were not sensible to moral arguments, because their economic interests were too bound up in maintaining the system. More-

over, the slaves felt that so long as abolitionists, or those who expressed antislavery sentiments, continued to use slave-grown articles, the slaveholder would continue to resist abolition. Some slaves felt that the only way to destroy the system was to undermine it, by underselling it in the world market. They argued that there would have been little problem in purchasing free-labor sugar or rice, but that the chief difficulty would be in procuring a sufficient supply of free-labor cotton. Yet, these slaves did not doubt that if proper encouragement were given, a very large quantity of cotton could have been procured from Africa, where it grew wild, and could be very cheaply cultivated, or from the West Indies, India, or Australia. John Brown claimed that many men were interested in this subject but felt the indifference of the antislavery public, who would not pay an increased price on an article, would thereby defeat the plan. Although they were indignant over the sufferings of the slave, many would not make the necessary financial sacrifice. Nevertheless, John Brown was one of those who were convinced that if slavery was to be put down, the most certain means was to reduce the value of its products in the markets by bringing into the United States as much cotton, sugar, and rice as could be raised by free labor. This, he felt, could not be done all at once, but could have been done slowly and systematically, and if accomplished, would have meant the end of slavery.[50]

Conclusion

The basic purpose of this study has been to present a picture of slavery in the United States as reported by those who lived it as the subject and object of its horror—it is, if you will, the story of the crime as related by the victim. The book presents only what the slave narratives say about slavery, without challenge or contradiction by the author.

Conc.

The central theme of the narratives, although not stated in so many words by the slaves, is the slaves' belief that slavery was a dehumanizing institution. That is, the narrators reflected what appears to have been a widespread belief among the slaves that those dedicated to and responsible for maintaining the system attempted, both consciously and unconsciously, to suppress and indeed to destroy those human qualities in the slaves which, if left unchecked, would eventually destroy the system. In the slaves' opinion the physical and psychological pressures of slavery were essential in order to stifle the desire for human freedom and the need for dignity. It was

this attempt at dehumanization, either conscious or due to the very nature of the system, which was, in the words of the slave, James Watkins, "the essence of the agony." It was not, said Watkins, the physical labor which was unbearable, but rather

the thousand immoralities that flow through the system—and in short, the fact that, in body and soul, a slave is made to feel that he is the property of a fallen human being, instead of the free agent that the Creator has designed him to be, free to serve Him where and how his own conscience, regulated by the divine will, dictates. This is the essence of the agony to my mind—that whatever might be the duty that I felt I had to do in the world, it depended upon the will of another, whether I had the opportunity. In fact, I hate the whole thing with a perfect hatred, and no consideration on earth shall ever induce me again to become a slave.[1]

Expressions of feeling such as this, together with expressions of innumerable other quite natural human reactions, desires, qualities, faults and frailties, may be found throughout the narratives.

There is discussion in the narratives of the "Uncle Toms" and the "Sambos," or what I classify as the pious or loyal slaves, which indicates that, in some instances, the attempt at dehumanization was successful. Indeed, the reports indicate that out of despair or anger or hatred, some slaves mutilated or killed themselves and/or members of their families, thus proving that some had lost the most basic of all human characteristics, that of the desire for survival. On the other hand there were reports of the militants and the fugitives—those whose very human desire for freedom and dignity led them to take action. For the most part, however, the narratives indicate that the slave was neither a militant nor a "Sambo." He was, according to most of the narrators, a human being forced into accepting a horrendous situation.

With the exception of the Nat Turner incident, actual insurrection or planned rebellion is rarely discussed in the

narratives. In the main, when they did discuss rebellion the slaves tried to show that emancipation of the slaves would not lead to retaliation against former masters. The narratives indicate that, in the slaves' view, massive and planned insurrection existed only in the minds of the masters. Nevertheless, they felt that the existence of this fear, exaggerated out of all proportion as they said it was, did dictate the oppressive actions of many slaveholding communities, and consequently, countless slaves suffered accordingly.

Furthermore, it appears from the narratives that the slaves regarded the popular notion of paternalism on the plantation to be as false as its accompanying rationale of "if you own it, you take care of it." The reports reflect, of course, the existence of some kind and paternalistic masters. But, for the most part, for reasons which they claimed included the necessity for absolute control, and others at which they only hinted but which might better be explained by a trained psychologist, the slaves felt that they were treated worse than the master's other beasts of burden. The alleged unmitigated abuse of the "chattel" is a constant theme of the narratives.

An interesting point, which is made quite clearly and emphatically in the narratives, is that despite the horror of their situation, their anger, and their hatred of many of America's institutions besides slavery, the slaves considered themselves Americans, and not Africans. With the exception of those sections that deal with the Dark Passage and the American Colonization Society, the narratives contain almost no reference to Africa either as a homeland or as the source of cultural heritage. Whether their almost complete identification with American culture was due to a lack of education about their heritage or otherwise, the fact is, as demonstrated by their vigorous anticolonization sentiment, that these people considered themselves completely American and had almost no cultural or historical identification with Africa.

In terms of moral and social attitudes, the narratives reveal

the slaves to have had the same variety of qualities that characterize all human beings. That is, they reflect the existence of informers, thieves, pious persons, law-abiding citizens, etc. The religious sentiments of the slaves appear from the narratives to have been in conflict. Most of them claimed that the religious training given by the master, and most of *his* slave preachers, was merely a device to maintain and perpetuate control over them. Nevertheless, the narratives reflect the fact that religious exercise played a very important social role, and as with most people, especially oppressed groups, the basic teachings of the church appealed to and comforted them. Indeed, in many cases they said salvation after death was all they had to which they could look forward.

During his lifetime, however, there appeared to be one fate which the slave dreaded above all else—that of being sold south. Although the narratives are quite clear about the fact that this fear existed, they do not reveal the specific basis for the fear. Not one slave said that he had been sold south and that the treatment or conditions there were harsher than in the more northerly plantations. And, conversely, there is not one report from a slave to the effect that he had been sold *north*, and that his lot was easier there.

The narratives indicate that, like all men, the slaves had their prejudices and their social strata. There appeared to be a universal bias against poor whites. Moreover, they seemed to discriminate among themselves on the basis of such criteria as lightness of skin color, position of employment on the plantation, and the wealth of their owner.

With respect to slavery and race, the narratives are in almost total agreement that the two were inextricably tied together. The slave was convinced that he was in his position because he was black and that even if slavery ended, future generations of blacks would feel the impact of the institution. Some even predicted that race conflict resulting in violence and bloodshed would take place. In any event, what comes

clearly resounding from the narratives is the protest against the cruelty and mistreatment of black by white. And it is to be hoped that someday, somehow, Americans, without regard to their color may, in the words of James Weldon Johnson, gain the freedom to consider every one, whether white or black, "merely a Man." [2]

Notes

NOTES FOR PREFACE

1. Benjamin A. Botkin, "The Slave As His Own Interpreter," *Library of Congress Quarterly Journal of Current Acquisitions* (November, 1944), Vol. II, No. 1, p. 37.

2. Sidney Fine and Gerald S. Brown, ed., *The American Past: Conflicting Interpretations of The Great Issues*, Vol. I (New York: The Macmillan Company, 1961), p. 369.

3. Samuel Eliot Morison, *The Oxford History of the American People* (New York: Oxford University Press, 1965), p. 505.

NOTES FOR CHAPTER I:
THE BEGINNINGS OF DEHUMANIZATION

1. Benjamin Drew, ed., *North Side View of Slavery, the Refugee; or, the Narratives of Fugitive Slaves in Canada, Related by Themselves* (Boston: John P. Jewett, 1855), p. 271.

2. William Wells Brown, *A Lecture Delivered Before the Female Anti-Slavery Society of Salem, at Lyceum Hall, November 14, 1847* (Boston, Massachusetts: Massachusetts Anti-Slavery Society, 1847), pp. 4–5.

3. *Ibid.*, p. 5.

4. Linda Brent, *Incidents in the Life of a Slave Girl* (Boston: by the author, 1861), p. 31. The name Linda Brent is a pseudonym used by Harriet Jacobs. Peter Still, *The Kidnapped and the Ransomed: Being the Personal Recollections of Peter Still and his Wife "Vina," After Forty Years of Slavery. Related to Kate Pickard* (Syracuse: W. T. Hamilton Press, 1856), p. 176.

5. Drew, p. 248.

6. Brent, p. 6.

7. *Ibid.*, p. 83.

8. *Ibid.*

9. *Ibid.*

10. *Ibid.*, pp. 83–84.

11. John Brown, *Slave Life in Georgia: a Narrative of the Life, Suffering and Escape of John Brown,*

a *Fugitive Slave, Now in England* (London: W. M. Watts, 1855), pp. 200–201.

12. *Ibid.*

13. Petition *To his Excellency Thomas Gage Esq Captain General and Governor in Chief in and over this Province. To the Honourable his Majestys Council and the Honourable House of Representatives in General Court assembled may 25, 1774.* Collections, Massachusetts Historical Society, 5th Series, III, pp. 432–433.

14. *Ibid.*

15. Andrew Jackson, *Narrative and Writings of Andrew Jackson of Kentucky Containing an Account of His Birth and Twenty-Six Years of His Life While a Slave. Narrated by Himself, Written by a friend* (Syracuse: *Daily and Weekly Star* Office, 1847), p. 40.

16. William Green, *Narrative of Events in the Life of William Green (Formerly a Slave), Written by Himself* (Springfield: L. M. Guernsey, Book, Job and Card Printer, 1853), p. 6.

17. *Ibid.*

18. Frederick Douglass, *Lectures on American Slavery by Frederick Douglass, Delivered at Corinthian Hall, Rochester, N.Y. December 1, 1850 and December 8, 1850* (Buffalo: Geo. Reese, 1851), p. 7.

19. *Ibid.*, pp. 14–15.

20. Reverend S. H. Platt, *The Martyrs and the Fugitive, or a Narrative of the Captivity, Sufferings and Death of an African Family and the Escape of Their Son* (New York: Printed by Daniel Fanshaw, 1859), p. 22.

21. *Ibid.*, p. 23.

22. *Ibid.*, pp. 25–26.

23. *Ibid.*

24. *Ibid.*, pp. 26–31.

25. *Ibid.*, pp. 28–33.

26. *Ibid.*, p. 34.

27. *Ibid.*, p. 35.

28. Zamba, *Life and Adventures of Zamba, an African Negro King, and His Experiences of Slavery in South Carolina. Written by Himself. Corrected and Arranged by Peter Neilson* (London: Smith, Elder and Company, 1847), p. 146.

NOTES FOR CHAPTER II:
LIFE ON THE PLANTATION—
THE ARENA OF DEHUMANIZATION

1. Jacob Stroyer, *Sketches of My Life in the South* (Salem, Massachusetts: Observer Book and Job Print, 1891), p. 44.

2. *Ibid.*, pp. 44–45.

3. Charles Ball, *Slavery in the United States: a Narrative of the Life and Adventures of Charles Ball, a Black Man, Who Lived Forty Years in Maryland, South Carolina, and Georgia as a Slave* (New York: John S. Taylor, 1837), pp. 274–275.

4. Jackson, pp. 27–28.

5. *Federal Writers' Project. Slave Narratives: A Folk History of Slavery in the United States from Interviews with Former Slaves.* Typewritten Records Prepared by the Federal Writers' Project, 1936–1938. Assembled by the Library of Congress Project, Works Projects Administration for the District of Columbia. Sponsored by the Library of Congress, 17 vols. (Washington, D.C.: 1936–1938), Microfilm Edition.

Georgia Narratives, IV, Part 1, Reel 5, p. 2.

6. Ball, pp. 53–54.

7. *Ibid.*, p. 54.

8. *Ibid.*, pp. 56–57.

9. John Brown, pp. 171–172.

10. *Ibid.*, p. 173.

11. *Ibid.*, pp. 173–176.

12. Solomon Northup, *Twelve Years a Slave, Narrative of Solomon Northup, a Citizen of New York, Kidnapped in Washington City in 1841 and Rescued in January, 1853, from a Cotton Plantation near Red River, in Louisiana* (Buffalo: Derby, Orton and Mulligan, 1853), p. 165.

13. *Ibid.*, p. 166.

14. Ball, pp. 140–141.

15. Henry Bibb, *Narrative of the Life and Adventures of Henry Bibb, an American Slave, Written by Himself* (New York: by the author, 1850), p. 116.

16. Ball, pp. 214–215; Northup, pp. 171–172.

17. John Brown, pp. 186–187.

18. *Ibid.*, p. 182.

19. *Ibid.*, pp. 182–183.

20. *Federal Writers' Project*, Florida Narratives, III, Reel 4, p. 2; J. D. Green, *Narrative of the Life of J. D. Green, a Runaway Slave from Kentucky, Containing an Account of His Three Escapes, in 1839, 1846, and 1848* (Eighth Thousand, Huddersfield: printed by Henry Fielding, 1864), pp. 7–9.

21. Thomas H. Jones, *The Experience of Thomas Jones, Who Was a Slave for Forty-Three Years. Written by a Friend as Given to Him by Brother Jones* (Boston: Printed by Daniel Laing, 1850), p. 7; also see 1871 edition, pp. 7–8.

22. *Ibid.*, 1850 edition, p. 7; 1871 edition, pp. 7–8; *Federal Writers' Project*, Georgia Narratives, IV, Part 1, Reel 5, p. 30.

23. *Federal Writers' Project*, Florida Narratives, III, Reel 4, p. 326.

24. Northup, p. 221; William Wells Brown, *Narrative of William Wells Brown, a Fugitive Slave, Written by Himself* (Boston: Anti-Slavery Office, 1847), pp. 87–89; Henry Watson, *Narrative of Henry Watson, a Fugitive Slave* (Boston: Bela Marsh, 1849), p. 18.

25. Peter Still, pp. 153–154.

26. Fisk University, *God Struck Me Dead; Religious Conversion Experiences and Autobiographies of Negro Ex-Slaves* (Nashville, Tennessee: Social Science Institute, Fisk University, 1945), pp. 156–157; *Federal Writers' Project*, North Carolina Narratives, XI, Part 2, Reel 8, pp. 434–435; *Ibid.*, p. 77; *Ibid.*, p. 78; *Federal Writers' Project*, Georgia Narratives, IV, Part 4, Reel 5, p. 189; *Ibid.*, p. 201; Reverend Jermain W. Loguen, *The Reverend Jermain W. Loguen, as a Slave and as a Freeman. A Narrative of Real Life* (Syracuse: Office of the *Daily Journal*, 1859), pp. 38–40.

27. Bethany Veney, *The Narrative of Bethany Veney, a Slave Woman*, 2nd ed. (Worcester, Massachusetts: George H. Ellis, 1889), pp. 18–22; *Federal Writers' Project*, North Carolina Narratives, VI, Part 1, p. 36; Bibb, pp. 38–39; Ralph Roberts, "A Slave's Story," *Putnams Monthly*, IX (June, 1857), 616–618.

28. Thomas H. Jones, *The Experience and Personal Narrative of Uncle Tom Jones: Who Was for Forty Years a Slave; also, the Surprising Adventures of Wild Tom,*

a Fugitive Negro from South Carolina (New York: C. G. Holbrook, 1858), p. 23.

29. Loguen, p. 38.

30. Daniel H. Peterson, *The Looking Glass: Being a True Narrative of the Life of the Reverend D. H. Peterson* (New York: Printed by Wright, 1854), pp. 15–16.

31. Drew, p. 122.

32. Sarah Bradford, *Harriet Tubman: The Moses of Her People* (New York: by the author, 1886), p. 69; Sam Aleckson, *Before the War and After the Union. An Autobiography* (Boston: Gold Mind Publishing Company, 1929), p. 19.

33. Bibb, pp. 43–44.

34. Thomas H. Jones, *The Experience and Personal Narrative of Uncle Tom Jones*, p. 8.

35. Stroyer, pp. 15–16; Bibb, p. 14; Francis Fedric, *Slave Life in Virginia and Kentucky; or, Fifty Years of Slavery in the Southern States of America. By Francis Fedric, an Escaped Slave* (London: Wertheim, MacIntosh, and Hunt, 1863), p. 25.

36. Joseph Vance Lewis, *Out of the Ditch: a True Story of an Ex-Slave, by J. Vance Lewis* (Houston: Rein and Sons, 1910), p. 155; William Grimes, *Life of William Grimes, the Runaway Slave. Brought Down to the Present Time. Written by Himself* (New Haven: by the author, 1855), pp. 24–26.

37. Fedric, pp. 41–44.

38. Austin Steward, *Twenty-Two Years a Slave and Forty Years a Freeman, Embracing a Correspondence of Several Years While President of Wilberforce Colony* (Rochester, New York: W. Alling, 1857), pp. 47–48; Annie L. Burton, *Memories of Childhood's Slavery Days* (Boston: Ross Publishing Company, 1919), p. 5.

39. Henry Box Brown, *Narrative of the Life of Henry Box Brown, Written by Himself* (Boston: Samuel Webb, Bilston, 1852), pp. 16–17.

40. William Wells Brown, *A Description of William Wells Brown's Original Panoramic Views of the Scenes in the Life of an American Slave* (London: Charles Gilpin, 1849), p. 105.

41. Reverend Peter Randolph, *From Slave Cabin to Pulpit: The Autobiography of Peter Randolph: The Southern Question Illustrated and Sketches of Slave Life* (Boston: James H. Earle, 1893), p. 205.

42. Lydia Maria Child, *Authentic Anecdotes of American Slavery* (Newburyport, Connecticut: Charles Whipple, 1838), p. 17.

43. Lewis and Milton Clarke, *A Narrative of the Sufferings of Lewis and Milton Clarke, Sons of a Soldier of the Revolution; During a Captivity of More than Twenty Years Among the Slaveholders of Kentucky, One of the So-Called Christian States of North America* (Boston: Bela Marsh, 1846), p. 111.

44. Fedric, pp. 42–45.

45. Peterson, p. 4; Northup, pp. 85–87.

46. Randolph, pp. 206–207.

47. Henry Box Brown, pp. 46–47.

48. Josiah Henson, *Truth Stranger Than Fiction. Father Henson's Story of His Own Life* (Boston: John P. Jewett and Company, 1858), pp. 104–105; Levi Coffin, *Reminiscences of Levi Coffin, the Reputed President of the Underground Railroad* (Cincinnati: Western Tract Society,

1876), pp. 252–264; Bibb, pp. 46–47.

49. Frederick Douglass, *Oration, Delivered in Corinthian Hall, Rochester, by Frederick Douglass, July 5, 1852* (Rochester: Lee, Mann and Company, 1852), p. 18; Douglass, *Lectures on American Slavery*, p. 12.

50. Booker T. Washington, *Up From Slavery*, Bantam Books (New York: Doubleday and Company, 1901), p. 5; James Roberts, *Narrative of James Roberts, Soldier in the Revolutionary War and Battle of New Orleans*, The Book Farm (Chicago: by the author, 1858), p. 111.

51. Lewis and Milton Clarke, p. 104.

52. *Federal Writers' Project*, Georgia Narratives, IV, Part 4, Reel 5, p. 189.

53. Jamie Parker, *Jamie Parker, the Fugitive. Related to Mrs. Emily Pierson* (Hartford: Brockett, Fuller, and Company, 1851), pp. 20–22.

54. Steward, pp. 82–83; Thomas H. Jones, *The Experience and Personal Narrative of Uncle Tom Jones*, pp. 13–14; Thomas H. Jones, *The Experience of Thomas H. Jones Who Was a Slave for Forty-Three Years*, 1850 edition, pp. 15–16.

55. John Thompson, *The Life of John Thompson, a Fugitive Slave: containing His History of Twenty-Five Years in Bondage, and His Providential Escape: Written by Himself* (Worcester: by the author, 1856), pp. 103–107.

56. *Ibid.*, p. 106.

57. Thomas H. Jones, *The Experiences of Thomas H. Jones Who Was a Slave for Forty-Three Years*, 1850 edition, pp. 11–13.

58. *Ibid.*, p. 16–18; Thomas H. Jones, *The Experience and Personal Narrative of Uncle Tom Jones*, p. 12.

59. Coffin, p. 71.

60. Peter Still, p. 40.

61. Coffin, p. 70; Peter Still, pp. 40–41.

62. Steward, p. 130.

63. James Roberts, p. iii.

64. John Hawkins Simpson, *Horrors of the Virginia Slave Trade and of Slave Rearing Plantations* (London: W. Bennett, 1863), pp. 39–40.

65. Henson, pp. 86–87; Brent., pp. 28–29.

66. Fisk University, *Unwritten History of Slavery; Autobiographical Account of Negro Ex-Slaves* (Nashville, Tennessee: Social Science Institute, Fisk University, 1945), p. 82.

67. Charles Ball, pp. 162–163.

68. *Ibid.*, p. 164; Northup, p. 98.

69. James Williams, *Narrative of James Williams, An American Slave: Who Was for Several Years a Driver on a Cotton Plantation in Alabama* (New York: American Anti-Slavery Society, 1838), pp. 72–73.

70. Fedric, p. 5; William C. Emerson, *Stories and Spirituals of the Negro Slave* (Boston, R. G. Badger and Gorham Press, 1930), p. 18; Bibb, p. 21.

71. Louis B. Hughes, *Thirty Years a Slave; from Bondage to Freedom, the Institution of Slavery as Seen on the Plantation and in the Home of the Planter* (Milwaukee: H. E. Haferkorn, 1897), p. 90.

72. *Ibid.*

73. *Ibid.*, p. 91.

74. Aleckson, pp. 28–29.

75. Drew, pp. 32–33, 79–80.

76. Charles Emery Stevens, *An-*

thony Burns: a History (Boston: John P. Jewett and Company, 1856), pp. 166–167.

77. Randolph, pp. 202–203.

78. Henry Clay Bruce, *The New Man: Twenty-Nine Years a Slave, Twenty-Nine Years a Free Man. Recollections of H. C. Bruce* (York, Pennsylvania: P. Anstadt and Sons, 1895), p. 72.

79. Henry Box Brown, pp. 3–4.

80. Stevens, p. 165.

81. Randolph, pp. 196–197.

82. *Ibid.*, pp. 197–198.

83. Henson, p. 132; Clarke, pp. 104–105; James Roberts, p. 12.

84. J. D. Green, p. 6.

85. *Ibid.*, pp. 6–7.

86. Lunsford Lane, *The Narrative of Lunsford Lane, Formerly of Raleigh, North Carolina* (Boston: by the author, 1845), p. 21; *Federal Writers' Project*, Georgia Narratives, IV, Part 4, Reel 5, p. 201.

87. Emerson, p. 18.

88. Robert Anderson, *From Slavery to Affluence. Memoirs of Robert Anderson, Ex-Slave* (Hemingsford, Nebraska: Hemingsford Ledger, 1927), pp. 23–24.

89. *Ibid.*, p. 24.,

90. Hughes, pp. 53–54.

91. *Ibid.*, p. 54.

92. Robert Anderson, p. 23.

93. Isaac D. Williams, *Sunshine and Shadow of Slave Life* (East Saginaw, Michigan: Evening News Printing and Binding House, 1885), pp. 66–67.

94. *Ibid.*, p. 67.

95. Israel Campbell, *Bond and Free; or, Yearnings for Freedom, From My Green Briar House; Being the Story of My Life in Bondage and My Life in Freedom* (Philadel-

phia: by the author, 1861), pp. 91–92.

96. Jupiter Hammon, *An Address to the Negroes in the State of New York. By Jupiter Hammon, Servant of John Lloyd* (New York: Samuel Wood, 1806), p. 19.

97. Drew, p. 136; *Ibid.*, pp. 331–332.

98. Stevens, pp. 174–175.

99. William Still, *Underground Rail Road Record, Narrating the Hardships, Hairbreath Escapes and Death Struggles of the Slave in Their Efforts for Freedom* (Philadelphia: People's Publishing Company, 1879), p. 120.

100. Charles Ball, p. 221.

101. William Wells Brown, *Description of Brown's Views*, p. 103; Stroyer, pp. 46–47.

102. Stroyer, pp. 46–47.

103. Fedric, p. 28.

104. *Ibid.*

105. Brent, pp. 179–180.

106. Northup, pp. 213–216.

107. Charles Ball, p. 267; C. G. Parsons, *Inside View of Slavery; or, a Tour Among the Planters* (Cleveland: John P. Jewett, 1855), p. 41.

108. Frederick Douglass, *Narrative of the Life of Frederick Douglass, an American Slave. Written by Himself* (Boston: Published at the Anti-Slavery Office, 1845), pp. 75–76.

109. *Ibid.*, p. 76.

110. William Henry Singleton, *Recollections of My Slavery Days* (Peekskill, New York: Highland Democratic Company, 1922), p. 6.

111. *Ibid.*

112. *Federal Writers' Project*, Arkansas Narratives, II, Part 5, Reel 3, p. 162.

113. James Williams, p. 47.

114. Drew, p. 74.

115. James Williams, p. 47.
116. *Federal Writers' Project,* Georgia Narratives, IV, Part 4, Reel 5, p. 200.
117. Robert Anderson, pp. 30–31.
118. *Federal Writers' Project,* Georgia Narratives, IV, Part 4, Reel 5, p. 200.
119. Robert Anderson, pp. 30–31.
120. Robert Anderson, pp. 24–25; Isaac D. Williams, p. 62.
121. Stevens, p. 167; Bibb, p. 118.
122. Watson, p. 19.
123. Randolph, pp. 180–181.
124. Steward, pp. 38–39.
125. *Federal Writers' Project,* Georgia Narratives, IV, Part 1, Reel 5, p. 127; Randolph, p. 181.
126. Stevens, p. 168.

NOTES FOR CHAPTER III:
THE MASTER'S BUSINESS

1. *Federal Writers' Project,* Arkansas Narratives, II, Reel 3, p. 10.
2. Fisk University, *Unwritten History of Slavery,* pp. 1–2.
3. Douglass, *Narrative,* p. 65.
4. James Roberts, p. 26.
5. Jane Blake, *Memoirs of Margaret Jane Blake. Related to Sarah R. Levering, Baltimore, whose father had owned Jane Blake* (Philadelphia: Innes and Son, 1897), p. 13.
6. Parker, p. 77.
7. Isaac D. Williams, p. 59.
8. Watson, pp. 10–12.
9. *Ibid.*
10. William Wells Brown, *Narrative,* pp. 50–51.
11. Fisk University, *Unwritten History of Slavery,* p. 169.
12. Loguen, p. 75.
13. *Ibid.*

14. Ball, pp. 36–38.
15. *Ibid.*
16. *Ibid.,* p. 38.
17. *Ibid.,* pp. 41–42.
18. John Brown, pp. 110–111.
19. *Ibid.*
20. *Ibid.*
21. Bibb, p. 101.
22. *Ibid.*
23. John Brown, pp. 111–113.
24. *Ibid.,* p. 114.
25. William J. Anderson, *Life and Narrative of William J. Anderson; or, Dark Deeds of American Slavery Revealed, Written by Himself* (Chicago: Daily Tribune Book and Job Printing Office, 1857), p. 14.
26. Watson, pp. 9–10.
27. Henson, p. 11.
28. Northup, pp. 79–80.
29. John Brown, pp. 115–116.
30. Ball, pp. 72–73.
31. Clarke, p. 75; Parker, p. 79.
32. Zamba, pp. 140–141.
33. Watson, pp. 8–9.
34. Hughes, pp. 7–8.
35. John Brown, pp. 123–124.
36. Veney, p. 30; *Federal Writers' Project,* Arkansas Narratives, p. 105.
37. Zamba, p. 142.
38. John Brown, pp. 116–117.
39. Stevens, pp. 157–158.
40. *Ibid.*
41. *Ibid.,* p. 159.
42. *Ibid.,* p. 158.
43. *Ibid.,* p. 159.
44. Douglass, *Narrative,* pp. 102–103.
45. *Federal Writers' Project,* Georgia Narratives, Part 4, Reel 5, pp. 128–129.
46. William Still, pp. 166–167, 170, 204.
47. Loguen, p. 110.
48. William Still, p. 299; Douglass,

Narrative, p. 98.

49. Clarke, pp. 126–127.

50. *Ibid.*

51. Randolph, p. 191.

52. Wilson Armistead, *Five Hundred Thousand Strokes for Freedom, A Series of Anti-Slavery Tracts of Which Half a Million Are Now First Issued by Friends of the Negro* (London: W. and F. Cash and William Tweedie, 1853), p. 165.

53. Douglass, *Narrative*, p. 37.

54. Randolph, p. 192.

55. Peter Still, p. 79.

56. *Ibid.*, p. 124.

57. Henry Box Brown, p. 15; *Federal Writers' Project*, Georgia Narratives, IV, Part 4, Reel 5, pp. 196–197.

58. Peter Still, pp. 46–47.

59. *The Liberator*, January 29, 1847.

60. John Brown, pp. 49–51.

61. Levin Tilmon, *A Brief Miscellaneous Narrative of the More Early Part of the Life of Levin Tilmon, Pastor of a Colored Methodist Church, New York City* (Jersey City: W. and L. Pratt, 1853), p. 73.

62. *Federal Writers' Project*, Texas Narratives, XVI, Part 2, Reel 2, p. 50.

63. Northup, pp. 61–62; Steward, p. 122.

64. Steward, pp. 116–123.

65. Ball, pp. 488–489.

66. Clarke, p. 111.

67. Douglass, *Narrative*, pp. 79–80.

68. *Ibid.*, pp. 25–26.

69. *Ibid.*, pp. 77–78.

70. Peter Still, pp. 48–49.

71. Bradford, pp. 40–41.

72. Ball, p. 500.

73. Simpson, pp. 22–23.

74. Ball, pp. 118–119.

75. *Ibid.*, p. 379.

76. *Ibid.*, pp. 378–379.

77. Northup, pp. 237–238.

78. Bruce, pp. 98–99.

79. Fedric, p. 29.

80. Clarke, p. 114.

81. Moses Grandy, *Narrative of the Life of Moses Grandy, Late a Slave in the United States of America* (Boston: O. Johnson, 1844), pp. 38–39.

82. *Ibid.*, p. 39.

83. Bruce, p. 96.

84. Steward, pp. 27–28; Drew, p. 249.

85. Northup, p. 158.

86. *Federal Writers' Project*, Arkansas Narratives, II, Part 1, Reel 2, p. 70; Bruce, pp. 96–97; Grandy, p. 38.

87. Brent, pp. 181–182.

88. Peter Still, p. 183.

89. Parker, p. 31.

90. *Ibid.*

91. *Ibid.*, p. 32.

92. *Ibid.*

93. *Ibid.*, pp. 32–33.

94. Stroyer, pp. 16–17.

95. Clarke, p. 122.

96. Stevens, pp. 170–171.

97. *Federal Writers' Project*, Alabama Narratives, Reel 1, p. 66.

98. Northup, pp. 226–227.

99. William Grimes, *Life of William Grimes, the Runaway Slave. Written by Himself* (New York: by the author, 1825), p. 18.

100. *Federal Writers' Project*, Texas Narratives, XVI, Part 3, Reel 2, pp. 212–213.

NOTES FOR CHAPTER IV:
TYPES OF SLAVES

1. Douglass, *Narrative*, pp. 49–50.

2. William Wells Brown, *Description of Brown's Views*, p. 112.

3. Clarke, p. 112.

4. Zangara and Maquama, *Slavery Illustrated; in the Histories of Zangara and Maquama, two Negroes Stolen from Africa and Sold into Slavery. Related by Themselves* (London: Simpkin, Marshall, 1849), pp. 28–29.

5. Ball, p. 21.

6. *Federal Writers' Project*, Arkansas Narratives, I, Reel 2, p. 73.

7. Douglass, *Narrative*, p. 51.

8. William J. Anderson, p. 19; Brent, pp. 9, 119.

9. William J. Anderson, p. 19.

10. James Williams, p. 48.

11. *Federal Writers' Project*, North Carolina Narratives, XI, Part 1, Reel 8, p. 360.

12. Isaac D. Williams, p. 63.

13. *Ibid.*, pp. 63–64.

14. Bradford, p. 18.

15. William J. Anderson, p. 19.

16. Brent, p. 55.

17. James Redpath, *The Roving Editor; or, Talks with Slaves in the Southern States* (New York: A. B. Burdick, 1859), pp. 93–94.

18. Louisa Picquet, *Louisa Picquet, the Octoroon; or, Inside Views of Southern Domestic Life* (New York: by the author, 1861), p. 50.

19. *Ibid.*

20. James W. C. Pennington, *The Fugitive Blacksmith; or, Events in the History of James W. C. Pennington, Pastor of a Presbyterian Church, New York, Formerly a Slave in the State of Maryland, United States* (London: Charles Gilpin, 1849), pp. vi–vii.

21. *Ibid.*, pp. vi–viii.

22. *Federal Writers' Project*, Kentucky Narratives, VIII, Reel 7, p. 53.

23. Peter Still, pp. 171–173.

24. *Ibid.*

25. Thompson, p.

26. William J. And

27. Fisk University, *Me Dead*, pp. 174–175

28. Fisk University, *History of Slavery*, p. 2.

29. *Federal Writers' Project*, North Carolina Narratives, XI, Part 2, p. 78.

30. Picquet, pp. 51–52.

31. William Wells Brown, *My Southern Home* (Boston: A. G. Brown and Company, 1880), pp. 91–97.

32. *Ibid.*

33. Bruce, pp. 38–39.

34. Henson, p. 32.

35. *Ibid.*, p. 54.

36. *Ibid.*, p. 51.

37. Veney, p. 10.

38. Abigail Field Mott and S. M. Wood, *Narratives of Colored Americans* (New York: Bowne and Company, 1882), p. 208.

39. Ralph Roberts, pp. 618–619.

40. Bibb, p. 200.

41. Peterson, p. 18; William Spottswood White, *The African Preacher; an Authentic Narrative* (Philadelphia: Presbyterian Board of Publication, 1849), p. 53.

42. White, p. 54.

43. *Ibid.*

44. *Ibid.*, p. 52.

45. Jupiter Hammon, p. 7; *Ibid.*, pp. 8–9.

46. William Spottswood White, p. 21.

47. Steward, p. 32.

48. *Ibid.*

49. Coffin, pp. 342–343.

50. *The Liberator*, September 17, 1858.

51. Coffin, pp. 343–344.

52. *Petition of Lewis Bolah, a free man of colour*. Legislative Petition,

Richmond City, Virginia. December 13, 1824.

53. Fisk University, *Unwritten History of Slavery*, pp. 255–256.

54. Northup, pp. 246–248.

55. *Ibid.*, p. 248.

56. Lewis, p. 166.

57. Douglass, *Narrative*, pp. 111–113.

58. *Ibid.*, p. 113.

59. Bruce, p. 91; Coffin, pp. 19–20.

60. Douglass, *Narrative*, p. 83.

61. Bruce, pp. 36–37.

62. *Ibid.*, p. 48; Isaac D. Williams, pp. 8–9.

63. John Brown, p. 48; Fisk University, *God Struck Me Dead*, p. 172.

64. Thompson, p. 27.

65. *Ibid.*, pp. 26–28.

66. William Wells Brown, *Narrative*, pp. 18–19.

67. *Ibid.*, p. 20.

68. Josephine Brown, *Biography of a Bondman by His Daughter* (Boston: R. F. Wallcut, 1855), pp. 32–33.

69. Steward, p. 107.

70. *Ibid.*, pp. 112–113.

71. Grandy, p. 41.

72. William Wells Brown, *Narrative*, p. 70.

73. Samuel Ringgold Ward, *Autobiography of a Fugitive Negro: His Anti-Slavery Labours in the United States, Canada, and England* (London: John Snow, 1855), pp. 160–161.

74. *Ibid.*, p. 163.

75. Isaac D. Williams, p. 12.

76. Jackson, p. 10.

77. Coffin, pp. 341–342.

78. *Ibid.*, pp. 254–256; Parker, p. 163; Ralph Roberts, p. 615.

79. *Federal Writers' Project*, Georgia Narratives, IV, Part 4, Reel 5, p. 43.

80. *Federal Writers' Project*, Florida Narratives, III, Reel 4, p. 295.

81. *Ibid.*

82. Jackson, p. 11.

83. Peter Still, pp. 188–190.

84. James Watkins, *Narrative of the Life of James Watkins, Formerly a Chattel in Maryland, United States* (Birmingham, England: W. Watton and Company, 1853), pp. 21–23.

85. Stroyer, pp. 64–71.

86. *Ibid.*

87. Ball, p. 74.

88. Brent, pp. 75–76.

89. Peterson, p. 22.

90. Bruce, p. 32.

91. Clarke, p. 117.

92. *Federal Writers' Project*, Alabama Narratives, VII, Reel 1, p. 263.

93. Ralph Roberts, p. 615.

94. Stroyer, pp. 64–71.

95. Ward, p. 165.

NOTES FOR CHAPTER V:
ATTITUDES, RELATIONSHIPS
AND CUSTOMS

1. William Wells Brown, *My Southern Home*, pp. 120–121.

2. Robert Anderson, p. 29.

3. Drew, p. 376.

4. Blake, pp. 11–12.

5. Bibb, pp. 39–40.

6. William Wells Brown, *Description of Brown's Views*, pp. 128–129.

7. *Ibid.*

8. Steward, p. 31; Parker, pp. 12–13.

9. Steward, p. 32.

10. *Ibid.*

11. *Federal Writers' Project*, Arkansas Narratives, II, Reel 3, Part 7, pp. 142–143.

12. Randolph, p. 160.

13. *Ibid.*, p. 161.

14. *Ibid.*

15. Ralph Roberts, p. 615.

16. William Still, pp. 69–70.

17. Bruce, pp. 37–38.

18. Aaron, *Light and Truth of Slavery, Aaron's History in Virginia, New Jersey and Rhode Island* (Worcester, Massachusetts: Colophon Press, 18–), pp. 17–18.

19. *Ibid.*, p. 45.

20. Douglass, *Narrative*, pp. 19–20.

21. Drew, p. 58.

22. William Wells Brown, *Narrative*, pp. 56–58.

23. Bibb, pp. 16–17.

24. *Federal Writers' Project*, Georgia Narratives, IV, Part 4, Reel 5, pp. 182, 195.

25. Campbell, pp. 37–38.

26. Northup, pp. 232–234.

27. Drew, pp. 29–31.

28. Douglass, *Lectures on American Slavery*, pp. 13–14.

29. *Ibid.*

30. *Ibid.*

31. Douglass, *Narrative*, p. 15.

32. *Ibid.*

33. Isaac D. Williams, pp. 58–59.

34. *Ibid.*

35. Douglass, *Narrative*, p. 54; *ibid.*, p. 17.

36. Ball, pp. 301–302.

37. Stroyer, p. 59.

38. *Ibid.*, pp. 59–60.

39. *Ibid.*, p. 61.

40. John Brown, p. 22.

41. Campbell, pp. 66–67.

42. Clarke, pp. 25–26.

43. *Ibid.*, p. 196.

44. John Brown, pp. 82–83.

45. Clarke, pp. 119–120.

46. Brent, p. 290.

47. Jackson, pp. 28–29.

48. Brent, p. 206; Jupiter Hammon, p. 10.

49. Jupiter Hammon, p. 10.

50. Henson, pp. 89–90.

51. Clarke, pp. 120–121.

52. Bruce, p. 130.

53. Ball, p. 260.

54. William Wells Brown, *My Southern Home*, p. 68.

55. *Ibid.*

56. *Ibid.*, pp. 69–70.

57. *Ibid.*

58. *Ibid.*, pp. 70–71.

59. Stroyer, pp. 54–55.

60. *Ibid.*, p. 56.

61. Bibb, pp. 25–27.

62. *Federal Writers' Project*, Georgia Narratives, IV, Part 4, Reel 5, p. 261.

63. *Ibid.*, p. 264.

64. *Ibid.*

65. *Ibid.*, p. 261.

66. Fedric, p. 91.

67. Bibb, pp. 117–118.

68. James Lindsay Smith, *Autobiography of James Lindsay Smith* (Norwich, Connecticut: Press of the Bulletin Company, 1881), pp. 2–3.

69. William Still, p. 114; Henson, p. 39.

70. Ball, pp. 205–207.

71. *Federal Writers' Project*, Georgia Narratives, IV, Part 2, Reel 5, p. 53.

72. Hughes, pp. 21–22.

73. Bruce, p. 99.

74. Washington, p. 13.

75. Aleckson, p. 78.

76. Bruce, pp. 85–86.

77. Bradford, p. 28.

78. Stevens, p. 156.

79. Brent, p. 198.

80. Brent, p. 190; Washington, pp. 5–6.

81. Washington, p. 5.

82. Robert Anderson, pp. 31–32.

83. Northup, pp. 222–225.

84. *Federal Writers' Project*, Georgia Narratives, IV, Part 1, Reel 5, p. 14.

85. Douglass, *Narrative*, pp. 23–24.

86. *Ibid.*

87. Ralph Roberts, pp. 615–616.

88. Henry Box Brown, pp. 24–26.

89. Northup, pp. 224–225.

90. William Still, p. 49; Watson, pp. 120–121; James Williams, p. 60.

91. *Federal Writers' Project*, Georgia Narratives, IV, Part 4, Reel 5, p. 182.

92. Stroyer, pp. 32–33; Parker, p. 22.

93. Ball, p. 308; Bruce, pp. 28–29.

94. Bruce, pp. 28–29.

95. *Ibid.*, p. 38.

96. Bibb, p. 24; *Federal Writers' Project*, North Carolina Narratives, XI, Part 1, p. 319.

97. Bruce, p. 30.

98. Bibb, pp. 24–25.

99. Bruce, p. iv.

100. Lewis, p. 158.

101. Bruce, pp. 30–31.

102. William Wells Brown, *The Black Man, His Antecedents, His Genius and His Achievements* (Savannah, Georgia: James M. Symms and Company, 1863), pp. 142-143.

103. Loguen, pp. 145, 16–17.

104. Bruce, pp. 76–77; Drew, p. 276.

105. William Craft, *Running a Thousand Miles for Freedom; or, The Escape of William and Ellen Craft from Slavery* (London: William Tweedie, 1860), p. 39.

106. Veney, p. 31.

107. Loguen, pp. 145, 16–17; *Federal Writers' Project*, Arkansas Narratives, II, Part 4, Reel 2, pp. 182–183.

108. *Federal Writers' Project*, Florida Narratives, III, Reel 4, pp. 264–265; William Wells Brown, *My Southern Home*, pp. 144–147.

109. Drew, pp. 205–206; *Ibid.*, p. 181.

110. Henson, pp. 6–7.

111. Clarke, p. 121.

112. Drew, pp. 29, 52.

113. Peter Still, p. 71; James Williams, p. 37.

114. Stroyer, pp. 42–43.

115. James Williams, p. 32.

116. Drew, p. 178; Campbell, p. 18.

NOTES FOR CHAPTER VI:
THE SLAVE'S INTERPRETATION
OF THE INSTITUTION

1. Pennington, pp. iv, x–xi.

2. *Ibid.*, pp. iv–v.

3. Isaac D. Williams, pp. 59–60.

4. Drew, p. 78; Pennington, p. v.

5. Jackson, p. 22.

6. Loguen, pp. 306, 241–242.

7. Ball, p. 69; Peter Bruner, *A Slave's Advances Toward Freedom; Not Fiction, but the True Story of a Struggle* (Oxford, Ohio: n.p., n.d.), p. 13.

8. Drew, p. 89.

9. Randolph, pp. 207–208.

10. Pennington, p. xii.

11. Zamba, pp. 158–159.

12. Drew, pp. 220–221.

13. James Roberts, p. iv.

14. Bruce, pp. 25–26.

15. Henry Box Brown, p. 19.

16. *Ibid.*

17. James Lindsay Smith, p. 30.

18. *Ibid.*, p. 31.

19. Jamie Parker, pp. 16–17.

20. Brent, pp. 98–100, 102.

21. *Ibid.*

22. *Ibid.*, pp. 98–99.

23. *Ibid.*, p. 102.

24. *Ibid.*, p. 103.

25. *Ibid.*, pp. 103–104.

26. Drew, pp. 44, 90–91.

27. Zamba, p. 248.

28. *Ibid.*, pp. 202–203.

29. Douglass, *Lectures on American Slavery*, pp. 31–32.

30. Grandy, p. 42.

31. *Ibid.*, pp. 283–284.

32. Parsons, p. 40; Drew, p. 198; *Ibid.*, pp. 129–130.

33. Jackson, p. 25.

34. *Ibid.*, pp. 25–26.

35. Drew, pp. 341–342.

36. Steward, p. 319.

37. *Ibid.*, pp. 319–320.

38. Coffin, p. 157.

39. *Ibid.*, pp. 158–159.

40. Louisa Picquet, p. 51; Bruce, pp. 130–131.

41. James Roberts, p. 22; Douglass, *Narrative*, p. 3.

42. Douglass, *Narrative*, pp. 3–4.

43. *Ibid.*

44. Clarke, pp. 20–21.

45. James Roberts, pp. 22–23.

46. *Ibid.*

47. Craft, pp. 16–17.

48. William M. Mitchell, *Underground Railroad from Slavery to Freedom* (London: W. Tweedie, 1860), pp. 61–63.

49. *Ibid.*

50. Coffin, pp. 28–31.

51. Steward, pp. 130–131; Douglass, *Narrative*, p. 4.

52. Ball, pp. 14–15; Henson, p. 15.

53. Steward, pp. 107–108.

54. Jackson, p. 2.

55. Northup, p. 205.

56. *Ibid.*, p. 206.

57. Blake, p. 14.

58. Washington, p. 12.

59. John Brown, p. 53.

60. *Ibid.*, pp. 55–57.

61. *The Liberator*, December 14, 1849.

62. *Ibid.*

63. Charles Nordhoff, *The Freedmen of South Carolina* (New York: Charles L. Evans, 1863), p. 3.

64. Isaac D. Williams, p. 50.

65. Steward, p. 33.

66. *Ibid.*, pp. 37–38.

67. Jamie Parker, pp. 161–162.

68. James Williams, pp. 26–27.

69. Grandy, pp. 35–36.

70. Ball, pp. 162–164.

71. Drew, p. 222.

72. *Ibid.*, p. 223.

73. Isaac D. Williams, pp. 49–50.

74. Ward, p. 279; James Roberts, pp. 12–17; Ward, p. 279.

75. William Greenleaf Eliot, *The Story of Archer Alexander. From Slavery to Freedom* (Boston: Cripples, Upham and Company, 1885), pp. 19–20.

76. *Federal Writers' Project*, Alabama Narratives, VI, Reel 1, p. 222; Peter Still, p. 159.

77. Peter Still, pp. 159–160.

78. *Ibid.*, pp. 160–161.

79. *Ibid.*, p. 161.

80. *Ibid.*

81. Campbell, pp. 71–74.

82. Fisk University, *Unwritten History of Slavery*, pp. 170–171.

83. Drew, pp. 239–240.

84. Zamba, pp. 155–160.

85. Jane Brown, pp. 47–49; William Wells Brown, *The Black Man*, p. 142.

86. Aaron, p. 8.

87. Jackson, pp. iii–iv.

88. *Ibid.*

89. *Ibid.*

90. Drew, p. 32.

91. Bibb, pp. 28–30.

92. Douglass, *Narrative*, p. 67.

93. Jupiter Hammon, pp. 14–15.
94. *Ibid.*, pp. 20–21.
95. Douglass, *Narrative*, p. 106.
96. William Wells Brown, *Lecture*, p. 10.
97. *Ibid.*, p. 11.
98. *Ibid.*
99. *Ibid.*, p. 13.
100. *Ibid.*, p. 14.
101. *Ibid.*, pp. 14–15.
102. *Ibid.*
103. Washington, p. 13.
104. *Ibid.*, p. 14–15.
105. Ward, p. 169.
106. *Ibid.*, pp. 169–170.
107. *Ibid.*, pp. 170, 190.
108. Steward, pp. 172–174.
109. *Ibid.*, p. 175.
110. *Ibid.*, p. 176.
111. *Ibid.*, pp. 327–332.
112. Brent, p. 68.
113. Blake, p. 20.
114. William Wells Brown, *The Black Man*, pp. 32–33.
115. *Ibid.*, pp. 35–36.
116. *Ibid.*, p. 36.
117. *Ibid.*
118. Randolph, pp. 155–156.
119. Ward, pp. 281–282.
120. James Roberts, p. 2.
121. *Ibid.*, p. vii.
122. *Ibid.*
123. *Ibid.*
124. William J. Anderson, p. 59.
125. *Ibid.*, p. 60.
126. Zamba, pp. 250–251.
127. *Ibid.*
128. *Ibid.*
129. *Ibid.*, pp. 249–251.
130. Elizabeth Keckley, *Behind the Scenes by Elizabeth Keckley, Formerly a Slave, but more Recently Modiste, and Friend to Mrs. Abraham Lincoln; or, Thirty Years a Slave, and Four Years in the White House* (New York: G. W. Carlton and Company, 1868), pp. xii–xiii.
131. William Wells Brown, *The Black Man*, p. 37.
132. *Ibid.*, p. 39.
133. Steward, pp. 326–327.
134. William Wells Brown, *The Black Man*, p. 42.
135. *Ibid.*
136. *Ibid.*, pp. 42–45.
137. *Ibid.*, pp. 45–46.
138. *Ibid.*, pp. 47–48.
139. *Ibid.*
140. *Ibid.*, p. 163.
141. *Ibid.*, p. 164.
142. *Ibid.*, pp. 45–46.

NOTES FOR CHAPTER VII:
SLAVERY IN A CIVILIZED SOCIETY

1. Steward, pp. 317–318.
2. *Ibid.*, pp. 318–319.
3. Thompson, pp. 37–38.
4. Eliot, p. 42.
5. *Ibid.*, pp. 42–43.
6. Aaron, p. 8.
7. *Ibid.*, p. 10.
8. Watkins, p. 61.
9. Grandy, p. 44.
10. James Williams, pp. 30–31.
11. William Wells Brown, *The Black Man*, p. 48.
12. *Ibid.*
13. *Ibid.*
14. James Wilkerson, *Wilkerson's History of His Travels and Labors in the United States, as a Missionary, in Particular that of the Union Seminary, Located in Franklin County, Ohio, since He Purchased His Liberty in New Orleans, Louisiana* (Columbus, Ohio: n.p., 1861), p. 27.
15. Steward, p. 327.

16. *Ibid.*, p. 330.
17. *Ibid.*, p. 331.
18. Peterson, pp. 74–75.
19. *Ibid.*
20. William Green, pp. 9–10.
21. *Ibid.*, p. 10.
22. Watkins, p. vi.
23. Watkins, p. vii; Fugitive Slave Act (United States Statutes at Large, IX, p. 472 ff.), September 18, 1850; Watkins, p. vii.
24. Watkins, pp. vii–viii.
25. *Ibid.*, pp. viii, 37–38.
26. Bradford, pp. 39, 46.
27. Steward, p. 325.
28. *Ibid.*, p. 326.
29. Brent, p. 286.
30. *Ibid.*, p. 287.
31. William Parker, "The Freedman's Story," *Atlantic Monthly*, XVII, March, 1866, pp. 280–281.
32. *The Liberator*, October 11, 1850.
33. John Brown, p. 212.
34. *Ibid.*, p. 212.
35. *Ibid.*, pp. 212–213.

36. Douglass, *Narrative*, p. 100.
37. *Ibid.*
38. *Ibid.*, p. 43.
39. James Williams, p. 99
40. Drew, p. 370.
41. Coffin, p. 153.
42. *The Anti-Slavery Bugle*, September 28, 1850.
43. Bruce, pp. 22–23.
44. Peter Still, pp. 267–268.
45. Douglass, *Narrative*, pp. 43–44.
46. Isaac D. Williams, pp. 54–55.
47. *Ibid.*
48. Douglass, *Lectures on American Slavery*, pp. 27–29.
49. *Ibid.*, pp. 29–30.
50. John Brown, pp. 206–209.

NOTES FOR CONCLUSION

1. Watkins, p. 40.
2. James Weldon Johnson, *Along This Way: The Autobiography of James Weldon Johnson* (New York: The Viking Press, 1968), p. 209.

Bibliographical Note

The narratives listed in the following bibliography include one published in 1704 and others as late as 1945, but the great majority, largely as a result of the abolitionist movement, date from the period 1830–1865.

The authors, or narrators, range from the totally illiterate and ignorant to the highly intellectual (although usually uneducated), and profound. They were engaged in activities which varied between skilled mechanic and house servant to ordinary field hand. Few, outside of Zamba, who claimed to be an African king, and Zangara and Maquama, who discussed their African antecedents, even mentioned Africa as the homeland or the base of their heritage. In most cases they were, as individuals, ordinary people whose only outstanding achievement was that, having once been slaves, they had gained their freedom.

Because it was easier to escape from the more northerly plantations, most of the narratives dated prior to 1865 came from slaves who lived in the upper south. After emancipation, the stories came from slaves who had lived in all parts of the south and southwest, and, essentially, these later narratives confirmed the earlier.

Finally, as for the narratives, many of the individual accounts such as those of Henry Bibb, Austin Steward, and William Grimes, were written by the slaves themselves, while the collections, such as Benjamin Drew's (1856), the Federal Writers' Project (1936–1938) and the Fisk University Volumes (1945) were dictated by the slaves or ex-slaves and written down virtually verbatim by the reporter.

The reader will note that the bibliography contains many titles not cited in the book. The reasons for this are that (a) the additional references basically repeat and confirm that which has been mentioned; and (b) the researcher who is seeking additional source material may find the expanded bibliography of some assistance.

Bibliography

SEPARATE SLAVE NARRATIVES

Aaron. *Light and Truth of Slavery. Aaron's History in Virginia, New Jersey, and Rhode Island.* Worcester, Massachusetts: Colophon Press, 18—.

Adams, John Quincy. *Narrative of the Life of John Quincy Adams, When in Slavery and Now as a Freeman.* Harrisburg, Pennsylvania: by the author, 1872.

Aleckson, Sam. *Before the War and After the Union. An Autobiography.* Boston: Gold Mind Publishing Company, 1929.

Alexander, Archer. *The Story of Archer Alexander, from Slavery to Freedom, March 30, 1863.* Boston: Cupples, Upham, and Company, 1885.

Allen, Richard. *The Life, Experiences, and Gospel Labors of the Right Reverend Richard Allen.* Philadelphia: Martin and Boden, 1833.

Anderson, John. *Story of John Anderson, Fugitive Slave.* Edited by Harper Twelvetrees, Chairman, John Anderson Committee. London: W. Tweedie, 1863.

Anderson, Robert. *From Slavery to Affluence. Memoirs of Robert Anderson, Ex-Slave.* Hemingsford, Nebraska: Hemingsford Ledger, 1927.

Anderson, Thomas. *Interesting Account of Thomas Anderson, a Slave "Taken from his Own Lips."* Dictated to J. P. Clark. N.p., 1854.

Anderson, William J. *Life and Narrative of William J. Anderson; or, Dark Deeds of American Slavery Revealed, Written by Himself.* Chicago: Daily Tribune Book and Job Printing Office, 1854.

Archer, Armstrong. *A Compedium of Slavery as It Exists in the Present Day.* London: J. Haddon, 1844.

Arthur. *The Life and Dying Speech of Arthur, A Negro Man.* A Broadside. Boston: printed and sold in Milk Street, 1768.

Aunt Sally; or, The Cross the Way to Freedom. Narrative of the Life and Purchase of the Mother of Reverend Isaac Williams of Detroit, Michigan. Cincinnati: American Reform Tract and Book Society, 1858.

Ball, Charles. *Slavery in the United States: a Narrative of the Life of Charles Ball, a Black Man, Who Lived Forty Years in Maryland, South Carolina, and Georgia as a Slave.* New York: John S. Taylor, 1837.

————. *Fifty Years in Chains; or, the Life of an American Slave.* New York: Dayton and Asher, 1858.

Bayley, Solomon. *Narrative of Some Remarkable Incidents in the Life of Solomon Bayley, Formerly a Slave in the State of Delaware, North America, Written by Himself.* London: Richard Hunard, 1825.

Bibb, Henry. *Narrative of the Life and Adventures of Henry Bibb, an American Slave, Written by Himself.* New York: by the author, 1850.

Black, Leonard. *Life and Sufferings of Leonard Black, a Fugitive from Slavery. Written by Himself.* New Bedford: Press of Benjamin Lindsey, 1847.

Blake, Jane. *Memoirs of Margaret Jane Blake.* Related to Sarah R. Levering, Baltimore, whose father had owned Jane Blake. Philadelphia: Innes and Son, 1897.

Boen, William. *Anecdotes and Memoirs of William Boen, a Colored Man, Who Lived and Died near Mount Holly, New Jersey.* Philadelphia: Printed by John Richards, 1834.

Bradford, Sarah. *Harriet Tubman: The Moses of Her People.* New York: by the author, 1886.

Brent, Linda. *Incidents in the Life of a Slave Girl.* Boston: by the author, 1861.

Brown, Henry Box. *Narrative of Henry Box Brown, Who Escaped from Slavery Enclosed in a Box Three Feet Long, Two Wide, and Two and a Half High. Written from a Statement of Facts Made by Himself. With remarks upon the remedy for slavery by Charles Stearns.* Boston: Brown and Stearns, 1849.

————. Manchester, England, 1851.

————. *Narrative of the Life of Henry Box Brown, Written by Himself.* Boston: Samuel Webb, Bilston, 1852.

Brown, Isaac. *Case of the Slave Isaac Brown. An Outrage Exposed!* N.p., n.p., 1847.

Brown, Jane. *Narrative of the Life of Jane Brown and Her Two Children.* Related to the Reverend G. W. Offley. Hartford: Published for G. W. Offley, 1860.

Brown, John. *Slave Life in Georgia: a Narrative of the Life, Suffering, and Escape of John Brown, a Fugitive Slave, Now in England.* London: W. M. Watts, 1855.

Brown, Josephine. *Biography of a Bondman by His Daughter.* Boston: R. F. Wallcut, 1855.

Brown, William J. *The Life of William J. Brown of Providence, Rhode Island*. Providence: Angell and Company, 1883.

Brown, William Wells. *Narrative of William Wells Brown, a Fugitive Slave, Written by Himself*. Boston: Anti-Slavery Office, 1847.

———. *A Lecture Delivered Before the Female Anti-Slavery Society of Salem, at Lyceum Hall, November 14, 1847*. Boston: Massachusetts Anti-Slavery Society, 1847.

———. *A Description of William Wells Brown's Original Panoramic Views of the Scenes in the Life of an American Slave*. London: Charles Gilpin, 1849.

———. *Life of William Wells Brown*. Boston: Bela Marsh, 1849.

———. *Three Years in Europe; or, Places I Have Seen and People I Have Met*. With a memoir of the author, by William Farmer. London: C. Gilpin, 1852.

———. *Places and People Abroad, by William Wells Brown, a Fugitive Slave, with a memoir of the author*. Boston: John P. Jewett, 1854.

Bruce, Henry Clay. *The New Man: Twenty-Nine Years a Slave, Twenty-Nine Years a Free Man. Recollections of H. C. Bruce*. York, Pennsylvania: P. Anstadt and Sons, 1895.

Bruner, Peter. *A Slave's Advances Toward Freedom; Not Fiction, but the True Story of a Struggle*. Oxford, Ohio: n.p., n.d.

Burton, Annie L. *Memories of Childhood's Slavery Days*. Boston: Ross Publishing Company, 1919.

Campbell, Israel. *Bond and Free; or, Yearnings for Freedom, from My Green Briar House; Being the Story of My Life in Bondage and My Life in Freedom*. Philadelphia: by the author, 1861.

Chandler, Charles. *The Story of a Slave*. N.p., n.p., 1894.

Clarke, Lewis. *Narrative of the Sufferings of Lewis Clarke, during a Captivity of More Than Twenty-Five Years among the Algerines of Kentucky*. Boston: D. H. Eli, 1845.

Clarke, Lewis and Milton. *Narrative of the Sufferings of Lewis and Milton Clarke, Sons of a Soldier of the Revolution; During a Captivity of More Than Twenty Years Among the Slaveholders of Kentucky, One of the So-Called Christian States of North America*. Boston: Bela Marsh, 1846.

Charlton, Dimmock. *Narrative of Dimmock Charlton, A British Subject, Taken from the Brig "Peacock" by the U.S. Sloop "Hornet," Enslaved While a Prisoner of War, and Retained Forty-Five Years in Bondage*. N.p., n.d.

Cooper, Thomas. *Narrative of the Life of Thomas Cooper*. New York: Isaac T. Hopper, 1837.

Craft, William. *Running a Thousand Miles for Freedom; or, the Escape of William and Ellen Craft from Slavery*. London: W. Tweedie, 1860.

Davis, Noah. *A Narrative of the Life of Reverend Noah Davis, a Colored Man, Written by Himself*. Baltimore: J. F. Weishampel, Jr., 1859.

Dinah. *The Story of Dinah, as Related to John Hawkins Simpson, after Her Escape from the Horrors of the Virginia Slave Trade, to London.* London: A. W. Bennett, 1863.

Dormigold, Kate. *A Slave Girl's Story, The Autobiography of Kate Dormigold.* Brooklyn, New York: n.p., 1898.

Douglass, Frederick. *Narrative of the Life of Frederick Douglass, an American Slave. Written by Himself.* Boston: Boston Anti-Slavery Office, 1845.

———. Boston: Bela Marsh, 1850.

———. Dolphin Books. New York: Doubleday and Company, Inc., 1963.

———. *Lectures on American Slavery by Frederick Douglass.* Delivered at Corinthian Hall, Rochester, N.Y., December 1, 1850 and December 8, 1850. Buffalo: Geo. Reese, 1851.

———. *Oration, Delivered in Corinthian Hall, Rochester, by Frederick Douglass, July 5 1852.* Rochester: Lee, Mann and Company, 1852.

———. *My Bondage and My Freedom.* Part I. Life as a Slave. Part II. Life as a Freeman. New York and Auburn: Miller, Orton, Mulligan, 1855.

———. *The Life and Times of Frederick Douglass.* Hartford: Connecticut Park Publishing Company, 1881.

Dubois, Sylvia. *A Biography of the Slave Who Whipt Her Mistress and Gained Her Freedom.* New Jersey: C. W. Larison, 1883.

Eldridge, Elleanor. *Memoirs of Elleanor Eldridge.* Providence: Printed by B. T. Albro, 1847.

Eliot, William Greenleaf. *The Story of Archer Alexander. From Slavery to Freedom.* Boston: Cripples, Upham and Company, 1885.

Equiano, Olaudah. *The Interesting Narrative of the Life of Olaudah Equiano, or Gustavus Vasa, the African. Written by Himself.* London: Stationers' Hall, 1789.

Fedric, Francis. *Slave Life in Virginia and Kentucky; or, Fifty Years of Slavery in the Southern States of America. By Francis Fedric, an Escaped Slave.* London: Wertheim, MacIntosh, and Hunt, 1863.

Franklin, Henry. *A Sketch of Henry Franklin and Family.* Philadelphia: Collins Printing House, 1887.

Frederick, Reverend Francis. *Autobiography of Reverend Francis Frederick, of Virginia.* Baltimore: J. W. Woods, 1869.

Grandy, Moses. *Narrative of the Life of Moses Grandy, Late a Slave in the United States of America.* Boston: O. Johnson, 1844.

Green, J. D. *Narrative of the Life of J. D. Green, a Runaway Slave from Kentucky, Containing an Account of His Three Escapes, in 1839, 1846, and 1848.* Huddersfield: Printed by Henry Fielding, 1864.

Green, William. *Narrative of Events in the Life of William Green (Formerly a Slave), Written by Himself.* Springfield, Massachusetts: L. M. Guernsey, Book, Job, and Card Printer, 1853.

Grimes, William. *Life of William Grimes, the Runaway Slave. Written by Himself.* New York: by the author, 1825.

————. *Life of William Grimes, the Runaway Slave, Brought Down to the Present Time. Written by Himself.* New Haven: by the author, 1855.

Gronniosaw, James Albert Ukawsaw. *A Narrative of the Most Remarkable Particulars in the Life of James Albert Ukawsaw Gronniosaw, An African Prince, as Related by Himself.* London: Davis and Booth, 1814.

Hall, Elder Samuel. *Forty-Seven Years a Slave; a Brief Story of His Life as a Slave and After Freedom.* Washington, Georgia: n.p., 1912.

Hammon, Briton. *A Narrative of the Uncommon Sufferings, and Surprizing (sic) Deliverance of Briton Hammon, a Negro Man,—Servant to General Winslow, of Marshfield, in New-England; Who Returned to Boston, after having been absent almost Thirteen Years. Containing An Account of the many Hardships he underwent from the time he left his master's house, in the year 1747, to the time of his Return to Boston.—How he was cast away in the Capes of Florida:—the horrid Cruelty and inhuman barbarity of the Indians in murdering the whole Ship's Crew;—the Manner of his being carried by them into captivity. Also, An Account of his being Confined Four Years and Seven Months in a closed Dungeon,—and the remarkable Manner in which he met with his good old Master in London; who returned to New England, a passenger, in the same ship.* Boston: Printed by Green and Russell, 1760.

Hammon, Jupiter. *An Address to the Negroes in the State of New York. By Jupiter Hammon, Servant of John Lloyd.* New York: Samuel Wood, 1806.

Hayden, William. *Narrative of William Hayden, containing a Faithful Account of His Travels for a Number of Years, Whilst a Slave in the South. Written by Himself.* Cincinnati: by the author, 1846.

Henson, Josiah. *Truth Stranger Than Fiction. Father Henson's Story of His Own Life.* Boston: John P. Jewett and Company, 1858.

Horton, George Moses. *The Home of Liberty, Poems: George Moses Horton.* Raleigh, North Carolina: J. Gales and Son, 1829.

Hughes, Louis B. *Thirty Years a Slave; from Bondage to Freedom, the Institution of Slavery as Seen on the Plantation and in the Home of the Planter.* Milwaukee: M. E. Haferkorn, 1897.

Jackson, Andrew. *Narrative and Writings of Andrew Jackson of Kentucky Containing an Account of His Birth and Twenty-Six Years of His Life While a Slave. Narrated by Himself, Written by a Friend.* Syracuse: Daily and Weekly Star Office, 1847.

(Jacobs, Harriet.) *Incidents in the Life of a Slave Girl. Written by Herself.* Boston: by the author, 1861. See Brent, Linda.

James, Reverend Thomas. *Life of Reverend Thomas James, by Himself.* Rochester: Post Express Printing Company, 1886.

Johnstone, Abraham. *The Address of Abraham Johnstone, a Black Man, Who Was Hanged at Woodbury in the County of Glochester, and*

State of New Jersey, on Saturday the Eighth Day of July Last. Philadelphia: Printed for the Purchasers, 1797.

Jones, Thomas H. *The Experience of Thomas Jones, Who Was a Slave for Forty-Three Years. Written by a friend as given to him by Brother Jones.* Boston: Printed by Daniel Laing, 1850.

———. *The Experience of Thomas H. Jones, Who Was a Slave for Forty-Three Years. Written by a friend as related to him by Brother Jones.* New Bedford: E. Anthony and Sons, 1871.

———. *The Experience and Personal Narrative of Uncle Tom Jones: Who Was for Forty Years a Slave; also, the Surprising Adventures of Wild Tom, a Fugitive Negro from South Carolina.* New York: C. G. Holbrook, 1858.

Joseph and Enoch. *Narrative of the Barbarous Treatment of Two Unfortunate Females, Natives of Concordia, Louisiana, by Joseph and Enoch, Runaway Slaves.* As told by Mrs. Todd and Miss Harrington. New York: by the authors, 1842.

Keckley, Elizabeth. *Behind the Scenes by Elizabeth Keckley, Formerly a Slave, but More Recently Modiste, and Friend to Mrs. Abraham Lincoln; or, Thirty Years a Slave, and Four Years in the White House.* New York: G. W. Carlton and Company, 1868.

Lane, Lunsford. *The Narrative of Lunsford Lane, Formerly of Raleigh, North Carolina.* Boston: by the author, 1845.

———. *The Narrative of Lunsford Lane. Formerly of Raleigh, North Carolina.* Boston: by the author, 1863.

Langston, John Mercer. *From Plantation to Congress.* Hartford: American Publishing Company, 1894.

Lewis, Joseph Vance. *Out of the Ditch: A True Story of an Ex-Slave, by J. Vance Lewis.* Houston: Rein and Sons, 1910.

Loguen, Jermain W. *The Reverend Jermain W. Loguen, as a Slave and as a Freeman. A Narrative of Real Life.* Syracuse: Office of the *Daily Journal,* 1859.

Maddison, Reuben. *A True Story.* Birmingham, England: n.p., 1852.

Marrant, John. *A Narrative of the Lord's Wonderful Dealings with John Marrant, a Black (Now going to Preach the Gospel in Nova Scotia) Born in New York, in North America. Taken down from his own relation, Arranged, Corrected, and Published by the Reverend Mr. Aldridge.* London: by the author, 1785.

Mars, James. *Life of James Mars, a Slave Born and Sold in Connecticut, Written by Himself.* Hartford: Case, Lockwood and Company, 1865.

Mason, Isaac. *Life of Isaac Mason, as a Slave.* Worcester, Massachusetts: by the author, 1893.

Meachum, John B. *An Address to the Colored Citizens of the United States, Prefaced by a Narrative of the Author as A Slave in Virginia.* Philadelphia: by the author, 1846.

Mountain, Joseph. *Sketches of the Life of Joseph Mountain, a Negro, Who*

Was Executed at New-Haven, on the 20th Day of October, 1790, For a Rape, Committed on the 26th Day of May Last. New Haven: T. and S. Green, 1790.

Northup, Solomon. *Twelve Years a Slave, Narrative of Solomon Northup, a Citizen of New York, Kidnapped in Washington City in 1841 and Rescued in January, 1853, from a Cotton Plantation near Red River, in Louisiana.* Buffalo: Derby, Orton and Mulligan, 1853.

Offley, Reverend G. W. *Narrative of the Life and Labors of the Reverend G. W. Offley, a Colored Man and Local Preacher, Written by Himself.* Hartford: by the author, 1860.

O'Neal, William. *Life and History of William O'Neal; or, The Man Who Sold His Wife.* St. Louis: A. R. Fleming and Company, 1896.

Parker, Jamie. *Jamie Parker, the Fugitive. Related to Mrs. Emily Pierson.* Hartford: Brockett, Fuller, and Company, 1851.

Parker, William. "The Freedman's Story," *Atlantic Monthly*, XVII (February, 1866), 152–156.

———. "The Freedman's Story," *Atlantic Monthly*, XVII (March, 1866), 276–295.

Pennington, James W. C. *The Fugitive Blacksmith; or, Events in the History of James W. C. Pennington, Pastor of a Presbyterian Church, New York, Formerly a Slave in the State of Maryland, United States.* London: Charles Gilpin, 1849.

Peterson, Daniel H. *The Looking Glass: Being a True Narrative of the Life of the Reverend D. H. Peterson.* New York: Printed by Wright, 1854.

Petition of Lewis Bolah, a free man of colour. Legislative Petition, Richmond City, Virginia. December 13, 1824.

Petition of a Grate Number of Blackes of the Province who by devine permission are held in a state of Slavery within the bowels of a free and christian Country. Collections, Massachusetts Historical Society, 5th Series, III, pp. 432–433.

Picquet, Louisa. *Louisa Picquet, the Octroon; or, Inside Views of Southern Domestic Life.* New York: by the author, 1861.

Platt, Reverend S. H. *The Martyrs and the Fugitive, or a Narrative of the Captivity, Sufferings and Death of an African Family and the Escape of Their Son.* New York: Printed by Daniel Fanshaw, 1859.

Randolph, Reverend Peter. *Sketches of Slave Life; or, Illustrations of the 'Peculiar Institution.' By Peter Randolph, an Emancipated Slave.* Boston: by the author, 1855.

———. *From Slave Cabin to Pulpit: The Autobiography of Peter Randolph: The Southern Question Illustrated and Sketches of Slave Life.* Boston: James H. Earle, 1893.

Roberts, James. *Narrative of James Roberts, Soldier in the Revolutionary War and Battle of New Orleans.* Chicago: by the author, 1858.

———. Hattiesburg, Mississippi: The Book Farm, 1945.

Roberts, Ralph. "A Slave's Story," *Putnam's Monthly*, IX (June, 1857), 614–620.

Roper, Moses. *A Narrative of Moses Roper's Adventures and Escape from American Slavery.* London: Harvey and Darton, 1838.

Seymour. *Life of Maumer Juno of Charleston, South Carolina.* Atlanta, Georgia: Foote and Davies, 1892.

Sheppard. *A Short Sketch of the Life of Mr. Sheppard While he was in Slavery, together with Several of the Songs Sung during the evening of the Jubilee Club.* Belleville, Ontario: Steam Press, 188–.

Simpson, John Hawkins. *Horrors of the Virginia Slave Trade and of Slave Rearing Plantations.* London: W. Bennett, 1863.

Singleton, William Henry. *Recollections of My Slavery Days.* Peekskill, New York: Highland Democratic Company, 1922.

Smith, Harry. *Fifty Years of Slavery in the United States of America.* Grand Rapids, Michigan: Western Michigan Printing Company, 1891.

Smith, James Lindsay. *Autobiography of James Lindsay Smith.* Norwich, Connecticut: Press of the Bulletin Company, 1881.

Smith, Venture. *A Narrative of the Life and Adventures of Venture, a Native of Africa; but Resident about Sixty Years in the United States of America. Related by Himself.* New London: Reprinted and Republished by a Descendant of Venture, 1835.

Spear, Chloe. *Memoir of Chloe Spear, a Native of Africa, Who Was Enslaved in Childhood.* Boston: James Loring, 1832.

Stevens, Charles Emery. *Anthony Burns; A History.* Boston: John P. Jewett and Company, 1856.

Steward, Austin. *Twenty-Two Years a Slave and Forty Years a Freeman, Embracing a Correspondence of Several Years While President of Wilberforce Colony.* Rochester, New York: W. Alling, 1857.

Still, James. *Early Recollections and Life of Dr. James Still.* Philadelphia: J. B. Lippincott and Company, 1877.

Still, Peter. *The Kidnapped and the Ransomed: Being the Personal Recollections of Peter Still and His Wife "Vina," after Forty Years of Slavery. Related to Kate Pickard.* Syracuse: W. T. Hamilton Press, 1856.

Stroyer, Jacob. *Sketches of My Life in the South.* Salem, Massachusetts: Observer Book and Job Print, 1891.

Thompson, John. *The Life of John Thompson, a Fugitive Slave: containing His History of Twenty-Five Years in Bondage, and His Providential Escape: Written by Himself.* Worcester: by the author, 1856.

Tilmon, Levin. *A Brief Miscellaneous Narrative of the More Early Part of the Life of Levin Tilmon, Pastor of a Colored Methodist Church, New York City.* Jersey City: W. and L. Pratt, 1853.

Truth, Sojourner. *Narrative of Sojourner Truth, a Northern Slave, Emancipated from Bodily Servitude by the State of New York, in 1828.* Boston: by the author, 1853.

Turner, Nat. *The Confessions of Nat Turner, The Leader of the Late Insurrection in Southampton, Va. As Fully Made To Thomas R. Gray, In the prison where he was confined, and acknowledged by him to be such, when read before the Court of Southampton: with the certificate, under seal of the Court convened at Jerusalem, Nov. 5, 1831, for his trial. Also, An Authentic Account of the Whole Insurrection, with Lists of Whites Who Were Murdered, and of the Negroes brought before the Court of Southampton, and there sentenced, &c.* Richmond: Thomas R. Gray, 1832.

Veney, Bethany. *The Narrative of Bethany Veney, a Slave Woman.* 2d ed., Worcester, Massachusetts: George H. Ellis, 1889.

Voorhis, Robert. *Life and Adventures of Robert Voorhis, the Hermit of Massachusetts, Who Has Lived Fourteen Years in a Cave. Secluded from Human Society. Comprising an account of his Birth, Parentage, Sufferings, and Providential Escape from Unjust and Cruel Bondage in Early Life—and His Reasons for Becoming a Recluse. Taken from his own mouth by Henry Trumbull, and published for his benefit.* Providence: Printed for Henry Trumbull, 1829.

Ward, Samuel Ringgold. *Autobiography of a Fugitive Negro: His Anti-Slavery Labours in the United States, Canada, and England.* London: John Snow, 1855.

Washington, Booker Taliaferro. *Up From Slavery: an Autobiography.* New York: A. L. Burt Company, 1900.

———. *Up From Slavery.* Bantam Books. New York: Doubleday and Company, 1901.

Washington, Madison. *The Heroic Slave, A Thrilling Narrative of the Adventures of Madison Washington, in Pursuit of Liberty.* Boston: Jewett and Company, 1853.

Watkins, James. *Narrative of the Life of James Watkins, Formerly a Chattel in Maryland, United States.* Birmingham: W. Watton, and Company, 1853.

Watson, Henry. *Narrative of Henry Watson, a Fugitive Slave.* Boston: Bela Marsh, 1849.

Webb, William. *History of William Webb, Composed by Himself.* Detroit: E. Hokstra, 1873.

Wheatley, Phillis. *Memoir and Poems of Phillis Wheatley, a native African and a slave. Dedicated to the Friends of the African.* Boston: Light and Horton, 1835.

———. *Letters of Phillis Wheatley, The Negro-Slave Poet of Boston.* Boston: Privately Printed, 1864.

Wheeler, Peter. *Chains and Freedom; or, The Life and Adventures of Peter Wheeler, a Colored Man Yet Living.* New York: E. S. Arnold and Company, 1839.

White, George. *Account of Life, Experience, Travels, and Gospel Labours of an African.* New York: J. C. Tottle, 1810.

White, William Spottswood. *The African Preacher; an Authentic Narrative.* Philadelphia: Presbyterian Board of Publication, 1849.

Wilkerson, James. *Wilkerson's History of His Travels and Labors in the United States, as a Missionary, in Particular that of the Union Seminary, Located in Franklin County, Ohio, since He Purchased His Liberty in New Orleans, Louisiana.* Columbus, Ohio: n.p., 1861.

William. *The Negro Servant. An Authentic Narrative of a Young Negro, Showing How He Was Made a Slave in Africa: and Carried to Jamaica, Where He Was Sold to a Captain in His Majesty's Navy, and Taken to America, Where He Became a Christian; and Afterwards Brought to England, and Baptised.* Kilmarnock: H. Crawford, 1815.

————. Boston: New England Tract Society; Tract No. 53, 1816.

Williams, Isaac D. *Sunshine and Shadow of Slave Life.* East Saginaw, Michigan: Evening News Printing and Binding House, 1885.

Williams, James. *Narrative of James Williams, An American Slave; Who Was for Several Years a Driver on a Cotton Plantation in Alabama.* New York: American Anti-Slavery Society, 1838.

Williams, James. *Life and Adventures of James Williams, a Fugitive Slave, with a Full Description of the Underground Railroad.* San Francisco: Women's Union Print, 1873.

Williamson, Passmore. *Narrative of Facts in the Case of Passmore Williamson.* Philadelphia: The Pennsylvania Anti-Slavery Society, 1855.

Zamba. *Life and Adventures of Zamba, an African Negro King, and His Experiences of Slavery in South Carolina. Written by Himself. Corrected and Arranged by Peter Neilson.* London: Smith, Elder, and Company, 1847.

Zangara and Maquama. *Slavery Illustrated; in the Histories of Zangara and Maquama, two Negroes Stolen from Africa and Sold into Slavery. Related by Themselves.* London: Simpkin, Marshall, 1849.

BOOKS CONTAINING SLAVE NARRATIVES

Adams, H. G. *God's Image in Ebony: Being a Series of Biographical Sketches, Facts, Anecdotes, Etc., Demonstrative of the Mental Powers and Intellectual Capacities of the Negro Race.* London: Partridge and Oakey, 1854.

Armistead, Wilson. *A Tribute for the Negro: Being a Vindication of the Moral, Intellectual, and Religious Capabilities of the Colored Portion of Mankind: With Particular Reference to the African Race. Illustrated by Numerous Biographical Sketches.* Manchester and London: Charles Gilpin, 1848.

————. *Five Hundred Thousand Strokes for Freedom, A Series of Anti-Slavery Tracts of Which Half a Million Are Now First Issued by*

Friends of the Negro. London: W. and F. Cash and William Tweedie, 1853.

Armstrong, Orland Kay. *Old Massa's People: The Old Slaves Tell Their Story*. Indianapolis: Bobbs-Merrill, 1939.

Barber, John Warner. *A History of the Amistad Captives: Being a Circumstantial Account of the Capture of the Spanish Schooner Amistad, by the Africans on Board . . . With Biographical Sketches of Each of the Surviving Africans*. New Haven: by the author, 1840.

———. *Interesting Memoirs and Documents Relating to American Slavery, and the Glorious Struggle Now Making for Complete Emancipation*. London: Chapman Brothers, 1846.

Botkin, Benjamin, ed. *Lay My Burden Down: A Folk History of Slavery*. Chicago: University of Chicago Press, 1945.

Brown, Hallie Q. *Homespun Heroines and Other Women of Distinction*. Xenia, Ohio: The Aedine Publishing Company, 1926.

Brown, William Wells, *The Black Man, His Antecedents, His Genius and His Achievements*. Savannah, Georgia: James M. Symms and Company, 1863.

———. *My Southern Home*. Boston: A. G. Brown and Company, 1880.

Catterall, Helen T., ed. *Judicial Cases Concerning American Slavery and the Negro*. 5 Vols. Washington, D.C.: Carnegie Institute, 1926–1937.

Child, Lydia Maria Francis. *The Duty of Disobedience to the Fugitive Slave Act: An Appeal to the Legislators of Massachusetts*. Boston: Anti-Slavery Tracts, No. 9, New Series, American Anti-Slavery Society, 1860.

———. *The Patriarchal Institution, as Described by Members of Its Own Family*. Boston: American Anti-Slavery Society, 1860.

———. *The Freedman's Book*. Boston: Ticknor and Fields, 1865.

Child, Lydia Maria. *Authentic Anecdotes of American Slavery*. Newburyport: Charles Whipple, 1838.

Coffin, Levi. *Reminiscences of Levi Coffin, the Reputed President of the Underground Railroad*. Cincinnati: Western Tract Society, 1876.

Colman, Julia, ed. *Child's Anti-Slavery Book*. New York: Carlton and Porter, 1859.

Curtis, Anna L. *Stories of the Underground Railroad*. New York: Island Workshop Press Co-Operative, 1941.

Drew, Benjamin, ed. *North-Side View of Slavery, the Refugee: or the Narratives of Fugitive Slaves in Canada. Related by Themselves*. Boston: John P. Jewett, 1856.

Emerson, William C. *Stories and Spirituals of the Negro Slave*. Boston: R. G. Badger and Gorham Press, 1930.

Fairchild, James H. *Underground Railroad*. Cleveland: Western Reserve Historical Society, 1877.

Fisk University. *Unwritten History of Slavery; Autobiographical Account* of Negro Ex-Slaves. Nashville, Tennessee: Social Science Institute, Fisk University, 1945.

——. God Struck Me Dead; Religious Conversion Experiences and Auto-biographies of Negro Ex-Slaves. Nashville, Tennessee: Social Science Institute, Fisk University, 1945.

Griffiths, Julia. Autographs for Freedom. Rochester: John P. Jewett and Company, 1853.

Howe, Samuel Gridley. The Refugees from Slavery in Canada West. Report to the Freedman's Inquiry Commission. Boston: Wright and Potter, 1864.

Johnson, Homer Uri. From Dixie to Canada. Romances and Realities of the Underground Railroad. Buffalo: Charles Wells Moulton, 1894.

May, Samuel. The Fugitive Slave Law and Its Victims, Anti-Slavery Tracts, No. 15. New York: American Anti-Slavery Society, 1861.

Mitchell, William M. Underground Railroad from Slavery to Freedom. London: W. Tweedie, 1860.

Moore, Frank. The Rebellion Record. A Diary of American Events, with Documents, Narratives, Incidents. New York: G. P. Putnam, 1861–1862.

Mott, Abigail Field. Biographical Sketches and Interesting Anecdotes of Persons of Color. New York: M. Day, 1826.

Mott, Abigail Field, and Wood, S. M. Narratives of Colored Americans. New York: Bowne and Company, 1882.

Nordhoff, Charles. The Freedmen of South Carolina. New York: Charles L. Evans, 1863.

Parsons, C. G. Inside View of Slavery; or, a Tour Among the Planters. Cleveland: John P. Jewett, 1855.

Redpath, James. The Roving Editor; or, Talks with Slaves in the Southern States. New York: A. B. Burdick, 1859.

Ross, Alexander. Recollections and Experiences of an Abolitionist; from 1855 to 1865. Toronto: Rowsell and Hutchinson, 1876.

Smith, E. Uncle Tom's Kindred: or, the Wrongs of the Lowly. Sketches and Narratives. 10 Vols. Mansfield, Ohio: Wesleyan Methodist Connection of America, 1853.

Still, William. Underground Rail Road Record, Narrating the Hardships, Hairbreath Escapes and Death Struggles of the Slave in their Efforts for Freedom. Philadelphia: People's Publishing Company, 1879.

Stowe, Harriet Beecher. A Key to Uncle Tom's Cabin. Presenting the Original Facts and Documents Upon Which the Story is Founded; Together with Corroborative Statements Verifying the Truth of the Work. Cleveland: John P. Jewett and Company, 1853.

(Weld, Theodore.) American Slavery As It Is: Testimony of a Thousand Witnesses. New York: American Anti-Slavery Society, 1839.

UNPUBLISHED COLLECTIONS

Federal Writers' Project. Slave Narratives; A Folk History of Slavery in the United States from Interviews with Former Slaves. Typewritten Records Prepared by the Federal Writers' Project, 1936–1938. Assembled by the Library of Congress Project, Works Projects Administration for the District of Columbia. Sponsored by the Library of Congress. 17 vols. Washington, D.C.: 1936–1938. (Microfilm Edition.)

NEWSPAPERS AND PERIODICALS

American Anti-Slavery Almanac, 1836–1846.
American Convention for Promoting the Abolition of Slavery, and Improving the Condition of the African Race, Minutes of the Proceedings at Philadelphia, 1794–1837.
American Anti-Slavery Reporter, 1834.
Anti-Slavery Bugle, 1850–1857.
Anti-Slavery Examiner, 1836–1845.
Anti-Slavery Record, 1835–1839.
Anti-Slavery Reporter, 1831–1832.
Anti-Slavery Reporter and Aborigines' Friend, 1840–1851.
Anti-Slavery Tracts, 1855–1861.
Christian Examiner, 1824–1869.
Emancipator, 1820.
Genius of Universal Emancipation, 1821–1825.
Herald of Freedom, 1835–1845.
Liberator, 1831–1865.
Liberty Bell, 1839, 1841–1849, 1851–1853, 1856, 1858.
National Standard, A Temperance and Literary Journal, 1840–1870.
Quarterly Anti-Slavery Magazine, 1833–1837.
Slave's Friend, 1836–1839.

OTHER SOURCES CITED

Botkin, Benjamin A. "The Slave As His Own Interpreter," *Library of Congress Quarterly Journal of Current Acquisitions,* II (November, 1944).
Fine, Sidney, and Brown, Gerald S. *The American Past: Conflicting Interpretations of The Great Issues.* Vol. I. New York: The Macmillan Company, 1961.
Morison, Samuel Eliot. *The Oxford History of The American People.* New York: Oxford University Press, 1965.

Index